Kundalini in the Physical World

Mary Scott was born in India where her father was Principal of Bahaddin College in Kathiawar. Both her parents were interested in comparative religion and Mary Scott feels that this background has made it easier for her to enter into Eastern modes of thought. After a short career in nursing, she took a degree in psychology and philosophy and a postgraduate diploma in social studies. She became a university teacher but gave up full-time employment after receiving a serious back injury. She worked as a part-time psychologist, lecturer and writer before retiring. She is currently concerned with working out a unified system of ideas which will make sense of the varied experiences of her working life, many of which science cannot yet explain. *Kundalini in the Physical World* was her first serious work in this area. It has been followed by *A Renaissance of the Spirit: A New Way to See Ourselves* which is more general and anecdotal but no less thoughtful.

KUNDALINI in
the physical world

Mary Scott

ARKANA

In memoriam

Professor Gardner Murphy
Itzak Bentov

ARKANA

Published by the Penguin Group
27 Wrights Lane, London W8 5TZ, England
Viking Penguin Inc., 40 West 23rd Street, New York, New York 10010, USA
Penguin Books Australia Ltd, Ringwood, Victoria, Australia
Penguin Books Canada Ltd, 2801 John Street, Markham, Ontario, Canada L3R 1B4
Penguin Books (NZ) Ltd, 182–190 Wairau Road, Auckland 10, New Zealand

Penguin Books Ltd, Registered Offices: Harmondsworth, Middlesex, England

First published by Routledge & Kegan Paul plc 1983
Published by Arkana 1989
10 9 8 7 6 5 4 3 2 1

Library of Congress Cataloging in Publication Data

Scott, Mary, 1906–
  Kundalini in the physical world.
  Bibliography: p.
  Includes index.
  1. Kundalini. 2. Tantrism. I. Title.

BL1215.K8S36 1983   294.5'43   82-22999
ISBN 014 01 9150 X

Printed and bound in Great Britain by
Cox & Wyman Ltd, Reading

Contents

Acknowledgments   ix

1 The object of the exercise   1

2 The Tantric background of Kundalini yoga   10

3 The Tantric cosmos   28

4 Evolution and the breath of Brahman   44

5 Organisation from above   58

6 Cosmic Kundalini   77

7 Kundalini as an Earth force   95

8 Ley lines and telluric emanations   111

9 Kundalini and the Pranas   127

10 The Sahasrara-Muladhara axis   136

11 Kundalini as Shabdabrahman   154

12 Tantric and Western psychobiology   169

13 Kundalini and physio-kundalini   182

14 The Linga Chakras   196

15 Theosophy and Tantra   217

16 Developmental stresses in the Chakras   239

Glossary   253

Bibliography   259

Index   264

Acknowledgments

A lot of research has gone into this volume and much of it would not have been possible without the assistance of the librarians of the Wiltshire County Libraries and Mr Launchbury of the Swindon Bookshop. Their unfailing helpfulness in chasing up recalcitrant references and procuring necessary textbooks is something for which I shall always be grateful. I would also like to acknowledge with gratitude the kindness of Mrs Jean Simister who offered to convert my amateur efforts into a respectable typescript; of Mrs Gladys Keable and Dr Sylvia Darke who took on the task of proof-reading; and of Dr Nicola Sutherland for helping me to grapple with the index. An author who enjoys research and writing can find these necessary chores extraordinarily laborious. I certainly did. Therefore the help of these friends and of the editorial and promotion staff of Routledge & Kegan Paul in getting this book into print was very much appreciated by me at every stage and is gladly acknowledged here.

The author and publishers would like to thank the following for permission to reproduce illustrations: Alice Bailey and Lucis Publishing Company (*A Treatise on Cosmic Fire*) for Figure 9; the Theosophical Publishing House (*Man Visible and Invisible*) for Figure 8.

1
The object of
the exercise

In philosophy there is something called the fallacy by naming. It means falling into the trap of thinking because we have given something a name we know what it is. We in the West seem to be in danger of falling into this trap over Kundalini. Everyone who is anyone in yoga circles has heard about Kundalini. We not only use the word, we can pronounce it properly, and even spell it. One might almost call it a cult word among meditators and consciousness researchers. But do we really know what the actual phenomenon is to which the sages of ancient India gave this name?

To explore this matter further was my first reason for writing this book.

Some years ago I came across a serious American journal, *Human Dimensions*, which had devoted an entire issue to Kundalini. My father spent his working life as a university teacher in India and I was born there. Both my parents were students of comparative religion. I had heard about Kundalini in my teens and knew something of what the great yogis of the past had meant by the term. I therefore greatly welcomed the opportunity of reading the views of a battery of contemporary students and practitioners of yoga in the West.

What struck me most about their various articles was how many Kundalinis there seemed to be. What I had thought a relatively clear-cut and limited phenomenon — the serpent fire of Hinduism, the caduceus power of the hermetic tradition — seemed to have become a mixed bundle of phenomena tied together and labelled 'Kundalini'. This intrigued me both as a psychologist and as a philosopher.

One did not doubt the sincerity of the writers; nor did one doubt that they had had the experiences they said they had. It was clear that the journal was a mine of information about sensations which cried out for explanation. Each person had had what was for him a 'Kundalini experience' and was offering it for evaluation. That he had attempted to interpret the happening for himself made the offering all the more valuable even if one did not necessarily agree with him. Most of the experiences reported were uncomfortable and some apparently permanently crippling, so that underlying many of the contributions was a *cri de coeur*.

It was the *cris de coeur* that I found most moving. What had happened to these people? Could a better understanding of human beings and their potentialities have spared them unnecessary pain? Or were their pains growing pains made distressing because Western bodies and Western ways of life are not conducive to the smooth evolution of the organs of spiritual perception and enlightenment? Or are they merely natural corollaries of a nervous system developing under accelerating evolutionary pressures? All these theories have been put forward and to go into them carefully was the second reason for this book.

I was all the more interested in these problems because I had no personal experience of yoga. When I was young I was very keen to know more about it and to practise meditation systematically. Today we talk about expansion of consciousness through meditation. Then the idea was to raise it on to high levels in order to advance spiritually. To do this in the West at that time one applied for membership of esoteric schools associated with one of the theosophical movements, such as that of the Theosophical Society, which had its headquarters in India, or the Arcane School founded by Alice Bailey whose teacher was a Tibetan lama. These were Raja yoga schools and one was not accepted into them lightly. In those days there was not the easy traffic between East and West there is now and it was far harder to find out about yoga. This was a good thing in a way because there was less risk of damaging oneself by too much experimentation or by practising it along unsuitable lines.

I was fortunate enough to get accepted by the Esoteric School of Theosophical Society only to make the humiliating discovery that I could not meditate as prescribed. When I tried I was somehow 'switched off'. I thought this was due to some serious shortcoming in myself and struggled to overcome it for a long time. My teacher was very patient but finally we came to realise that there was some centre of control deep in myself which was inhibiting this particular activity. It 'allowed' me to use my mind and will quite freely in other ways. In fact I found reading about spiritual and psychological matters easy and absorbing then as now.

As time went on I became increasingly familiar with being guided by this switching-off method, being allowed to do some things but having doors shut firmly in my face if I tried to do others. I did not have visions or hear voices but, over the years, I gradually became aware of an inner, wiser self which seemed only to interfere when I tended to stray from some invisible path along which I was apparently being directed. It was only comparatively recently that I found a reference to this negative way as one well known in Raja yoga. Alice Bailey's Tibetan master writes of the closing of doors as being associated with the development of intuition. This makes good sense because, in dealing with problems and choices, it is not always possible to reason one's way through dilemmas. Some can only be resolved by waiting patiently for doors to close. If this can be done without fretting it all too often turns out that the only door remaining open does in fact lead to where one should be. This is not a discovery that comes all at once, of course, but over the years one finds that it is true and that, by behaving in this way, many mistakes and disappointments can be avoided. Also that what 'mistakes' are made prove to be extraordinarily fruitful in the long run.

The way of meditation as this term is usually understood is chiefly concerned with controlling and enriching the mind. People drawn to it are, for the most part, seeking inner experiences, and meditative techniques are directed at improving the quality and extending the range of consciousness. In spiritual terms meditators who cannot meditate in this way tend to feel not only deprived but spiritually deficient. I certainly did for many years until I realised there seemed to be a way of contemplation and a way of action. This insight grew on me as I came to recognise that my unseen companion, the 'senior partner' in my adventures, seemed less interested in my conscious state than in what I attended to and how I acted. What seemed important was that I did the right thing, and often the good I did was not at all what I thought. In fact sometimes my failures seemed more necessary to some invisible pattern than the success at which I aimed.

It is not easy for those of us who have trained minds and strong personalities to realise that we may be far less in charge of our lives than we like to think. It is even more disconcerting to discover that we do a great deal better if we can develop a partnership between the ego-self with which we identify and some other greater self which is completely transcendent as far as our personal consciousness is concerned and yet seems thoroughly cognisant of what we should be and do. (73)

Those of us who develop through this sort of partnership are seldom aware of improvements in spiritual consciousness, but are continually being surprised by the manner in which we are enabled to say, do or think the right thing. One has an impulse to go somewhere and there we find someone who needs our help or we theirs. We pick up a book and a door opens in the mind so that whole tracts of our thinking are changed. We do not so much feel we are developing as discovering in ourselves the ability to do better. Some people lose themselves in a great ocean of Being, the small I slipping like 'a dewdrop into a shining sea'. Others of us seem to move outwards into what Martin Buber called 'the world of the Between', the great network of interrelationships which is the universe as a field of action. (74)

One of the religious disciplines which deals with action rather than consciousness is, of course, Zen Buddhism which emphasises the Doctrine of the Act. Here the object of meditation is to bring the pupil's mind to the Laya centre, a neutral point from which one can act out in all directions with equal facility. The ideal is the right man in the right place doing the right thing at the right time. One might say the Zen master's raps and koans are the analogues of life's closed doors and the blows of fate.

Since the Kundalini experience is so often reported to be uncomfortable if not downright painful, must we not also ask ourselves whether there may not be some ways of meditating which are better than others or better for certain people or better at certain times? Maybe there is some relation between the stage we are at and the sort of yoga we should be practising. And what about the likes of me who get switched off when we try to meditate at all? Are we in a phase or are we a type or are we in some way spiritually retarded so that the prize of the risen Kundalini, which is enlightenment, is not for us?

Trying to answer these questions was a further aim of this book.

My final aim was to explore the physiological implications of the Kundalini experience. Though usually discussed in a context of yoga and meditation, many such experiences appear to relate to the body almost more than the mind. When things go wrong the health of both is disturbed in ways which suggest that we may be up against an actual psycho-biological entity. The impression is of a force operative in organisms which can be activated by mental processes involving imagination and directed attention and also by physical movements and postures. It is commonly assumed that meditation is required to raise Kundalini into and up the spinal canal. This is not always the case. Spontaneous arousals have been reported as a result merely of holding one's breath while coincidentally finding oneself in certain postures.

Once roused, all the problems of what to do about it are present whether the arousal has been accidental or due to the unwise practice of yoga. This is brought out vividly in Gopi Krishna's autobiographical account of the great bodily distress which followed an upsurge of Kundalini before his system was properly prepared for it. Not only did he find he had a tiger by the tail but he was unable to find a single yogi able to help him tame it. Medical diagnosis of an acute psychosomatic disorder would have been accurate, but what doctor would have been able to prescribe for it in the present state of our ignorance? Fortunately for us Gopi Krishna made good use of his misfortunes. His detailed descriptions of his symptoms and subjective states were written with research in mind. At his Kundalini Research Institute he has not only continued to work with this end in view, but he has done much to interest scientists and medical men in what some are calling 'the Kundalini syndrome'. In preparing his book, *Kundalini: The Evolutionary Energy in Man*, he collaborated with James Hillman, then Director of the C.G. Jung Institute in Zurich, who produced a commentary analysing Gopi Krishna's experiences along Jungian lines. His autobiography, Hillman's commentary, and the findings of the Sannella-Bentov group which produced the Kundalini syndrome theory, are largely responsible for the biological emphasis in my treatment of this subject.

I have never been happy with Jung's tendency to reduce the Chakras of Tantric yoga to symbolic objects of meditation unrelated to the body and its mechanisms. Not only Jung but depth psychologists in general tend to perpetuate the split between psyche and soma, which originated in philosophy, by concentrating on the one as if it operated independently of the other. This has been unfortunate both for psychology and the philosophy of science. It has also reinforced, by this approach, science's predisposition to divide mind from matter for methodological convenience. Fortunately research is carrying science well beyond the limits of the five senses. Its sophisticated instruments now regularly probe levels of matter regarded as 'ethereal' or 'supernatural' by earlier generations. Moreover it is now almost impossible to draw a line between physics and metaphysics because of the behaviour of elementary particles which cannot be seen but must be assumed.

The boundaries between psyche and soma are getting blurred in much the same way. Biologists, however, have yet to find themselves sharing the experiences of those physicists who, attempting to understand the nature of particles, find themselves turning into mystics. Or perhaps one should say find themselves explaining mysticism in terms of physics. It is something which only happens, it seems, when intuition is playing round elements on the border where matter appears to disappear either into another dimension or another state.

Kundalini could be just such an element in the field of psychobiology.

Preliminary exploration of it lures one into foreseeing some such possibility. My search for a conceptual framework which could contain all the relevant data and make biological sense has not been an easy one. It has involved many periodic lapses into confusion while ideas were reorganising themselves round some new insight. The whole subject of Kundalini is fascinating in its ramifications. There have been frequent occasions when the attempt to synthesise science and Hindu thought led to formulations which seemed adequate until some new piece of information came along. Various possible models have presented themselves only to be discarded. The present one has stabilised sufficiently for me to feel it is worth offering for others to try out. It has brought me, via biology, to the same frontier to which sub-atomic physics has brought such scientists as Capra. It has done more than that. It has helped me to see the body's mystic participation in its cosmic environment and its mystical union with Jung's self-beyond-the-ego as completely matter of fact and down to earth, as open to scientific as to religious examination.

In so far as the way of yoga is a search for enlightenment, my own path would seem to have been a combination of the yoga of action or Karma yoga and the yoga of knowledge or Jnana yoga. (75) In fact there is a sense in which it could be said that the element of discipline one associates with yoga was exerted through mental processes allied to learning rather than to meditation. Both sorts of activity demand sustained concentration and focused attention. Possibly my experience of being switched off when trying to still the mind in meditation may have stemmed from disparities which exist in the spiritual needs of those on different yoga paths or at different stages of a yoga path.

In India it is well understood that religious life has a worldly as well as a spiritual dimension. Only after fulfilling one's role as a member of society is one free to withdraw from it and seek for liberation within the world of the psyche. It was because of their understanding of individual differences in spiritual development and the variety of available approaches to enlightenment that the founding fathers of the yoga schools laid so much emphasis on the importance of seeking a guru and choosing him with care.

Nowadays finding one's guru, as Gopi Krishna learned, is no easy matter even in India. This may be because, as Sri Aurobindo suggests, those who are ready for the master to appear will find him within more readily than was once the case. Certainly it seems true that those who seek human gurus tend to follow them more from the need to give their lives a spiritual dimension than because they are ready for the rigours of the transformation process through which alone the crown of yoga is attained. There is no easy road to Nirvana and no short cuts via Kundalini are either recommended by wise teachers or successfully negotiated by impetuous students. Yoga means literally union, and enlightenment is essentially fruit of the union of the seeking ego-self and a transcendent greater self into which it is finally elevated and absorbed. Earthly gurus are only surrogates deputising more or less adequately for the guru within to whom, if we are lucky, they may introduce us.

As, like Gopi Krishna, my fate seems to require that I try to find answers from within myself, this enquiry into the nature of Kundalini has been a contrapuntal affair. As junior partner I have 'devilled' for my senior partner. I have attempted to find the most relevant sources and study them. I have tried to make available in the association areas of my brain as many facts and ideas as possible. I have worked to develop sensitivity in recognising what is the right book to read, the right conference to attend, the right time to work and the necessary time to let brain and mind lie fallow. Throughout this process I have been aware of the guiding presence which has quietly opened and shut doors and has, almost miraculously it seems now, prevented me wasting time and effort exploring unnecessary bypaths. I am also aware that anything of value which may emerge as a result of our joint endeavours will be designed to meet the needs of strangers about whom I only know one thing: their needs must in some way reflect my own.

I have long felt that the search for truth is not just a search for facts but involves also a search for the meaning which gives coherence to all the facts we collectively know. I cannot personally rest until the bits of a jigsaw have been put together so that pieces, pattern and meaning are united in a single whole. The bits collected in three nursing trainings; those gathered reading and teaching psychology, philosophy and social science; unusual experiences met in practice as a psychologist which set me exploring parapsychology; the happenings of my personal life; all these cannot be allowed to lie about as so many isolated bits and pieces. Somehow one must try to fit them into an overall pattern. At present Western science appears to have no existing framework to help me with my jigsaw so, in the course of my enquiry into Kundalini, I have cast my net wide. In part the subject itself made this necessary. In part I did it because I could see as I went along that, by extending the scope of my investigation here and there, I could construct a theoretical model of greater coherence. Maybe even one that will enable me to complete my jigsaw puzzle.

At first sight it almost looks as if it might, but even if, on closer scrutiny, this proves not to be the case the intellectual adventure has been exciting and rewarding in itself.

2
The Tantric background
of Kundalini yoga

Kundalini science and Kundalini yoga are dealt with in most detail in the Tantras, which is why Kundalini yoga is sometimes called Tantric yoga. The Upanishads, Puranas and Tantras are the major Shastras or sacred writings of the Hindus and all derive from the ancient Vedas. They differ in emphasis and in some of their terminology, but a common cosmology and psychology runs through them all. It therefore seemed best to approach the subject of Kundalini as a possible force in nature by way of the Tantric texts to see what I could make of what the founding fathers of its science and practice had to say. Thanks to the mammoth labours of Sir John Woodroffe many of the Tantras are available in English translations. The most familiar are those in his classic, *The Serpent Power*, first published in 1919 under his pseudonym of Arthur Avalon, but enlarged and revised later. Since his death his publishers, Ganesh & Co. of Madras, have been at pains to make it easier for Western students to understand the Sanskrit references. Serious readers are therefore advised to use the more recent editions. For a modern exposition from an Indian point of view the fullest and most systematic treatment of Tantric yoga is probably to be found in the writings of Sri Aurobindo. (1, 2) In some usages Sri Aurobindo and Sir John Woodroffe deviate from one another somewhat but rather than being confusing this forces one to analyse more closely and to make more subtle distinctions.

It is impossible to arrive at any clear conception of what Kundalini meant to the Rishis, the sages and seers who first defined it, without going back to the Sanskrit source material. The whole subject has been tremendously overlaid down the centuries and can readily be misunderstood, as I have found to my cost in wasted time. Two factors are chiefly responsible for the confusion surrounding it. One was radical misconceptions in the West about the true nature of Tantric religious practices, misconceptions which came to be shared by many Westernised Indians. The other was the fact that many Hindu philosophical ideas were introduced into Western occult literature by Europeans less familiar with Sanskrit than Sir John Woodroffe and so liable to mistranslations of basic terms.

Tantric science and therefore also its yoga was, and still is, a body-affirming system. Unlike yogas advocating its denial and seeing bliss and enlightenment as involving the transcendence of physical limitations, the Tantric yogi seeks to raise up the quality of natural forces so that enlightened states can be experienced within the body. Sri Aurobindo makes this plain. The joy associated with yoga, union with one's own spiritual essence, should not be conceived as something other-worldly but as something in which the body could and should share. Tantric yoga from the beginning laid great stress on the bliss side of spiritual experience and it is this, combined with the positive value given to the body's participation in all its rites, which has been most misunderstood.

Yogas, as ways in which union can be sought, are of various kinds depending on their emphasis on one or other aspect of the general Way. All share in common the idea that the Sadhaka, the man preparing to walk the yoga road, must reach a certain moral and spiritual standard before he can hope to be taken on by a guru for special training in the arts of Pranayama (breathing exercises), Asanas (ritual postures) and Dhyana (meditation). Hatha yoga, which is a discipline of the body alone, was never much practised as a yoga in its own right. Theoretically, if one carried out Asanas and Pranayamas in a context of devotion and participated in all the prescribed rituals, it could lead one to bliss and the experience of expanded consciousness associated with Samadhi. This, however, could only be done by so much hard work over so long a period that one might well die before reaching one's goal. It would, moreover, be an exclusively bodily achievement and, as Sri Aurobindo points out, physically acquired skills die with one — a powerful argument against using Hatha yoga alone in a country where the belief in reincarnation is general.

Yogas in which wisdom and understanding are sought are Jnana yogas or yogas of knowledge. Yogas for the devotee are Bhakti yogas or yogas of devotion and worship. Yogas of action or Karma yogas aim at union with the Divine through service and sacrifice, by the way of works and the exercise of compassion.

Discussing various religions as yoga paths, an Indian friend described Christianity as a mixture of Bhakti and Karma yoga. It has never been a Jnana yoga. There have been great thinkers who have tried to resolve the philosophical arguments which have gone on since the days of the early Church Fathers, particularly those concerning the nature of Jesus, his immaculate conception and his miracles. The multitudinous sects within the Christian Church show how impossible it has been, in spite of the efforts of the great systematisers like St Thomas Aquinas, to arrive at a consensus on these matters. In modern times science has shattered literalistic interpretations of Genesis and, unfortunately, fundamentalists have seemed unable to see its story as an allegory of the Creation as magnificent in its imagery as any creation myth ever produced. It is the fact that it is not a Jnana yoga which lies at the root of the split between science and religion, for if science is anything it is a Jnana way.

As a Bhakti yoga Christianity is one of the greatest of its kind. In spite of all its factions, its tortured history of dissensions and persecutions, the devotion to Christ of untold millions down the centuries has never failed. Even the attempts to diminish the Jesus of history have only served to make him more challenging and contemporary. The Bhakti yogas of Christianity and Buddhism are unique in that the objects of contemplation and worship have been actual human beings. They are paradigms, the one of how God can be incarnate in man in the world; the other of how man can transcend the world while still in it. Their transfiguration, their enlightenment, were things achieved in life and their compassion something which encompassed the world. They walked, in Tagore's beautiful words, 'among the poorest, and the lowliest, and the lost'. Humanity needs such heroes even more than it needs scientists and welfare states. It is the spirit of man which droops in adversity, and explanations and material comforts alone can never lift up the heart. It needs the encouragement of those who have known suffering and remained undefeated by humiliation. In this Jesus has no equal among the great religious figures, which is perhaps why he appeals so much to Africans and the indigenous peoples of South America. Christianity is not a Jnana way, but it can nevertheless bring what Hindus call Vijnana, Brahman knowledge, knowledge of God. Of this its mystical literature gives abundant proof.

I have expatiated on this at some length because it may seem strange to Christians that I shall seem to be offering science models from Hinduism as if Christianity were a failed religion. Not at all. Like others before me, I do not think it has failed so much as never been tried. As a Karma yoga Shastra the New Testament offers the pilgrim an example of how life should be lived which all Christians venerate but few copy. It is only because it provides little for those who are interested in how the world came to be as it is and how things come to behave as they do that Christianity is less use to science than Hinduism. Like my senior partner, Christ seems more concerned about what we are and do than what we know. It is good to know but even better, it seems, to be the right person in the right place doing the right thing at the right time. He is at one with the Zen Buddhist in this. What the Western world needs is not science as a substitute for religion but a science which complements religion. Modern man needs both. In earlier times and among simpler people Jnana may not have been necessary. For us it is.

To return now to my main theme. In all yogas there is the goal of ego-transcendence since that is what union really is, transcendence of one's small personal self by the transposition of consciousness into the all-inclusive spiritual entity which is at once our deepest self and the all-encompassing being of the universe. In practice most gurus make use of a mixture of yogas depending on the needs and temperament of the pupil. Sri Aurobindo illustrated this when he called his own system 'Integral Yoga'.

Yogas can also be differentiated as yogas of withdrawal and yogas of mastery. In yogas of withdrawal the emphasis is on detachment. One detaches oneself from just about everything, living in what is sometimes called 'the witness Purusha', the soul as a spectator. One becomes essentially a watcher of a drama in which one wants no part. The great aim is to free oneself from the ever-revolving wheel of birth, suffering and death. Liberation is sought through retreat into the inner world in order to find the Divine in meditation and trance. By contrast, in the yogas of mastery the soul does not merely observe the play of nature, it affirms its value. It sees consciousness and nature as interdependent and evolving together. The yogi is prepared to play the creator within nature and then rise above it both within himself and in the world. Tantric yoga is of this sort.

In its pure form Tantric yoga is a Jnana yoga of a very advanced kind. Its practice requires a detailed knowledge of the Chakras and of the Mantras associated with their functioning. The science of Mantra is in itself an extremely complex and difficult subject, and one that cannot be understood without an intimate knowledge of the doctrines underlying Hindu religious thought. The idea of anyone attempting to raise Kundalini through the Chakras without this knowledge rightly fills those really qualified to judge with the utmost alarm. Kundalini yoga, involving as it does both body and mind, has to be embarked on with the greatest caution. Even under the guidance of a guru who is himself fully competent in all its practices and who has thoroughly tested the quality of his pupil, the risks are considerable and the difficulties beyond the scope of all but the very few.

Competence (Adhikara) for yoga is something which is not taken very seriously in the West where the general idea is that yoga is just a matter of some form of meditation and a few Hatha yoga exercises. In India, where religion is a way of life, Sadhanas or religious disciplines vary according to the disposition, abilities and spiritual qualities of the Sadhaka. Their common aim is, ultimately, union (Yoga) with the Brahman self within through identification with it and, through this union, to experience the bliss of liberation (Mukti) from the lesser self. It is, however, recognised that all men have not reached the same stage on the path to yoga with Brahman and, since all cannot be yogis, each must discover the level of his own competence and follow the Sadhana most appropriate for him.

From this standpoint the Hindu sees each life as representing his present Dharma or place in the universal scheme of things, and a preparation for a higher Dharma at the same time. His personal Sadhana is selected accordingly. Sadhana comes from the root word Sadh meaning to strive. Siddhi is the name given to success through striving. Thus a Sadhaka, in the case of a man, or a Sadhika, in the case of a woman, is one who strives to become Siddha, which means accomplished or successful in what one has undertaken. A Sadhana is therefore a discipline, a form of training. It can be either religious or secular but will be used here in a religious sense.

Religious Sadhanas recognise three basic types of Sadhaka, Divya, Vira and Pashu, roughly translated as divine, heroic and animal. This is much the same as the Gnostic classification of people into those with material, mental and spiritual dispositions. The divine or spiritual man is a rarity. Most Sadhakas are a mixture so that the Sadhana for this class is yoga as a preparation for the divine state rather than one designed for those who have already achieved ego-transcendence and enlightenment. The divine man is thus really the goal at which all Sadhakas aim rather than a stage many have actually reached.

The great bulk of humanity falls into the animal or material category so that many Tantras deal with the various kinds of Pashu and their spiritual needs. Pashu is not a word which derives from animal in any derogatory sense, but comes from a word which means to bind. The Pashu is a person who tends to be in bondage to the material world and his animal nature. The great bonds, due to our subjugation to Maya at this level, are ignorance, seeing ourselves as isolated and separate from all other created things, and seeing our actions as things we control more than we actually do. There are also lesser Pasha or bonds. Some are not readily seen as such.

One such, for instance, is pity of the sort Taoists call 'inferior benevolence' to distinguish it from compassion. Others are ties of family, class or caste which put limitations upon our capacity to understand and feel for all people equally; codes and customs which lead us to divide groups into Them and Us; prejudices which produce intolerance and cruelty. Fear, shame and disgust are Pasha we can more easily feel as bonds but which are, in fact, emotions which can help us to rise into the heroic class. This is because they are uncomfortable and spur us to fight and fighting is of the essence to the heroic Sadhaka provided we can learn to fight the right things. Being heroic in the religious sense means facing our limitations squarely with a view to overcoming them. The hero's great enemies are the faults which blind and depotentiate: ignorance, laziness, complacency and weak acquiescence for the sake of a quiet life, habits which can grow on us in so insidious and negative a way that they are readily overlooked.

As Sir John Woodroffe brings out clearly in his book on the Tantra Shastras, *Shakti and Shakta*, this view of Tantric Hinduism is seldom found in the West, where something called 'The Tantra' is most often thought of as a debased form of Hinduism smacking of magic, eroticism and the left-hand path. Far from there being just one dubious Tantra there are more than five hundred, and nearly as many other Shastras. The bulk of all we know of Mantra Vidya, the science of Mantra, is derived from the Tantras. So true is this that the Tantras are sometimes referred to as the Mantra Shastras. The so-called 'lay' Tantras cover most of our systematic knowledge of Indian chemistry and medicine. The major part of the Tantras are, however, descriptions of religious ceremonies and disciplines devised for different types of Sadhaka and appropriate to a variety of occasions. Tan comes from a word which means 'to spread' and Tra from a suffix which means 'to save'. The idea is therefore to spread knowledge which saves.

All the Indian Shastras, including the Tantras, regard the Vedas as the final authority against which to assess their own validity. And here again it is important to understand that the Indian scriptures are meant to be practical guides for the seeker and productive of actual spiritual experience. You do not argue about a Shastra, you try it out. The Vedas and Upanishads have stood the test of time because those who have themselves entered Samadhi can confirm the experiences described by the Rishis who compiled them. In the Tantras, as in most Shastras, it is the Divine who speaks. For this reason the Tantras are sometimes called Agamas, from the word meaning to listen. In the Tantras all are listeners who read them or hear them recited while the Devata or divinities listened to are Shiva, Vishnu and Shakti. It is the Shakti Agamas of which Sir John Woodroffe has made a special study and from which most of the modern Indian worship of the Mother derives. Nevertheless, whether it is Shiva, Shakti or Vishnu who speaks, it is the workability of the practices advocated which is the test of the validity of a Shastra, not the divine status claimed for its author.

This makes practical good sense because even the most accomplished yogi who has closely identified with the Divine in himself can misinterpret or mistranslate when it comes to putting into words what are essentially ineffable experiences. And the Indian makes no mistake about who the writer is behind the Devata, for it seems quite in order that the Gods should speak through men and men avow the God who so inspires them. This is because a basic tenet of Hinduism is that 'All is Brahman', 'All is Shiva', 'All is Shakti', and so it is not blasphemous for him to say 'So'ham' (He I am) and 'Sa'ham' (She I am) and try to feel its truth. Nevertheless, the Indian also knows that living men and women can be led into error because of the limitations of the body as an organ of spiritual perception. Hence the need to test a Shastra to see if it lives up to all that is claimed for it.

Another error common among Westerners is that of regarding modern Hinduism as predominantly Vedic with Tantricism as a sort of mongrel offshoot. Due to the great waves of invaders who overran India, the old Vedic civilisation of the sub-continent was completely disrupted. The Brahmin caste of hereditary priests became demoralised as their authority was eroded and their roles disappeared under the pressures of alien cultures. The tradition of the high Rishis of the Golden Age of Veda survived only as a thread preserved by a line of yogis who retired to the forests to practise their religion in isolation from society. The true history of Tantricism is the story of the struggle of this native Vedic teaching to re-assert itself in a completely new setting. There is an unfortunate tendency for historians to jump from the Vedic to the Buddhist phase of Hinduism as if this long struggle, carried on piecemeal in villages scattered all over India, had never occurred. Buddhism was ancillary to this process rather than being an entirely new religion. This can be gathered from the way it rapidly declined in India. Even in Tibet, where it became the official religion, it became so imbued with Tantric elements that it was called Tantric Buddhism to distinguish it from the Taoist Buddhism of China and Japan. In its pure form it was too austere to appeal to the general mass of the Indian people, nor did it satisfy their temperamental need for a transcendental dimension to their religious life. To find this through Samadhi is not easy and can be achieved only by the few. To make it real for the many it must be brought to them from outside through rites and ceremonies which stir the heart and vivify the spirit.

This is what the promulgators of Tantra set out to do; to spread the knowledge that saves; to devise rituals that made the transcendental come alive in the consciousness of individuals according to their temperaments and their ability to apprehend it. The vast number of Tantras, almost all of which are suggested forms of Sadhana, show how much the richness and variety of human personality was taken into account. Shiva, Shakti and Vishnu spoke in many idioms, offering this method here and that there for the listener to ponder and from among which to find the one best suited to his character and situation.

The revival of Hinduism ran along two lines. The first was a revival of Vedic metaphysics. There has always been a philosophical side to Indian religion. It is rich in rational analyses of its doctrines and practices. Collectively these analytical commentaries are referred to as Sankhya. Sankhya represents the intellectual as opposed to the existential school of Vedanta. One of the great systematisers of this period was Shangkara, sometimes called the Conqueror of Buddhism because of the effectiveness with which he upheld the classical tradition of the Vedas against the arguments of the Buddhist Non-conformists. Modern Vedanta as it is understood in the West is largely based on the principles formulated by Shangkara, though it is important, as we shall see, to distinguish between Vedanta as 'the culmination of the Veda' and Vedanta as Shangkara interpreted it.

The second reviving force was the influence of the Tantric Shastras upon the religious practices of the people. The origins of Tantric worship seem to be incredibly remote. Woodroffe traces practices in it which pre-date the Vedas, going beyond India and Chaldea to ancient Egypt. Some of its rituals have much in common with the mystery religions of classical Greece, especially those in which the Great Mother plays a central role. It is essentially a religion which places emphasis on the equality of the male and female principles in nature as dual aspects of the immanent Creator, and its use of sexual imagery to illustrate this is largely responsible for the criticism that the Tantras are obscene.

The Shastra which is most often cited to demonstrate the depravity of Tantric worship is the Panchatattva or secret ritual. This ritual appears to be similar to that of the Eleusinian mysteries of ancient Greece. It was open only to initiates of high degree who were able to participate in it as a spiritual experience in which all the elements involved were regarded as aspects of the Divine. To regard them in any other way not only debased the ritual but worked against the person who degraded it. For this reason the details of the rite were kept secret. One can readily understand why many critics find it difficult to accept that the Panchatattva has Vedic antecedents. It is in many ways a strange form of worship to find in India where meat and alcohol are taboo and sexual continence so highly prized for, as in the rites of Demeter, wine, meat, grain and women were seen as elements not only to be worshipped but actually enjoyed in a series of ceremonial acts. There is, of course, no doubt that the rituals came to be abused as time went on and as secrecy became more lax, but this is the fault of the practitioner and not inherent in the Panchatattva Shastra itself. Whether or not we approve of the Greek, Vedic or Tantric initiates who worshipped in this way, we should at least try to understand what they were trying to do and the spirit in which they were trying to do it. As Woodroffe says of the Tantras as a whole, 'Let those condemn this Shastra who will. That is their affair. But let them first study and understand it.' This he set out to do himself and found the exercise so rewarding that he claimed later that he had never really understood the Vedanta until he had investigated the Tantras.

The view that the Tantras are not Vedic he found to have no basis in fact. On closer examination of the texts and their historical background it is discovered that they are adaptations of Upanishadic Shastras made by the forest anchorites and their successors. At the time their new practices were being devised the direct heirs of the Vedic ritual tradition had become a small minority among a horde of non-Aryan immigrants. The hereditary castes which had maintained the older system in its orthodox form were unable to Aryanise the mixed population of the new India and, if it had been left to the Brahmins of that time, the Vedic teachings would have disappeared. What saved them was the knowledge of Vedic principles and of the Vedic yoga practices among the monastic communities in the forests who, abandoning unworkable rituals and regulations, set to work to contrive means of Aryanising the polyglot masses by reformulating the doctrines of the Upanishads. Their aim was to establish communal forms of worship which could carry the essence of Veda into the lives of the immigrant people who were swarming all over India and were without spiritual guidance. To Aryanise in this sense had nothing to do with race purity. It was a spiritual endeavour towards re-establishing the religious continuity of Hinduism in the way best suited to the times.

This was the Tantric contribution. It needs to be contrasted with that of the hereditary Brahmin caste which tried, with diminishing success, to maintain the 'pure' Hindu orthodoxy with all its customary exclusiveness. It was against the ritual formalism of this latter group that the followers of Buddha rebelled. What survived was Tantric Hinduism with its temple worship for the masses, its rituals for family devotions in the home and its new formulations of the old teachings for those wishing to tread the yoga path. Indian Buddhism only survived against this background because it became itself considerably Tantricised, emerging finally in its

Mahayana form. For all its shortcomings at various times in its long history, Tantric Hinduism cannot be separated from the Vedic tradition which could not have endured unless it had been preserved by the promulgators of the Tantras.

Woodroffe found the criticism that the Tantras were treatises on black magic largely rested on the fact that the Indian Shastras aim at giving practical advice. This meant that there was inevitably a great deal of incidental occultism taught in order that the experiences sought might actually be gained. This is as true of the Upanishads as of the Tantras. In itself such knowledge is not good or bad. The religious assumption would be that the knowledge being imparted only to initiates would be well used. It is undoubtedly true that this was not always the case. The debasement of occult powers, however, was not encouraged by the Tantrika, the followers of Tantra, any more than it would have been by the compilers of the Arthavaveda. This Veda is equally full of magical lore and describes very similar practices.

The modifications in practice introduced by the Tantrika included a widening of the conditions of entry into its Sadhanas to include women and members of the Shudra caste, the so-called 'untouchables'. This was a very radical departure from orthodox Vedic exclusiveness which confined its initiation rituals to men of the three superior castes, the priests, warriors and businessmen. It is due to Tantric influence that there are women gurus and that women are so much honoured in India today. The Shakta branch of Tantric Hinduism so respects the Divine in the feminine that it is claimed that greater benefit accrues from initiation by a woman and that this is enhanced eightfold if she is a mother. Those familiar with the life and work of Sri Aurobindo will know what an honoured place was reserved for the Mother in his Ashram and how impressive was her contribution to the spiritual life of their community in Southern India.

There are always those who are unable to make a ritual 'come alive' and those who cannot see that an image can 'stand for' a divinity without being an actual physical incarnation of it. Such people can never really understand religion as a spiritual activity. To understand Tantric ceremonial practices one must accept the Hindu view that matter has two aspects, one physical and one mental, and to be able to regard thought as a force which can influence gross matter and be influenced by it. Unless one can do this Indian religion must remain a closed book. In Eastern thought spiritual reality is primary. In it all is One, eternal and unchanging. It is the transcendental world of the Gods and Goddesses, the Devas and Devis. In their own proper forms (Svarupa) Devas and Devis are all aspects of the one Brahman, latent aspects in transcendental Brahman, potent aspects in immanent Brahman. This is why the devotee can say in one breath 'All is Brahman' and in the next 'All is Shiva. All is Shakti. All is Vishnu.' Brahman as transcendent is changeless. Brahman as immanent is the changeless cause of all the changes created by the Devas and Devis who are His emanations. Man as a spiritual being has similarly a transcendental side to his nature. By virtue of this he is part of unchanging Brahman as well as part of the immanent Brahman who is the universe. Because of this the humblest untouchable as well as the holiest sage can say 'I am Brahman.' The aim of the Hindu Sadhaka is to find this Brahman in himself and so be freed from the need to experience the world as a place of suffering. Unless one realises this one cannot properly understand what the Hindu who has real 'competence' is doing when he worships, when he meditates and when he recites the prescribed Mantras.

Let us take some examples. In Indian psychology what a man thinks about shapes the mental matter of his mind and modifies its quality. Since the minds of most of us are never empty, the important thing is to fill them with the right things. Thus to dwell upon the Divine is to shape one's mind in a lofty mould. The more often this is done the more easily the mind falls into this mould. Hence the value of the regular practice of meditation (Dhyana) and the recitation of Mantras (Jappa). Moreover, because mind and body interact they can reinforce one another in attempts to realise the Brahman within. Worship should be not only a matter of words and thoughts but also of bodily movements. The Tantras have therefore contrived a complex system of Mantras, Asanas (postures) and Mudras (gestures), allocating to each aspect of the Divine what the worshipper may seek to embody in his own nature through its own special pattern of worship.

The Indian worship of images is therefore not only a more subtle affair than most Westerners give it credit for, but also far more selective. The devotee is helped to find the divinity most suited to his needs and this then becomes his Ista Devata, his personal divinity. His aim is to try to put life into a representation of his Ista Devata and, this done, to draw the vitalised thought-form back into himself. This is called the rite of 'giving life'. It is not the same as the Catholic's adoption of a saint as an intercessor. The God sought is not remote but within. Thus prayer is not a device the Sadhaka uses to remind God of his needs. God is presumed to know these already. It is a device to remind the mind that 'All is Brahman' or, in specific circumstances, 'All is Ista Devata.' The procedure, therefore, is one of using the life of the mind to create with the help of the concrete image a vital inner image of a living Deva or Devi and then to bring this divine essence into one's very body. This enables it to influence the quality of one's entire inner being. It is the height of arrogance and unimaginativeness for Christians to assume that 'heathens' actually worship sticks and stones either in India or Africa as so many tend to do.

A typically Tantric rite is a Mantra form of Sadhana called Nyasa. Nyasa means 'placing' and the ritual consists of literally using the fingers or the palm of the hand to place the thought of a Devata in different parts of the body. The thought is embodied in a special Mantra, the Bija or 'seed-mantra' of the chosen Devata. Only a body-affirming religion would have conceived such a practice and, once again, the idea is to remind both mind and body that the Divine is already present there. Seed-mantras need to be given to the Sadhaka because Mantra Vidya, the science of Mantra, has evolved a complete system in which each divine aspect has its own Bija and only those with special training can use such Mantras safely. The repetition of Mantras (Jappa or recitation) was never meant to become a mechanical activity. Mantra comes from 'man' and 'tra' and so means thought that saves. Unless the mind is involved, therefore, Jappa is just a meaningless movement of the mouth.

This element of reminding is brought into all aspects of

Indian life and the simpler the devotee the more he needs the
help of concrete symbols and ritual acts to aid his imagination and so bring the Divine into the life of every day. The
dressing and tending of 'dolls' so decried by critics of Indian
popular religion is a daily reminder that Brahman is ever-
present and no least thing one does is done apart from him.
Properly the offerings made to these inanimate things are
sacrifices of oneself made in gratitude for this knowledge.

To understand Kundalini and Kundalini yoga we must
think of them against this background. Kundalini is a Shakti,
a manifestation of the 'feminine' side of Brahman. It is therefore part of the Great Mother out of whose womb the
universe emerges as a continuous unfolding of immanent
Brahman. Its importance in Tantric yoga is that Kundalini is
the Shakti with particular responsibility for physical forms. It
is sometimes called Shabdabrahman in bodies. Shabda means
sound, but not sound as generally understood and which
Tantrikas call the sound of two things knocking together. It
is sound as a causal agency within the creative process; sound
which, like speech, has both power and significance. It is
because it is a manifestation of meaning that a Mantra is a
formative force. It is essentially a significant sound which
loses its efficacy if said without understanding or repeated
parrotwise. Knowledge of the way Kundalini works in the
body and how it is related to sound is basic to the safe and
effective use of Kundalini yoga. This knowledge has largely
been lost in recent times which may well explain why Gopi
Krishna was unable to find a guru to help when he found
himself struggling with a sudden upsurge of uncontrollable
forces from the base of the spine.

A further reason why there is currently so much confusion,
particularly in the West, about what Kundalini is is that
Indian theories about Kundalini and the Chakras or force
centres in the subtle body through which it works, have been
filtered through one or other of the 'Theosophies'. Indeed it
was to books about them written by clairvoyants and
occultists of various Theosophical persuasions that I first
went for information. It was only when I found myself
confused by discrepancies between their usages and those in
translations from the Sanskrit that I decided to go to sources

before confusion became worse confounded. From reading Sri Aurobindo, that greatest of modern Tantric yogis, I also realised how great some of these discrepancies were. Some terms now current in Theosophical literature are, in fact, used in quite other senses in Hindu writings. Deva is a case in point. Other deviant usages will be noted as we go along. It is important to do this because, valuable as has been the Theosophical contribution to widening our ideas, in trying to integrate Kundalini into Western science we need to use terminology as unambiguously as possible. Otherwise our Eastern friends will misunderstand our science as we have apparently misunderstood theirs.

To see how Tantric yoga can be reinterpreted for modern consumption by someone with first-hand experience of how to bring risen Kundalini down for use in daily life, Sri Aurobindo's books are invaluable. His Integral Yoga is not only a reformulation of Tantric yoga in a form which can be safely practised, it also deals with a stage in which many of us find ourselves and which we need to understand better. This is the stage when, in the first glow of dawning enlightenment, the ego becomes aware of the ever-present self and its greater potential but does not know how best to relate to it.

Innumerable teachers of yoga have stressed that attempts to raise Kundalini by meditating on individual Chakras is dangerous, indeed 'disreputable' yoga practice. This is not merely due to a dislike of Tantra in general. It is practical good sense. Too much knowledge has been lost, and in any case it is not the best or simplest way for modern man to achieve ego-transcendence. Those who know about the behaviour of the Jivatman, the embodied spirit in man, say that Kundalini wakes of itself as we develop in ourselves qualities and attitudes conducive to its arousal. The illumined guru can tell where it is and how awake it is from a person's moral and spiritual condition. Only those not ready will try to force its pace and only the unwise or the unfortunate will raise it prematurely. There will be time enough to play master to nature when we can manage ourselves. Just trying to do this in the circumstances of today is the best yoga path for most of us in the West, for nowhere is the ego so strong and yet so constricted by a too-materialistic humanism than in our affluent and so-called advanced societies.

Not trying to raise Kundalini is not the same as not trying to understand what it is and how it is said to work by those who once claimed to know how to manipulate it systematically. No one has yet devised instruments which will enable us to study the Chakras by current scientific methods. All attempts to trace them instrumentally have so far failed, though many clairvoyants have claimed to see them. The same is true of the acupuncture points and lines which for thousands of years have been used diagnostically and therapeutically in China. If Kundalini is a natural force we have as yet only the accounts of the seers to go to for clues as to how it might work.

From studying the texts it seems likely they were written by men who had the extended vision still to be found among practised clairvoyants. Most of us seem not to have this or, alternatively, to have lost the use of it due to the dominance of the cerebral cortex and evolutionary pressures to develop the rational mind. It is, however, relatively common among children and primitive peoples. Many yogis seem to have it. Dr Karagulla's study (34) of similarly gifted subjects in the United States indicates that a considerable number of them exist among professional people and business executives some of whom are not even aware that they perceive more than those around them. Ryzl's work (67, 68) on the trainability of ESP raises the possibility that our perceptive capabilities may be wider than our use of our faculties presently suggests. Possibly biofeedback techniques to extend human acuities as tools for research only await science's willingness to admit that other-dimensional realities may exist and may conceivably become perceptible as evolution proceeds. It would be a beginning if we could hear as much as bats or see ultra-violet light like bees. We might not then need to put electrodes on our roses to become aware of the quiet music they apparently produce, nor use Kirlian photography to see the coloured cloud of particles and micro-organisms surrounding them. There is nothing in the nature of matter to suggest this is inherently impossible. On the contrary, advances in microbiology confirm at every stage the infinite plasticity and responsiveness of living cells. One only has to consider the miracles of diversification performed in the womb sparked off by only two of them. Even our genetic mechanisms are less rigidly programmed than was once thought. A virus infection of sufficient virulence can bring about a mutation. Who knows? We may yet have to bring Lamarck out of mothballs and evaluate the concept of the inheritance of acquired characteristics all over again.

If we did find we could train up suitable sensitives and use them in research, we should, of course, be landed with massive problems of interpretation. These may prove no greater, however, than those facing a man born blind suddenly confronted with the visual world. Or, indeed, those faced by scientists using electron microscopes for the first time. Extended senses in all these cases would be operating within an environment already familiar in other ways. We would not be working in territory completely without landmarks. In biology a sensitive could not be expected to interpret scientifically the things he sees going on in the body and come up with the right answers without specialist training. But if he described them to a physiologist we might have better luck. A partnership of this sort could be very fruitful, as the work of Payne and Bendit showed. She had been clairvoyant from birth with all the attendant problems of distinguishing between the things everyone sees and the things she saw that other people did not. He was a doctor. Together they worked diagnostically in a medical group and also produced several books about the energy organisation of the body's subtler counterpart. (80, 56) That they got all the answers right is doubtful, but, if we focused several such human microscopes on our inner workings, their interpretations could be used to correct and amplify one another. We might in this way get material for hypotheses which could later be explored experimentally.

It was with some such idea of combining the insights of seers and scientists that I went back to the Tantric texts concerning Kundalini. I felt strongly that we were dealing with something more than images and symbols to be meditated upon merely as meaningful abstractions unrelated to human physiology and the working of nature. I hoped to find out how justified this feeling would prove to be on closer examination.

3
The Tantric cosmos

Before one can write meaningfully about specific texts one must first set the Chakras (force centres) and the Nadis (force channels) of the Kundalini system within the wider framework of Indian theories of man and nature. As far as the Tantras are concerned, this means never forgetting that man is an embodied soul and therefore part of nature and at no level isolated from the cosmic dance.

This would seem to be an eminently sensible approach since every exercise of our minds, whether it be looking at a map or contemplating Nirvana, is taking place within our embodied selves. When one sits and lets one's imagination roam the world, it is still firmly anchored in the body to which the projected self returns as is also the memory which records the journey. The same is true when one dreams or has an out-of-the-body experience. The body only appears as something separate on the bed or the operating table. In Tantric yoga the enlightenment sought by the Sadhaka is similarly one to be experienced by him in the flesh. He recognises that, while living, to know what disembodied states of enlightenment are like is impossible.

The dichotomy between soul and body, between mind and matter, so characteristic of Western thought is quite absent from Indian philosophy. The dualism which tends to arise in Eastern thought is not between mind and matter but between the natural world, seen as an illusion created by the senses, and reality, seen as Brahman; between nature and God. This is the basis of the Hindu philosopher Shangkara's distinction between true and false knowledge and his equation of the phenomenal universe, or Maya, with illusion. It caused, within classical Hinduism, a dichotomy between the creator and the creation which neither Shangkara nor any of his followers has managed entirely to overcome. A similar split between God and the phenomenal world never arose in Tantric cosmology. As a nature-affirming system, it set phenomenal reality within and not over against Brahman. In experience veils of Maya render our perceptions of ultimate reality in varying degrees partial rather than false. As the soul evolves, Avidya, knowledge of the phenomenal world, does not have to be rejected but transformed, until finally Maya is transcended and it no longer sees through a glass darkly. Avidya then becomes Vidya, complete knowledge of the essential nature of things.

In Hinduism and the various forms of Buddhism which stem from it, cosmology starts with Brahman. Brahman is God as the One which is also the All. In this Absolute nothing is differentiated but all is latent. It is into this Brahman state of being that the Mahayogi, the truly enlightened yogi, is lifted at the height of his meditation. A similar state is described in different language by the mystics of other religions. The Tantricist would recognise that all references to Brahman would denote not Brahman as he is in himself, but Brahman as experienced by an embodied bit of himself. The Brahman we know is therefore in a sense the product of our own experience of something vast and vital to which we give this name. It is important to remember this because it enables us to conceive enlightenment and the bliss associated with the Divine as something our bodies can encompass. To say this is not to say there is no Brahman apart from us. This is something we cannot possibly know one way or the other. Nor does this really matter either to us or to science. What does matter is that looking at religious experiences in this light makes it easier to accept rationally the fact that many people have them and that science should attempt to account for them along with other phenomena which it is currently disregarding, largely because it does not know how to classify them. Just because people feel dissociated from their bodies does not mean that they are actually resident in their disembodied minds. The problem is rather where are they in relation to the body and what is the 'they' we are talking about.

Indian psychology makes it easier to avoid such a mind-body dichotomy. Its tendency to personalise forces, however, has given its terminology a mythological flavour which has made it difficult for Western scholars to recognise the scientific value of its findings. Cosmic forces disguised as gods and goddesses are not readily seen as polarities in nature by hard-headed scientists. Moreover, a mixture of puritanism and a religious preoccupation with monotheism inclines many of us to regard polytheism of any sort as benighted and tied up with all sorts of excesses. Consider the dubious behaviour of the members of the Greek pantheon and the shocking sexuality of temple carvings in India. All that is austere and intolerant in the Judaic, Christian and Islamic traditions has often prevented us from taking seriously the insights which lie behind the stories of the Gods and their traffic with men. Like the 'Tantra' the ancient gods have fallen into disrepute. We fail to see how skilfully ritual and imagery were used to convey the manifoldness of the universe as well as its underlying unity.

On closer inspection the religions of India, Greece and Egypt do not appear any less monotheistic than our own. The personalising of natural forces is a common human tendency and the average man still thinks concretely and anthropomorphically. Subtleties readily elude him. This may well have been why their priests embodied religious truths in stories and taught through rites and ceremonies. With gods abounding, however, one can see how easily a scientist could assume that such subjects as Kundalini were matters for yogis and the theologians rather than for psychobiologists.

Ascribing to Brahman the role of first cause of the created universe, the Hindu sees the process of manifestation as the work of Brahmanic emanations. The creative impulse is associated with Brahman as Ishvara. The One-ness, the element of uniqueness in created things, is preserved throughout the universe by Brahman as Atman. The Jivatman is thus the divine Self in the Jiva, the individual human being. The actual work of manifestation is carried on through Mahashakti and her hierarchy of lesser Shaktis. She is the power of Brahman at work in the cosmos.

The difference between the masculine and feminine emanations of Brahman appears to be a difference between forces generating experience and forces generating energy. For this reason gods and goddesses are often shown in pairs and are often given the same name with different endings. Thus when referring to Brahman in the act of creation Ishvari or Ishvarashakti may be used to stress the active mode. Elements in which consciousness, awareness, predominate are regarded as passive and their names have masculine endings as, for instance, Purusha (the conscious self in man) and Maya (nature in its phenomenal aspect). Elements in which the form, the pattern of forces, is prepotent are regarded as active and are given names with feminine endings as in Shakti (energy or power) and Prakriti (nature as an active field of forces).

The created universe is interpenetrated at all points by Brahman and all his emanations in a way which makes it essentially a hologram. For the purposes of analysis, however, it can be divided into two interacting aspects. There is phenomenal subjective consciousness which is Maya and phenomenal objective nature which is Prakriti. As Ishvara-Ishvari together create layer upon layer of increasingly complicated forms in the natural world of Prakriti so increasingly thick veils of Maya surround consciousness. In this process matter becomes progressively more solid and opaque. Maya is seldom understood in this sense. This is because the Swamis who most influenced the way in which Hinduism has reached the West have mostly been followers of Shangkara, tending to equate Maya with illusion. Many Theosophical writers use the two words as synonymous. This would not be the Tantric view.

In both the Upanishads and the Tantras knowledge is divided, as we have seen, into Vidya and Avidya. According to Sri Aurobindo, Vidya is knowledge of Being and the underlying unity of all things. Avidya is knowledge of Becoming and the diversity of the manifested universe, knowledge of Maya and Prakriti. Shangkara and his followers read the Upanishads as implying that only Vidya was real knowledge which led them to conclude that Avidya was only a semblance of knowledge and essentially misleading. Sri Aurobindo, on the other hand, regarded both Vidya and Avidya as equally real, differences depending upon where at any given stage in evolution consciousness is mainly focused. Thus, as one rises through Maya insights deepen, transforming Avidya progressively into Vidya. In his Integral form of Tantric yoga it is possible to think of these transformations as gradually cleansing our perceptions at sensory, instinctive, emotional and intellectual levels of mind. What is involved is metanoia, seeing the familiar world in new ways.

All parts of the individual are thus conceived as participating in what amounts to an evolution of awareness within an increasingly sensitive and responsive physical vehicle. Tantric psychology, unlike our own, can therefore remain unitary. It can retain within its province what Western science pushes into neuropsychology at one end and parapsychology at the other. It avoids breaking up what should be humanology into bits which science, as currently organised, cannot readily fashion into a coherent whole.

The part of man which experiences Maya is called the Mayapurusha and it reacts differently to different densities of matter. It is therefore given distinguishing prefixes to indicate at what level consciousness is mainly concentrated at any given time. Only the Parapurusha, the Supreme Purusha, transcends the limitations of Maya. This Purusha is sometimes called Shiva and is an aspect of Brahman embodying truth and preserving it at the core of our being. Only this part of the Jiva is capable of Vidya, pure knowledge of the essence of things. Vidya is sometimes called Vijnana or Brahman knowledge to distinguish it from the form of Avidya which is called Jnana or mental knowledge. The distinction is between the truth-knowing soul and the truth-seeking soul; between the Parapurusha and the Jnanamayapurusha and their respective approaches to reality. It is the in-dwelling Shiva, the divine Purusha at the level Sri Aurobindo calls supramental, which enables us, in Samadhi states of enlightenment, to experience Brahman as the One and the All. He is individualised Brahman in souls as Kundalini is individualised Brahman in bodies. It is because they are both surrogates of

Brahman that they are personalised as divinities.

In Kundalini yoga Shiva is associated with the Chakra at the crown of the head and Kundalini with the Chakra at the base of the spine. As we shall see, the partnership of these two Brahmanic emanations and the polarity of the energies connected with them are basic assumptions of Tantric science. Kundalini yoga is the systematisation of the practical knowledge of the ancient Rishis who elaborated the study of the Chakras and Nadis as nodes and energy channels in the subtle body. They taught that before one could hope to become one with Shiva one must first learn to understand and work with Kundalini-Shakti, the Kundalini system of forces. This is because the matter of the body must be refined until it is in a state called Bodhi and Kundalini is the major synthesiser of forces while the Jivatman is in the flesh. The Bodhi body is the most spiritual vehicle used by the Jivatman, the embodied divinity in man. It is sometimes called the causal body by the Hindus because it is it, and not the mind, which ultimately determines all that we are and do. It is in Bodhi bodies that the Bodhisattvas of Compassion are said to remain incarnate while they wait, voluntarily staying to help humanity until all beings can be freed from the bondage of birth, suffering and death. Kwan Yin is perhaps the best known and best loved of these Bodhisattvas. Because the Bodhi body is a causal one she can at will clothe herself in grosser forms if her missions of mercy should require it. Only the Purusha in the Bodhi body can become one with Shiva, which is why even the most saintly of us cannot remain permanently in states of enlightenment.

Compared with the Bodhi body which is composed of a single type of substance, the mental body of Indian psychology is a much more complex affair. It is called the Suksma Sharira or subtle body to distinguish it from the gross body or Sthula Sharira. The causal, subtle and gross bodies together constitute the structural components of man's tripartite organisation.

In the Tantric system mental matter is conceived as having variable densities comparable with those of physical matter and, like solids, liquids and gases, blending in different ways in mixed operations. It assumes four kinds of mind-stuff.

Taking them in descending order as emanations from Bodhi, the first to manifest is Buddhi. This is the form of energy which makes thought possible. It mediates generalised, impersonal conscious processes. In spite of their nominal similarity, Bodhi and Buddhi are quite distinct material categories. The former, being the stuff of the causal body, is a supramental form of matter. Buddhi is not supramental at all but a refined form of purely mental energy. At its most evolved Buddhi enables the Jivatman to think abstractly, but even at less developed stages it gives thought the quality of detachment.

Ego-centredness and self-awareness permeate thought processes via a form of mind-stuff called in Sanskrit Ahangkara. This energy modifies Buddhi, making consciousness personal by introducing I-ness. With it arises the capacity to be a subject, an experiencer, distinct from the world of objects experienced. Buddhi and Ahangkara constitute the two distinctively human levels of mind. Animals are not deemed to be self-aware or capable of detached intelligence. In children one can watch them developing as they turn from little animals into people. At first they do not seem to be conscious of needs as personal, and the way they designate themselves shows incomplete ego-distinction. To begin with they refer to themselves by the names given to them by others. It is only later that Tommy and Jenny become I and You. In the same way thought is at first concrete and instinctive. As every teacher knows, the capacity for objectivity and abstract thought comes later if, indeed, it comes at all. In other words, in some people the higher energies latent in their mental bodies may never be employed.

It is the Buddhi-Ahangkara energies in man which mediate self-determination and self-control and so make spiritual progress possible. It is into them that the Jivatman infuses the formative energies from above, correcting the distortions in our basic nature made by impacts from the phenomenal world. These energies are forever descending into Buddhi which is itself an emanation of Bodhi and therefore the carrier of the divine intention for a particular Jiva from causal into mental matter. This intention is an inherent and immutable part of ultimate reality so that it imposes laws equally inherent and immutable. What seems random and changeable is not in Buddhi but in the Purusha's interpretation of reality as he sees it. Pure Buddhi is that aspect of mental matter most akin to Atman, the means by which the universal can be individualised and yet remain detached from the rest of Maya of which it is a part. The Buddhimaya-purusha is a witness Purusha, a spectator of the play of nature, sanctioning it and enjoying it but taking no part in the action.

Ahangkara is that which makes individualising forces personal. It mediates the sense of I-ness. It is the form of mental matter associated with Shiva-Shakti as divine partners. In the Bodhi body the Shiva-Shakti combination of principles qualifies the true self so that it is experienced as a person, a doer as well as a spectator. Carried down into Buddhi, the personal element, one stage further from the Brahman self, becomes human and therefore more vulnerable. It loses touch with its own identity with the One and the All. The I begins to experience nature, Prakriti, as something separate. As this personal element descends, universality seems to pass from the Purusha, the Shiva aspect, into Prakriti, the Shakti aspect, until man comes to feel himself more subject to natural law than in command of the phenomena consciousness creates and sanctions. Thus the Purusha progressively falls away from the Shiva state of 'resting in the self' as it leaves the causal body and enters the Sukshma Sharira. The Shiva state is even more difficult to hold on to once it becomes embodied in the gross matter of the Sthula Sharira and Maya's densest veils surround it. This is because the self contracts into the ego, the Parapurusha into Purushas which feel more isolated and more governed from without the thicker the veils of Maya which surround them. Finally, at the level of physical matter each Purusha experiences itself as alone, subject to people and objects to the behaviour of which it must adjust. This alienation of I from Other, not Maya as such, is the great illusion and the prime cause of the distortions which it is the purpose of yoga to correct. And it is the presence of the Brahman self, as the magnet which induces the field within which this all happens, that ensures that this correction is not only possible but an evolutionary necessity.

Kundalini yoga puts the human predicament into the image of the separation of Shiva and Shakti and their reunion through the activities of Kundalini. In the lowest Chakra Kundalini waits upon the time when the Purushas under bondage to Maya seek her aid. As she rises from Chakra to Chakra up the spine, her cleansing presence brings new insights. The Purusha increasingly becomes able to see the Other as less alien and the way is paved for the reunion of Purusha and Prakriti, Shiva and Shakti, which culminates finally in the limitations imposed on the self by the ego being transcended. Kundalini will by then have sufficiently refined matter for the Purusha to rise into the Bodhi body. It is then that Kundalini, as the Shakti above all other earthly Shaktis, can reunite with Shiva, the Purusha above all other earthly Purushas. The Samadhi experience of this yoga is the result of the body being able to encompass this state of 'resting in the self'. Hindus sometimes call this state simply Shiva and it is the work of Kundalini which enables us to achieve it while still in the flesh.

The Ishvara-Ishvari aspect of Brahman works in mental substance as the creative imagination, reflecting within Maya the powers of divine ideation which brought the universe out of the void of absolute latency. Its energies suffuse all types of mind-stuff and are responsible for the patterning of phenomena in nature and in subjective states of consciousness.

Sri Aurobindo categorises three grades of Buddhi all of which are infused with I-ness. Lowest is what he calls elementary reason. At this primitive level the mind is dominated by the senses and biological drives. Its capacity to manipulate data is limited as is the ability to foresee and plan. Intermediate reason is still predominantly based on needs and drives. It is largely instinctive, leaning heavily on stereotypes and norms current in the community. It produces the conventionally conditioned person. It is not until the highest level of mind-stuff can be used that the individual can free himself from stereotypes and apprehend reality in ways which are not sense-bound. It is only with the development of higher reason that the truth can be sought for its own sake. This is the realm of the Jnanamayapurusha where knowledge of the kind found in science and philosophy becomes possible. Vijnana or divine wisdom is not Buddhi-knowledge as some Theosophical writings suggest. From the Tantric standpoint such cosmic truth is only available to the Purusha in the Bodhi-body, to the self operating at levels which transcend both ego and mind. The similarity of the terms Bodhi and Buddhi may account for the elevation of Buddhi to Bodhi status by some Theosophists. Sanskrit is a subtle language and the two words may well derive from a common root.

Manas is the next form of mental matter to arise in the involutionary process whereby Brahman descends through Maya and Prakriti. For neither Sri Aurobindo nor the scholars consulted by Sir John Woodroffe is this Manas the same as the Manas of Theosophical literature. (3, 8, 38) In these latter it is divided into higher and lower Manas and associated respectively with abstract and concrete thought. These, as we have seen, would be allocated to the intermediate and higher reaches of Buddhi in the Indian system. Manas in Tantric psychology animates the sensory mind. It is responsible for organising sensations into perceptions and needs into instinctive and reflex response patterns. The senses or Indriyas belong here and are to be distinguished from the sense-organs of the dense physical body. The Indriyas are divided into the knowledge senses (Jnana Indriyas) and the action senses (the Karma Indriyas) corresponding in the subtle body roughly to the sensory and motor divisions of the physical nervous system. That sensations are essentially of the mental and not the gross body is demonstrated by the fact that all of them can be experienced by yogis without any stimulation of the sense-organs at all. The same is true of ordinary people under hypnotic suggestion. For this reason the Hindus distinguish more clearly than we do between physical objects and their supersensible counterparts. These supersensible counterparts are conceived as purely mental constructs and are called Tanmatras. The Tanmatra corresponds to what philosophers call universals, things as members of a general class of objects rather than particular instances.

In human beings sensations selected out and synthesised automatically by Manas are not registered until Ahangkara makes them personal and Buddhi makes them conscious.

Responses depend largely on how they are systematised and presented to the Purusha at the Buddhi level where they are perceived as meaningful gestalts. What the Purusha makes of them is influenced by the thickness of the Maya veil surrounding it, in other words whether one can think for oneself, can think only through conditioned ideas or thinks blindly from one's instincts.

According to Indian psychology and contrary to appearances, all our real decisions are made by the Jivatman, the embodied spirit, and not the conscious self at ego level. This is because it is the self in the causal body which is the agent of Brahman and custodian of the form on which each life is based. It activates Buddhi, and it is to it and not to us as egos that Buddhi is answerable. Buddhi is influenced by ego-reactions, but it only presents its findings to us — little as we may welcome this idea — when higher authority considers our awareness is required. The wisdom of this arrangement is demonstrated on the one hand by the disturbances of behaviour which can result from misguided ego-intervention and on the other by the efficiency of the many unconscious processes upon which our physical and mental health depend. Indians also view Buddhi as the medium through which karmic influences, effects of our actions in past lives, are brought to bear on us as predispositions. This is done by inducing biases at various levels of personality which then operate reflexively as characteristic types of proneness.

The densest kind of mental matter is Chitta. Sri Aurobindo and Sir John Woodroffe describe the nature of Chitta rather differently but both are in agreement that it is the stuff of memory and recall. Sri Aurobindo calls it the basic mind-stuff which supports all mental operations while Sir John Woodroffe stresses the priority of Buddhi since it permeates all the mental instruments emanating from it. The difference proves more apparent than real on closer inspection. In one sense Chitta is indeed basic since without memory our development as thinking beings would have been impossible. Ontologically, however, Chitta, Manas and Ahangkara are all modifications of Buddhi. In this sense Buddhi is basic, as Sri Aurobindo and Sir John Woodroffe's scholarly advisers all agree.

In Sri Aurobindo's account Chitta has two modes. As a passive principle it acts as a subconscious memory store, receiving impartially impacts from the environment. These can come up vertically from the sense-organs and the life-vehicle, or be received horizontally as telepathic impressions. As an active principle it meets the demands for recall by producing the required information. It binds together bundles of habits, physical, nervous and emotional. In this role it helps to preserve the integrity of personality and maintain the mind-body connection. It operates at the level of the Kamamayapurusha, the desire soul, so called because of the way Chitta ensures that the needs and drives of the instinctive nature are met through its agency. In terms of nature in general Chitta maintains the continuity of forms as habits held together by a primitive kind of memory. The cell memory of which biologists speak would be of this sort. Also the atomic memory of the physicist and the molecular memory of the chemist. Teilhard de Chardin's (18) conception of consciousness and matter evolving together and Max Planck's (57) mentoid particle make better sense once memory is thought of in this way.

Chitta is readily modified by association with other kinds of matter, as we have seen. It receives impacts from the gross body and from the life-vehicle or Prana sheath. It organises them into bundles of habits which form the basis of instinctive and reflex responses. It stores subconscious memories for use in higher mental processes. It is the desire level of mind operating, with nervous and Pranic energies, to give instinctive drives their psychological components. It combines with physical and psychic Pranas, which in turn are modified by Manas, to turn sensations into perceptions. It is not until the Purusha is beginning to function at the level of Buddhi, however, that the ability to manipulate this data conceptually can start to emerge. Reason is at first practical and relatively elementary with little infusion of Ahangkara or self-awareness. Pragmatic thinking in terms of norms and stereotypes is seen as giving way gradually to high-grade self-critical thought and sensitivity of response to presenting situations. Judgments are progressively freed from stereotypes and values from self-interest.

In Indian psychology these four types of mind-stuff taken together, penetrating one another and combining in a wide variety of mixed operations, constitute the Antahkarana. Literally Antahkarana means internal instrument and the term is used in contradistinction to Bahyakarana or the external instruments which are the five knowledge senses, the five action senses and the basic sensory categories by means of which we distinguish one kind of sensation from another. Antahkarana as thus used should be particularly noted by students of Alice Bailey's Tibetan writings. Here the Antahkarana and Bahyakarana are natural constituents of all subtle bodies. The Tibetan's Antahkarana seems to be a bridge entity between ego and self which is not given but has to be fashioned by human effort. The common denominator would seem to be the idea of the mind as an instrument which is also the link between the divine self within and the gross body through which it manifests in the physical world. What the Tibetan master appears to be stressing is that, in its natural state, it is a crude instrument the refining of which cannot be left to the forces of evolution alone. We must ourselves contribute to its tempering. Which is, of course, essentially the yogic view. In Tantric science the fact that the natural instruments must be refined is implicit not only in the practice of Kundalini yoga but in its whole theory of evolution.

In using the term ego-transcendence it is important to note that one is doing so in the way the word is used in the West. In Hindu psychology Ahangkara only confers I-ness. It is not a structure but an element in all self-conscious processes. The sense of identity we associate with our egos or conscious selves has two sources: the uniqueness of each Jivatman as a differentiated fragment of Brahman and the separateness of bodies from one another in the physical world. The I-ness deriving from the Jivatman is real and keeps us in touch with our true selves. It is the separateness of bodies and the way memories cluster round them because they go with us everywhere that creates the illusion of a structural ego-complex. It is the illusory ego-complex which yoga aims to disperse so that the I-ness deriving from the Brahman within can suffuse our whole being. Only then can we be truly ourselves, knowing our proper tasks and when and how to do them. Until such time, the further the Purusha is separated from the Brahman self the more isolated and vulnerable it feels and the more self-protective and self-seeking the behaviour of the individual. Extreme egotism is in fact a function of alienation from the rest of the cosmos with its concomitant sense of insecurity. Ego-transcendence is sought, however unconsciously, as a means of healing the rift between the One and the All. The desire for it is an evolutionary urge. It ensures that the One which goes off to explore the Many can never get lost. Like the prodigal son, it will surfeit and become homesick. Life in the small self will be found wanting in the end and a larger self be craved for and ultimately found.

Linking gross and subtle bodies is the life-vehicle or Prana sheath. Prana is another complex subject because the term is used in several senses. In Theosophical literature it is generally confined to what is called the etheric body and is identified with the energy deriving from the Sun which vitalises the physical body. The etheric body is therefore sometimes referred to as the vital body. Sri Aurobindo differentiates between physical and psychic Prana relating the one to vivifying the gross body or food sheath and the other to bringing together life-force and consciousness in the subtle body as it functions within the food sheath.

The connection between Prana and the life principle has led some scholars to talk of finer Pranas energising matter at all levels since all matter is thought of as being alive as well as conscious. This makes it necessary to try to disentangle the relationships between consciousness, mind, life and matter.

In Hindu cosmology the Absolute, Parabrahman as the Unknowable, comes over as an infinite void, a sort of silent Is-ness of Being. Out of this emerges the Absolute as Knowable and to this cosmic state of Brahman is given the composite name of Satchitananda usually translated Being-Consciousness-Bliss. Neither mind nor matter exist at this level. There are no forms. All these arise as creation proceeds. The emergence of the phenomenal world of Maya draws consciousness away from the state of Satchitananda and divides it into Purusha and Prakriti, subjective consciousness manifesting as the experiencer and objective consciousness manifesting as the universe of objects experienced. The evidence for Sat and Ananda lies in the fact that things exist and appear to enjoy existing sufficiently to struggle to survive.

Sri Aurobindo sometimes calls life Chit-Shakti, allying it to active Prakriti rather than to passive Purusha. It is a dynamic power, Brahman at work. Its job is to help build, maintain and dissolve forms, working with nature to create the manifold of entities which is the multidimensional universe. Thus in so far as Prana is equated with life, it must be conceived as a force which operates at all levels of matter and not only in the life-vehicle which would confine it to the border between gross and subtle matter in bodies. As thus conceived Prana is an undifferentiated universal force which only becomes differentiated after entering and vivifying forms. Sir John Woodroffe points out that it is held to have a special relation with Atman which is an undifferentiated spiritual force which becomes differentiated by embodying itself in individual selves. A form, whether spiritual, mental or physical, is, from this point of view, both a nexus of universal forces and an agent of differentiation.

In Tantric psychobiology only human personality to the level of Chitta survives bodily death. The gross body and the life-vehicle are both regarded as transitory, holding together by grace of a combination of Prana and Chitta which unites them to the higher bodies for the duration of a single lifetime. This conception makes the distinction between physical and psychic Prana very important. It means that at death only the former returns to the general store of universal Prana. The life of the subtle body would be unaffected since psychic Prana would go on working in it undisturbed. The Self decides the time of death, withdrawing from the two lower bodies, the Sthula Sharira and the life-vehicle, which, separated from their organising field, simply disintegrate. Their constituents become once more part of the general pool of vital energy and organic molecules available for recycling. The survival of Chitta, however, ensures that there is no loss of personal memories which is presumably why, under appropriate conditions, there can be recall of past lives. What these conditions are reincarnation researchers like

Professor Ian Stevenson have yet to discover. Chitta must also play a mini-reincarnational role during each separate physical incarnation since, in spite of the body itself being constantly changed as cells die and are replaced by new ones, our sense of bodily continuity remains. Presumably this is because of the unbroken chain of conscious and subconscious memories which we associate with it. Memory in one form or another is involved in all types of continuity.

The absence of Kundalini from non-physical forms is especially to be noted in this context since it explains why Kundalini yoga is a yoga in which the physical body, the body of this life, plays an essential role. It also accounts for its nature-affirming character. The terrestrial world in which we find ourselves is not an enemy of the spiritual life. The heavy matter through which we move is not the antithesis of cosmic consciousness but its densest and most inert expression. The space-time we know is not a singular creation but a way of perceiving a multidimensional universe enjoined upon us by the nature of the bodies we inhabit while in physical incarnation. At this level Maya-thickness and Prakriti-density are such that we tend to see the universe as three-dimensional. That, however, is not to say there are no other ways of perceiving it. Science itself has found it necessary to postulate multidimensional space in physics; yoga practice assumes that the matter of our multiple sheaths can be worked on in such a way that perceptual conditions can alter radically. We can so live that our perceptual range can be infinitely widened and the penetrative capacity of our insights infinitely extended.

Such transformations, while directed from the Jivatman within each one of us, could not be achieved in the flesh without the co-operation of Kundalini-Shakti as the representative of Brahman in gross matter. This accounts for her primacy in Tantric yoga, that most this-worldly of all the Raja yoga systems to reach us from the East.

4
Evolution and the breath of Brahman

Prana is sometimes translated by Sanskrit scholars as 'life' and sometimes as 'breath', so that Prani is a term which can mean all living things or all breathing creatures. The life of a universe is said to be one breath of Brahman. On his out-breath it comes into being. When he breathes in all returns to the void. Between one breath and the next is Pralaya, a lull between one creation and the next.

As one would expect in these circumstances, evolution is conceived as circular not linear. First there is an involutionary arc during which Brahman in manifestation descends progressively deeper into matter, generating layer upon layer of Prakriti, proliferating forms in nature of increasing density and structural complexity. Simultaneously the experiencing consciousness is surrounded by a thickening mist of Maya, ensuring an equal richness and diversity of inner states. The seemingly linear phase of evolution starts only when, as far as this planet is concerned, the creative impulse reaches its nadir at the level of dense physical forms and minimal self-awareness. Once the curve of the circle passes its nadir we are on the arc of return, and evolution proper is said to begin, with man spearheading the creation back into the mouth of Brahman. No doubt as millennially slowly as it descended into matter the spirit reascends. In all this process the two have evolved together, matter as the body of spirit and spirit as the soul of matter and both equally Brahman.

From this point of view evolution is seen as a trend which, once established, will involve a thinning of both matter and

Maya as the ascent progresses. This is true both in man and in the cosmos as a whole. If there are intelligent beings else-where in the universe who are ahead of us on the evolutionary path, there may be areas where the rarification process has already started. More backward planets may still be solidify-ing. It is interesting to speculate about our solar system from this standpoint. Could black holes, for instance, be vortices sucking matter out of our physical universe into one which is only our own one floor higher up in a multi-storey cosmic edifice?

Human evolution has a similar circularity. Consciousness descends stage by stage into three bodies under orders from an encapsulated fragment of Brahman seeking manifestation as something to be enjoyed. Stress on the joy of the creator in generating and sustaining the universe is characteristic of Tantric yoga. Indeed, this idea permeates Hinduism generally and is the experience of the Divine which is the lure of yoga. It is bliss, Ananda, even more than enlightenment which is sought in meditation, as can be inferred from the frequency with which the names adopted by Swamis end in 'ananda'. Brahman, it would seem, is no harsh will-to-power forcing us all to be good the hard way. It is our clogged senses which perceive as suffering what could be sustained cheerfully as growing pains had we but eyes to see. It is in order that our eyes may see again that the spirit which became matter sets about dematerialising itself and evolution begins the upward climb. Progressively the Purusha, the experiencing soul, is able to rise above the denser levels of Prakriti where it is blinded by the thickness of Maya into realms where it can enjoy greater freedom and penetrate further into truth. This is the process through which Avidya becomes Vidya, veils of ignorance falling away slowly one by one. The last veil falls when our lesser selves are transcended and our centre of identity becomes the Self. This is when we can experience the blissful state of Satchitananda and know we are home.

This cyclic evolution is seen as encompassing not only creatures but also the creation. Not only does each living thing evolve, but the Earth and the universe as well. Indeed, the Earth,Prithivi, is regarded as being itself a creature, one in which all terrestrial forms inhere like cells in an organism.

Some scientists have come to see the world in this way from their studies in microbiology, but their numbers are still few. Oriental sages have long done so, in both India and China, as the result of direct experiences in the practice of seership and the exercise of intuition. Different tools bringing men to the same conclusions suggest a common basis of facts waiting to be confirmed.

Dr Lewis Thomas in his fascinating set of essays, *The Lives of a Cell*, exploring nature imaginatively as a scientist, speculates about the role of mankind as a cell-system in the body of the Earth. He suggests we probably function as its nervous system. As he points out, there is evidence that we operate in response to more signals than we are conscious of and co-operate in ventures determined by forces we do not control, directed towards ends we do not set. Taking an historical view, it is certain that many important changes are not deliberately willed by anyone, but are the outcome of many apparently unco-ordinated group activities. Human social behaviour resembles the social behaviour of insects in this respect.

It is noteworthy that ideas like this have come to scientists working on the fringes of the imperceptible and far beyond the scope of ordinary sense perception. We can now examine not only the behaviour of sub-atomic particles but also of the micro-organisms which are the minutest living things. Our instrumentally extended vision is bringing home to us that nature is a single system of intricately related sub-systems ultimately dependent on one another. For instance, we have to thank chloroplasts, tiny organisms in the photosynthesising cells of plants, for the oxygen we breathe in from the atmosphere. In addition we have within our own cells an army of mitochondria, micro-organisms which enable us to process oxygen and direct it to the tissues where it is most needed. In respiration we owe as much to the one as to the other.

Mitochondria are not just organelles, minute cell components, they are distinct organisms with their own genes, replicating themselves quite independently of the cell divisions which go on under orders from our own nuclear DNA. They are separate little creatures and how they got into us is a mystery. They behave like amoebas and must have formed a symbiotic partnership with cell cytoplasm millions of years ago and found the arrangement so cosy and mutually rewarding they have made their home in animal tissue ever since. They perform for the animal kingdom the same sort of respiratory function that chloroplasts do for plants. They act in us like billions of tiny supplementary lungs.

Between them mitochondria and chloroplasts have served evolving nature in a way out of all proportion to their size. Plants, with the help of their chloroplasts, take in carbon dioxide in the process of photosynthesis, giving out oxygen and water vapour as waste products. Chloroplasts must have evolved before plants and made possible the growth of vegetation first in the sea and then as mosses and later stiff-stemmed plants on land. Gradually this will have changed the balance of carbon dioxide and oxygen in the oceans and in the atmosphere until more and more life-forms were able to develop and survive on the Earth's surface. The interrelation between the environment, plants and animals is thus seen to be a finely balanced one. Living things do not only depend on the environment; in a very real sense they create it.

It is a moot question which came first, plants or animals. The first minute living entity was probably an equipotential micro-organism capable of being either. Mutation will then have sent some one way and some the other. Unless nature had produced such a creature our own environment could not have developed as it did. As we now know from the experimental work of Stanley Miller and his successors working on the origins of life, (14, 23) the constituents available on Earth at the time the first organic molecules appeared were probably hydrogen, water vapour, methane and ammonia. There was no free oxygen and little or no carbon dioxide, both vital for sustaining life. Somehow the atmosphere had to be changed to one in which the oxygen in suspension in water vapour was freed and the amount of hydrogen in the atmosphere reduced. Somehow also carbon, which forms 99 per cent of living material, had to be disentangled from metal carbides and converted into organic compounds. As we have seen, animals and plants can make profound changes in atmospheric conditions, but what no experiments have yet shown is how they themselves came into being. Miller and his successors, by putting together their 'primal soup' mixture and simulating in various ways the heat, electric storms and ultra violet radiation of the early atmosphere, have produced organic molecules from inorganic ones but never a living organism. Somewhere along the line a new factor must have come in.

Western science, in tackling this possibility, starts out with the assumption of a purely material planet the constituents of which are the products of chemical and physical forces. This means trying to explain phenomena of a higher order in terms of phenomena of a lower one. It is an effort more productive of ingenious than satisfying theories, not only of life but also of mind. Eastern science, asking the same questions, would make very different basic assumptions. In its multi-dimensional world the problem would appear less intractable and the arrival upon the scene of an equipotential micro-organism much easier to explain.

As I understand it, the Hindu explanation would involve the incursion into dense matter of a Pranic element bringing with it a small quantity of Chitta. This would produce minute energy vortices, sites for the transformation of inorganic into organic forms. At these catalytic points equipotential organisms could develop. In other words, minute fields of the type Harold Saxton Burr (12, 13) called life-fields would be generated at electromagnetic levels, patterning chemical substances in the primal soup in new ways. Enzymes would probably then appear, tiny message-carrying molecules which act as catalysts, operating both to transform and to accelerate the pace of change. Theories of the origin of living things which do not include the conception of patterning processes breaking into randomness can never take us far enough. It is not its components which distinguish an organic from an inorganic molecule, but its arrangement. Pasteur saw the connection between life and arrangement long ago, but we tend to overlook the implications of this for evolutionary theory. The problem which needs explaining is not how matter produced life but what is responsible for patterning.

Natural selection is clearly only part of the story. For instance, it can account for the variety of species but it does not really account for the origin of species, for the first primitive organism. Also, as at present understood, it deals primarily with the effect of the environment on living things. We tend to exclude from its ambience the subtle differences made to environments by the activities of those they support so that we readily fail to recognise the essential circularity of the relation between parts of nature and nature as a whole. It is because of this that we have broken into so many ecological systems and are busily altering the balance of oxygen and carbon dioxide in the atmosphere with so little insight into the long-term consequences of what we are doing.

New data is still coming in to make scientific theorising more difficult. The theory that life was somehow generated in flashes of lightning or in the intense heat of the atmosphere while still lacking any ozone-shield against ultra-violet radiation, for instance, must now be looked at again. Deep-sea diving experiments by the Marine Biology Laboratory, Woods Hole, Mass., off Darwin's famous Galapagos Islands, have come up with the discovery of gigantic and extraordinary life-forms more than two miles below the surface. Down there in pitch darkness there would have been no lightning or ultra-violet radiation. There would, however, have been the intense explosive heat which Cyril Ponnamperuna found so effective in his repetition of Stanley Miller's experiments with the primal soup mixture. It is true he added adenine, one of the DNA bases, but he used no electron bombardment or electric charges. Heat and water seem to be more important than electrical energy, which suggests that there is more to a life-field than the electrodynamic forces discovered by Northrop and Burr (53) and measurable by Burr's voltmeter. Scientists have synthesised many organic proteins, those building blocks of living tissue, since Miller made his crucial discovery, but the genesis of organisms remains as baffling as ever.

I use the word genesis advisedly because, since the 1960s, there have been many interesting theories about how organisms may have arrived on Earth from space. Fred Hoyle, for instance, has shown that both organic molecules and viruses are to be found in the interstellar dust. Meteorites could well have brought them to earth from outside, but that would only explain their presence on the earth's surface. It would not explain the strange teeming jungle two miles down off the Galapagos Islands. Nor does it answer the question of how molecules came to be so intricately organised, particularly the nucleic acids of DNA and RNA which have learnt how to replicate. Science assumes that they organise themselves randomly as they joggle about and that natural selection does the rest, but this still leaves us with the residual problem of how they learnt to replicate.

Dr Leslie Orgel (54) of the Falk Institute in California, working in this field, has argued that the nucleic acid molecules must have been the first form of organic matter, since the basic characteristic of living tissue lies in the capacity of its cells to replicate. In other words genes are primary lifeforms. The secret of replication is a particularly challenging problem for Western scientists because they will be trying to explain how in the physical world physical entities have learnt to violate the laws of physics. Strictly speaking molecules joggling about should shake themselves to pieces and, under the terms of the second law of thermodynamics, assist in the general running down of the earth's energy supply. It would seem, therefore, that the laws of life are not physical laws in the currently accepted scientific sense. Invoking the principle of parsimony, it might be simpler at least to toy with the idea that there may be field-forces other than physical field-forces rather than discount it out of hand only to be driven to it by one's data in the end. For if the living world does indeed turn out to be a being, its force-field system must be as multidimensional as our own. To insist on trying to describe its multifarious activities in terms of physical laws alone may well be to put it into a strait-jacket and to sentence our probing minds to the same fate.

Chloroplasts and mitochondria, benign and pathogenic viruses and similar self-replicating unicellular micro-organisms are parts of the earth no more visible to the naked eye than sub-atomic particles. Like sub-atomic particles they are also parts of us, living in symbiosis with us in varying degrees of intimacy. Mitochondria colonise our every cell. Benign bacteria browse harmlessly on our skin and numerous other membranes. Many reside permanently in our bowels without our being any the worse for it. Viruses and bacteria of all sorts pass in and out of our lungs in the air we breathe and heaven alone knows how many such simple organisms enter the alimentary tract with the food we eat. The air swarms with life as well as particles. It is not just so much space around us; it is part of the body of the Earth, vibrant with inert and living matter, streaming forces and interacting fields; it is a communication medium for more than sound. Yogis would say that not only Prana but Chitta, Manas and Buddhi are everywhere, in living things and between living things. That is why it is easier for them to explain phenomena such as telepathy, telekinesis and even teleports, than it is for us. They do not have to invent a set of para-sciences to deal with them any more than they need a concept of supernature. Their view of nature, Prakriti, is wide enough to accommodate all phenomena, sensible and supersensible, material and psychological. The level of nature we tend to confine ourselves to is only one of her many spheres.

Shakti, the power of Brahman at work in the universe, is protean in its manifestations. It can work as spiritual force, consciousness-force, life-force or physical force, all equally forces of nature. The Goddess or Divine Shakti has many names depending upon where, within Prakriti, she is seen to be operating. And because her working is everywhere divine she can be represented in Hindu cosmology by any number of goddesses each with their own distinctive name and sphere of influence. This makes it difficult for the secular and scientifically based Western mind to translate the Shaktis into forces at work in specific areas. The same goes for interpreting the Tantras, as the student soon finds out. Nevertheless to try to do so is well worth the effort even though it means going over the texts many times.

In the physical world Hindu science postulates five states of matter — all material things resulting from combinations of them and all sensory experience depending on them.

The breath of Brahman reaching the world of gross matter first appears as Akasha. Akasha is usually translated 'ether', but Sri Aurobindo in *The Life Divine* and Sir John Woodroffe in *The Serpent Power* describe it in such a way that the more appropriate translation would appear to be 'space' — not space as empty but space as a modification of all the subtler forces which preceded it in order of generation, teaming with spirit, life and thought. This is an idea, incidentally, quite compatible with modern developments in physics.

Akasha, then, is the primary state of physical substance and is conceived as pure extension, unobstructed and so radiating in all directions equally freely. Inherent in it, characteristic of it, are vibration and sound. Vibration carries into dense matter through movement (Spanda) and meaningful sound (Shabda) the first suggestion of possible forms. Vibration and meaning alone cannot produce forms so that out of Akasha there emerges a secondary force-field which introduces into space the ability for energies to interact. By impinging upon one another they offer resistance to the uninterrupted radiation of forces in primary space. Interacting forces, however, do not constitute forms as these are understood in our physical sensory experience. There must be demarcation lines and these demarcation lines are brought into being by the appearance of light and heat, the one outlining forms to the sense of sight and the other to the sense of touch. The arrival of light and heat constitute a third modification of Akasha. Physical forms are not just static in our experience of the world. They expand and contract, repel and attract one another. The ancient Hindu seers associated expansion and diffusion with liquidity and contraction and cohesion with solidity. For them these were the fourth and fifth modifications of Akasha.

These states of matter must not be confused with the elements of modern science. They are essentially ways of perceiving the physical universe, not characteristics of its substance independent of the way in which it is known. The cosmic reality is matter as pure energy. This is non-existent for us until it is converted by the instruments specially designed for the purpose into the changing, transitory, growing and decaying phenomena of sense experience. These instruments, in addition to the Indriyas and Tanmatras of the subtle body, are the sense-organs of the gross body. Together these produce Bhutas or the things the senses perceive as existing in the physical world.

The Tanmatras, as we have seen, are not senses as are the

Indriyas. They are categories of sensation — sight, sound, touch and so on as classes into which sensory experience can be divided. Categories in the Kantian sense, not specific instances of things seen, heard or touched. As Tanmatras are ways of perceiving, Bhutas are categories of things perceived. Thus Akasha is space as that in which we perceive forces operating and which gives forms their context. It is interesting that the ancient Indian physicists associated it with sound, since Western science is now discovering that everything is subtly musical. Radio astronomy and sonar diagnosis in medicine are rapidly expanding branches of scientific research and technology.

In Indian psychobiology touch precedes sight cosmologically as it also does in the development of primitive lifeforms in orthodox theories of evolution. It is associated with the way we know objects by contact with them and so with the perception of resistance and pressure. Light and heat are grouped together as ways of recognising outlines by sight and touch respectively. Liquidity is related to the sense of taste and solidity rather interestingly to the sense of smell. Indians consider smell as an emanation from the dense matter of minerals, plants and animals so that it would be the minute solid elements in such gases as chlorine which provide their odour. Odour is not itself gaseous. Students of Indian physics need, therefore, to be careful how they understand Sanskrit terms such as Akasha which is generally translated as ether, Vayu which translates as air and sometimes breath, Tejas which can be translated as either light, heat or fire, Apas which is water and Prithivi which is earth. None of these are elements in the same sense as earth, air, fire and water would be understood by us normally. Similarly, they need to be clear about the distinction between Tanmatras and Bhutas. Tanmatras are the various major sensory categories imposed on us by the way we are made. Bhutas are categories of physical forces as we find them operating in the objective world and which combine to produce the innumerable forms which impinge upon our sense.

As we have seen already, the impacts received by our sense-organs are worked on by Manas and Chitta together with the Indriyas and Tanmatras before they can become perceptions of objective reality. These may remain unconscious and mediate behaviour of a reflex or instinctive nature. Alternatively, they may be made personal by Ahangkara and conscious by Buddhi and become the basis of voluntary reactions. The test of whether we are perceiving external material objects or figments of our own imagination is whether or not others present can share our experience. Bhutas are at work in a shared physical environment and the objects constructed from them should be perceived by all occupants of gross bodies in roughly the same way, allowing of course for such individual differences as angle of view and sensory deficiences such as deafness or colour blindness.

The Indian view of the physical universe is not a phenomenological one as Western philosophers understand the term. They do not hold that there is no objective reality outside our own consciousness. The outside world exists but it is the product of cosmic consciousness, not of yours or mine. In us cosmic consciousness is divided as far as the outside world is concerned into a contribution from us, our internal and external instruments of perception, and a contribution from nature, the Bhutas in all their manifold combinations. Bhutas belong in a public world and we can compare notes about them. Hallucinations and the eidetic images produced in hypnotic states are private and we have to take one another's word for them.

Now let us return to Hindu evolutionary theory to recapitulate briefly. The universe comes into being with Brahman as the unified field of cosmic consciousness in which all forms of matter and all states of awareness are latent. This field or ocean of consciousness emerges from Parabrahman, the Unknowable, the void. Brahman is a constant, the background and at the same time the static organiser of the whole creative process. It is pure Being from which all proceeds and to which all returns. Everything else is cycles within the great cycle of Becoming. The All becomes the multiplicity of nature, of Prakriti. The One becomes innumerable Purushas which experience themselves as separate from one another and from nature. Maya is phenomenal consciousness which, in · the cycle of Becoming, loses its identity with cosmic consciousness in the descent into matter finally to find it again as the veils of enshrouding substance fall away. The Mayapurusha in man has different names depending on the level of matter in which consciousness is centred at any given time. Thus when the centre of consciousness is in the life-vehicle it is called the Pranamayapurusha; when at the sensory level of mind it is called the Manomayapurusha and so on. The most common translation of Purusha is soul, but the soul as observer, as subject rather than agent. As agent Brahman manifests through the Jivatman and the Shaktis.

The ignorance into which the Purusha falls becomes greater the further it is from contact with the Jivatman, the embodied spirit, the Brahman element at the core of personality. The contact, however, is never entirely lost because the Jivatman remains the organiser of our whole field whether we are aware of it or not. It is our pure Being in which the One and the All are eternally united. It could be regarded as a magnetic centre round which our whole personality lies like an induced field. There are lesser magnetic centres inducing lesser fields, but the Jivatman is organiser-in-chief ensuring that each body and each Purusha comes into manifestation in due order, that involution and evolution proceed according to Brahman's grand design.

On this theory every process is controlled from above. Matter as we know it is the densest substance into which spirit descends. It is created in order that the Purusha may experience life down to the level of Prithivi. Nor is it any good to ask why this is necessary since only the Parapurusha in the true self knows the answer. We must wait upon the transcendence of our limitations as a complex of lesser Purushas before we know also. This is the goal of yogas of enlightenment — to know at least at the end of the journey what it has all been about.

Meanwhile the world we are in is there to be understood; to be enjoyed too if we are lucky; to be made the most of in any case. Trying to understand it is a Jnana yoga way which some of us manage to tread with considerable interest and even pleasurable excitement. In this one finds oneself in the Aurobindo camp rather than that of Shangkara. None of our knowledge may be Vidya, knowledge of ultimate reality, the true being of things; but it is real knowledge nevertheless.

This is because both being and becoming are phases of Brahman. Our scientific and philosophical probings may only produce Avidya, partial knowledge of reality, but this does not mean our findings must inevitably be false. Indeed it ensures the future of knowledge as a system of changing and ever-expanding fields.

This conception of nature as a phenomenal whole controlled from above and involving an integral evolution of mind, life and matter, seems potentially more useful as a model for science than any we have so far contrived in the West. It would appear capable of containing physics, biology and psychology within a single multidimensional framework. It also has the advantage that it can encompass religious experience without forcing it upon those who, like Freud, can find in themselves no evidence of a spiritual self. It would be sufficient for all practical purposes if such scientists were prepared to keep an open mind on the subject. The important thing is for them to review their data from the angle of control from above and the possible need to extend the energy spectrum to include non-physical forces.

Historically science has so far proceeded from what can be seen to what must be inferred from what is seen; from experimental certainties to mathematical speculations. What it has incorporated has been selected methodologically. It has included the life sciences more reluctantly than the physical sciences; psychology and sociology more reluctantly still. It can hardly be said to hear religion knocking on its door. The result of this has been tremendous advances in technology without accompanying advances in our knowledge of human personality, the full range of experiences and behaviours it can mediate and the needs they generate. Our knowledge of nature is similarly hampered. We stumble upon its multidimensionality by accident, mathematics and our microscopes and not by our own perceptiveness forcing it upon our attention. Nor are the implications of what they show us at all easily assimilated because we do not have on hand frames of reference into which they readily fit. We tend to assume creation must always move from the seen to what arises out of the seen and so comes to be seen in its turn. It is this which leads us to think of evolution as a linear physical progress through historic time.

This is surely a Flatlander's view of the world not easily transcended, it seems, even by mathematicians. (69) It is not necessary to divide body from mind nor man from nature in order to attribute causal properties to force-fields generated at levels beyond the reach of our existing instruments. It is enough to entertain the idea and see what it does to data otherwise difficult to explain. In some form magnetic and gravitational attraction may operate in mental as well as physical matter in both man and nature. At least let us look at such a possibility. We have enough empirical data to experiment with. They can surely be arranged in some more integral schema than Western science has evolved so far. This would enable us to do more effective multidimensional and interdisciplinary research than we are doing at present because our efforts would be supported by a wider and more coherent cosmological framework.

5
Organisation from above

What strikes one most forcibly in studying Hindu cosmology is its suggestion that magnetism is the dominant organising force in nature, operating through a hierarchical system of fields induced in descending order through the various levels of manifested Brahman. It preserves the One and stabilises the Many. Each separated thing is distinct and yet it cannot escape from the universe which, in its turn, is forever contained in Brahman. Brahman generates Prakriti to create the Many out of his All-ness, but Prakriti as nature herself remains always within his magnetic field. All created things are, as it were, so many iron filings and she the magnet which determines the patterns they make. Brahman, however, remains the magnetic source and from that point of view Prakriti and all the other Shaktis, Maya and all the Purushas, Atman and all forms of separateness, are the iron filings he holds within his field, as Prakriti holds within hers the universe of natural things.

Looked at in this way, the Shaktis form a force spectrum which stretches from Brahman's will to produce a cosmos down through levels of matter each with its own wave-band. It is not necessary to confine ourselves to the electromagnetic spectrum of physics. Nor is it likely to be fruitful to assume that forces operate in 4D, 5D and 6D space under 3D world limitations. This is again to make the Flatlander's error, hard though it is to avoid doing so, our senses being what they are.

We are already accepting a view of the physical universe as a system of interlocking fields patterned by magnetic and gravitational forces. As long ago as 1935 Burr and Northrop introduced the concept of life-fields exerting an organising influence on reactions in organisms. In 'An Electro-dynamic Theory of Life' they offered the model of a primary body-field controlling a complex of interacting secondary fields which ultimately determined the structure, function and life-cycle of tissue cells. The Hindu model merely enlarges this conception to include fields induced at finer levels of matter. From the Tantric standpoint, Burr's L-fields would become physical Prana fields and his primary body-field the life-vehicle. Control of these fields would, however, be traced back to the Antahkarana or subtle mental body and its system of sub-fields.

This would involve a higher level of control in that the forces influencing physical events would belong on a super-physical part of the Shakti spectrum. This means that prior to and dominating control by life-fields are thought-fields, which in turn means that the way we think, however subconscious or even unconscious such thinking may be, determines the way we direct our vital energies, thus influencing, at one remove, the way our tissues function. The power and scope of thought-fields were studied first by a group of Russian scientists at the Institute of Brain Research in Leningrad in the 1930s. An interesting account of their experiments can be found in L.L. Vasiliev's book *Experiments in Mental Suggestion* recently republished in its English translation.

Vasiliev and his colleagues found that fields induced by concentrated thought could attach themselves to matter of any shape or kind. They were of the opinion that their place of origin was some point in the brain. This can, of course, be questioned without in any way discounting the importance of cerebral participation. From the Tantric as well as from a scientific standpoint, the interaction of mental and physical processes must necessarily be assumed. Since spirit, mind and life are all embodied in the Sthula Sharira, the gross body, its involvement is inevitable. However, before it can act upon objects in the physical world, the Hindu would consider that elements from the subtle body, the Suksma Sharira, must also come into play. Thought-fields would require a good deal of organisation by Shaktis of the Antahkarana as a whole. Mental structuring of Vasiliev's T-fields would have to take place before the brain could be appropriately stimulated. Burr's L-fields would also have to act as intermediaries between mind and body in the transmission of impulses. What was valuable about Vasiliev's telepathy experiments was their implication that forces generated by thought could establish almost instantaneously fields covering immense distances. They also indicated that transmitted thoughts could be picked up at any point within the field by suitable human receivers, a fact which goes a long way towards explaining why discoveries can be made simultaneously by great thinkers who have no direct contact and share only a common interest. It is unfortunate that Soviet scientists seem bent on fitting Vasiliev's findings into brain theories of mind. The Hindu model would seem to contain them better.

In *The Cycles of Heaven*, G.L. Playfair and Scott Hill imply that Prana, as the vitality principle associated by Theosophists with the etheric body, is essentially an electromagnetic force. Burr's work seemed to them to confirm this. After a comparative study of Theosophical writings on the subject in 1974, (59, 38) I found myself concluding that much covered by the term 'etheric' fell within the electromagnetic spectrum. For instance, there were clearly electrophysical components in the auras round human bodies investigated by Walter Kilner (35) in the Radiography Department of St Thomas's Hospital in London in the early 1900s and described by many clairvoyants before and since. The same is true of the changing emanations from plants and people's hands detectable by Kirlian photography. (36, 48) However, it now seems to me that there is more to a life-field than electricity and that the auras perceived round living things cannot be accounted for in electromagnetic terms alone.

When writing on the subject of subtle bodies in 1975, (76) I was already beginning to see that the etheric body of the Theosophists must involve at least two distinct types of energy at work. There seems to be one which is inseparably associated with the functioning of the dense physical body and this could well be a complex of field-forces detectable by one or another of a wide range of instruments. The primary and secondary L-fields picked up by Burr's voltmeter must have been of this kind in so far as they were registered at all. However, since they could be used prognostically, the patterns predicting illness antedating the appearance of symptoms, it seems likely that energies operating in another space-time were also present. These could not be detected instrumentally but his findings implied something of the sort.

If one takes a psychosomatic view of medicine, as increasingly it seems we must, the way we use ourselves, our prevailing attitudes, our emotional predispositions and physical habits will make us prone to symptoms which match our characters long before they manifest themselves externally. Hereditary traits according to Tantric teaching, as well as what biologists call cell memory, are imprinted on Chitta which, as we have seen, interacts with physical Prana from the mental side. Looked at in this way, Burr's L-fields are probably structured by a mixture of physical and psychic Prana, the physical Prana responsive to impacts from the gross body and the psychic Prana to those from mental levels. In other words T-fields are involved with L-fields but escape notice because not perceptible instrumentally. On this theory the L-fields of plants would be accompanied by very simple T-fields, while those of animals would contain in addition Manasic forces associated with sense perception and instinctive behaviour. In the case of human beings elements of Buddhi and Ahangkara would be present as well.

An interesting piece of evidence indicating that not all phenomena theosophically defined as etheric are electromagnetic is connected with the Chakras. These centres or 'lotuses' are often described as lying along the etheric counterpart of the spine and a number of scientists have tried to confirm this experimentally. A great deal of work in this area has been done by Professor Motoyama of Japan, (50) without success. Nevertheless many clairvoyants have claimed to see them and a lot of healers claim to work through them. However, like acupuncture lines, they continue to elude scientific detection. Their fields, if they exist, are clearly not L-fields in the Burrian sense. Discussing this some time ago with Professor Hasted of King's College, London, (28) he proferred the view that Chakras were psychic and not physical entities. He based this statement on the fact that he had been unable to locate them with any of a wide range of instruments but that they were clearly visible to some of the children he had been testing for metal-bending propensities of the Uri Geller type.

In 'Science and subtle bodies' in 1975, I suggested that there must be a vitality vehicle which could not be safely separated from the physical body even in sleep. At the same time the version of the body so often claimed to go 'astral travelling' under anaesthetics and in trance states seems to need to be attached to the gross body also. The connection between traveller and sleeper is apparently one that must not be broken as the many reports of a cord linking them indicate. The presence of this cord seems also to imply that the mobile body in these cases is not just a mobile centre of consciousness of the sort postulated by Puharich in *Beyond Telepathy*. Such a mobile centre could go to the Moon and back without the aid of more than trained clairvoyance. It is the cord which requires explanation, for it suggests that consciousness remains very much an embodied phenomenon during life on earth. The Tantric model of a subtle body composed of mental matter which is permanently part of one's enduring personality but which temporarily co-opts a life-vehicle and physical body for a single life-time may be more useful, as an explanatory concept, than the more complex Theosophical one with which I struggled during 1974.

As we have seen, Hindu science does not separate gross from subtle physiology. Its allocation to the Jiva, or living human being, of three bodies which are interdependent and interpenetrating during life is because, in life, there can be some degree of dissociation between them. Out-of-the-body experiences (OOBE) are cases in point. In the fully waking state all three bodies, spiritual, subtle and gross, are in alignment. During OOBE the centre of consciousness moves into the subtle body which can then move out of alignment with the gross body in its vitality sheath. It is in this state that the cord tends to be reported. Since the subtle and gross bodies and the life-vehicle are melded into a substantial unity by a combination of Chitta and Prana (physical and psychic), it is probably the attenuation of this binding substance as the bodies become dissociated which gives rise to the cord. This substance seems to be highly elastic. The degree of its elasticity is so extraordinary that it cannot be a property of physical matter alone. Its constituents must derive in part at least from elements belonging to another space.

This theory of the cord being formed by withdrawal and attenuation helps to account for another problem associated with it, the various places on the subtle body to which it is attached in different reports of OOBE. This is something I have previously found hard to explain. Theosophical versions of occult physiology lead one first to try to find answers in terms of Chakras as points of entry into and exits from the physical body. Empirical evidence, however, lends such attempts no support. Muldoon, (51) for instance, maintains that its proper position is between the shoulder blades. It was here that Robert Monroe, in *Journeys out of the Body*, said he found it when his attention was drawn to its possible existence. Joan in White's *The Betty Book* experiments was not consistent in this respect, however, and on one occasion it was found attached to one of her hands. It is possible that the ectoplasm extruded in physical mediumship may be composed of the same mixed material. Whatever substance the cord may be made of, its role seems related to maintaining an unbroken connection between bodies. It seems to have nothing to do with the Chakras as possible ports for the departure and return of consciousness.

The mechanisms by means of which the gross and subtle bodies are interlocked may elude our instruments, but there are concepts already within science which may not be without relevance. Once one allows oneself to entertain the idea of organisation from above which would give T-fields priority in the order of generation over L-fields, it is only a small step to speculate about how these fields determine chemical changes in the next level down. And it seems to me the answer must lie down among the imperceptibles, among Prithivi's minute building blocks, the elementary particles of physics and tiny 'handed' molecules of chemistry. To explain the strength of the forces which bind the gross and subtle bodies together, in spite of the different space-time in which each operates, one finds oneself looking at the primary forces of physics in a new way, particularly the strong and weak nuclear forces.

If the nucleus of the atom is only there to exert an electro-magnetic pull upon electrons and provide them with a positive pole, why has it been necessary to endow it with such internal binding force that to split it is a near lethal undertaking? From the standpoint of Nature to hold the nucleus together seems worth enormous risks demanding proportionate built-in safeguards. One wonders why.

Nuclear binding forces and electromagnetism are together regarded as primarily responsible for matter as we know it. They operate to give elementary particles form. Nuclearisa-tion of elementary particles seems to be the first step in the formation of dense matter. It leads to the structuring of the atom. This normally consists of neutrons and protons held together to form the core of the atom by the powerful nuclear binding force to which we have already referred. As their names imply, the neutron has no charge, while the proton is positively charged electrically. Both have spin and therefore magnetic properties. Electrons are infinitely small, negatively charged particles which move round the nucleus like planets round the sun. Electromagnetism is the force which binds the electrons to the nucleus as it also binds atoms together in molecules.

The interesting question is where the particles came from in the first place. Karl Pearson, as long ago as 1894, (23) suggested they were points at which 'ether' is squirted into 3D from 4D space. This is a fascinating idea, especially now when the term ether is regaining some measure of scientific respectability. It suggests a possible 'mechanism' of cohesion related to interdimensionality.

If one thinks of nuclear particles as a mixture of electro-magnetic and psychopranic entities, they could be sites at which subtle and dense matter meet. This in turn could explain the tremendous binding power of the force which holds the proton and neutron together. It could also account for the devastating effects nuclear explosions have on all forms of organic life. It is possible that the disruption of the bond between psychomagnetic and electromagnetic elements in the organism prevents it from remaining functionally intact in the 3D world, if indeed it can survive at all. The consequences of a nuclear holocaust are horrible to contemplate, especially by those who regard life as an evolute of dense matter. In the multidimensional Tantric universe only gross forms would be destroyed. Subtle matter and subtle bodies would remain, hopefully to reincarnate in some more enlightened age.

While strong nuclear forces bind, weak nuclear forces may operate to release. They are still something of a mystery. They have been called nuclear forces because it is necessary to posit them in order to account for the behaviour of quarks in protons and neutrons. None of the forces already isolated by science seemed to apply. If the nuclei of atoms are anchorage points maintaining the cohesion of physical and psychic forces at the particulate level, it is very important to have forces which partially release as well as forces which strongly bind.

In Robert A. Monroe's detailed account of his experiences in *Journeys out of the Body*, he distinguished several locales in which he found himself. In the first of these, Locale I, the laws of physics still applied to a considerable extent. For instance, once in this locale he found himself trapped in a Faraday cage in which he had been placed as part of an experiment. Until the current was switched off he could not get past what felt to him like a flexible but impenetrable net. Interestingly this was a region without colour. In the second locale, Locale II, he found not only colour but much greater freedom of movement. Mental and not physical energies were apparently prepotent. Thoughts and desires operated as forces so that in order to be in a place he had only to think himself there. He said of this locale, 'Please check all physical concepts here.'

Monroe was born into an academic family, is well-educated, a successful businessman and an electronic engineer of wide experience, especially in communication theory. Having through a series of chances found himself able to leave his dense body at will, he decided to experiment systematically and keep records. He was also sensible enough to do this under medical supervision and there seems no reason to doubt the accuracy of his account of what happened. Interpreting his experiences, however, is something else again.

From the standpoint of science it is Locale I which is of most interest, because here he was moving about in a region where the laws of physics were to some extent applicable. His 'second body' in this state appeared to have weight and to be in some measure responsive to gravity. On one occasion, for example, he speaks of his body falling like a feather but head first as if the head were heavier than the rest of the body. Though it had weight and therefore mass, his second body had little density for it passed readily through walls. A Tantric scholar might interpret his state as one in which the centre of consciousness was in the sensory mind, the Manomayapurusha. At this level, though detached from the sense organs, perceptions would still be governed by the categories of sense experience relating them to the laws of physics. In other words he would be moving about partially dissociated from the gross body but not sufficiently to be free from the conditions governing it. In Locale II the centre of consciousness would be in the Antahkarana, the mind proper, where it would be operating according to the laws of psychic and not physical matter.

What mechanisms are responsible for shifts of this sort present science with a challenging problem. It is here that the weak nuclear forces may come into play. By small, judicious doses of particle emission changes of electrical charge at the interface between physical and mental matter may trigger off a partial slackening of the binding forces in nuclei. All dissociated states and not only OOBE may involve some such process. So also may deep thought. For instance, an interesting finding of one of Burr's colleagues, Leonard J. Ravitz Jr., (64, 65) was that L-fields in states of deep concentration are similar to those produced in hypnotic trance. This suggests that physiological mechanisms which induce shifts in the centre of consciousness away from external reality are the common factor. Bearing in mind that all fields are bodily fields, such shifts of level would take place within an integral field but would involve changes in the interaction patterns of its various sub-fields. Both trance and concentration place the focus of attention in the subjective world of the subtle body.

Sensation and motor activity place it in the objective world of the gross body. This would seem to imply that changes of level could depend on whether one's activities are primarily physical or psychological. Physiologically the difference between concentrating or being in trance could thus presumably be less than the difference between solving a problem and playing tennis.

Another relevant mechanism operating at the particulate level may be related to a kind of asymmetry which runs through the universe, a bias to the left or right called 'handedness'. Handedness was first discovered at the frontier between organic and inorganic matter. It has since been found to exist in elementary particles as well. Handedness in molecules was discovered by Pasteur when he was working with polarised light. If atoms are the smallest units which have the property of matter, molecules are the smallest units of chemical substance. When atoms are all of one kind they form an element. Most substances are made up of two or more kinds of atoms, though some rare gases, like helium, consist of only one. Molecules can be simple, consisting of only two or three different atoms. Complex ones, like the proteins which give so much diversity to living forms, can be made up of chains of literally thousands of atoms. In solids atoms and molecules tend to be arranged in lattices of various sorts. These are 3D geometrical patterns which are fixed and constantly repeated so that their uniformity gives each substance its individual character. Lattices have varying degrees of symmetry. The relevant type for the purpose of this discussion is reflective symmetry.

Reflective symmetry is sometimes called superposability. This is because it implies that if a thing is superimposed upon its mirror image it coincides with its reflection point by point. If the coincidence is perfect a form is said to be symmetric; if it does not it is said to be asymmetric. 3D objects have only limited symmetry. Animals and humans, for instance, have only a superficial bilateral symmetry. Their bilateral symmetry is reflective in that coincidence can be achieved if they face their mirror images. This applies only to their mirror images, however. In actual fact the two sides of our bodies resemble one another but our ears, hands and feet 'go the other way round'. The same is true of spirals and that is what is important here.

In his work with polarised light, Pasteur found that when a beam of light passes through some minerals their lattices only permit it to undulate through them along a single plane, not back and forth as is usually the case. Light is then said to be polarised. Earlier a French biochemist called Biot had found that quartz, in addition to polarising light, gave it a twist. At first he thought all forms of quartz would do this. This did not prove to be the case, however. He found that when the quartz was dissolved it lost this property. In other words he found that the twist was not inherent in the molecules of quartz but depended on the way they were arranged. Pasteur, in carrying on Biot's work, found that this was not invariably the case; in some cases the twist was indeed in the molecule. In fact he discovered that certain molecules differed only in the twists they gave to polarised light. Working with two forms of tartaric acid, for instance, he found that only one polarised light with a consistent handedness. The other did not polarise light at all and this proved to be due to its lattice containing an equal number of right-handed and left-handed crystals whose twists cancelled one another out. When he dissolved the second form of tartaric acid, separating out the right- from the left-handed crystals, he found each set could now polarise light but that each kept its characteristic handedness.

Pasteur carried on to work with moulds and micro-organisms and discovered that organic substances polarised light in a way that made them more selective by enabling them to react to their mirror images of opposite handedness in consistent ways. For instance, he found that certain moulds would destroy molecules of only one handedness and leave the others intact. This suggested to him some sort of asymmetry in the mould which was governing its eating habits. He experimented with a variety of organic and inorganic substances and found that only living things could produce asymmetric molecules that 'all went the same way' in terms of handedness. This led him to conclude that 'the only well-marked line of demarcation that can at present be drawn between the chemistry of dead and the chemistry of living matter' is just this specific inherent property. The capacity to polarise light is said to make a substance 'optically active' and this particular activity in living things seems to be related to both asymmetry and spiral formations. The significance of this in relation to Kundalini's serpentine characteristics is something we must presently explore.

Later physicists came to realise that a similar handedness is to be found among elementary particles and is relative to the way they spin. This was discovered as part of research into parity. Parity is a conservation law which assumes that one of the invariances in nature is mirror symmetry — the assumption, in other words, that nature has no bias in favour of either form of handedness.

First doubts about parity in physics came with the discovery of anti-particles. (23) Their existence was first presumed by a mathematical physicist called Dirac, who calculated in 1931 that there must be a particle with the same mass as an electron but with an opposite charge. He christened it an anti-electron. The following year just such a particle was found by Carl D. Anderson in the cloud chamber at the California Institute of Technology. Not knowing of Dirac's work, he called it a positron, an electron with a positive charge. Anderson assumed that the complementarity of its charge was due to the other-handedness of the magnetic moment, the magnetic field produced by its spin. It is now known that not only the electron but every elementary particle has its anti-particle.

Dirac, in addition to anticipating anti-matter, suggested that particles sometimes changed spaces. Like Karl Pearson, he felt that particles were tied up with 4D space in some way. In other words four spaces were needed to account fully for the way they behaved. He envisaged nature as a vast sea of particles jostling one another in 3D space. The situation was such that any particle squashed out of this dense mass had nowhere to go but up into another space. Only the existence of a fourth space would ensure that there was room for such transactions to occur just as some transactions cannot take place in linear space but require a third dimension to accommodate them.

Matter itself is composed of stable atoms, (14) those

whose positive and negative charges are in balance. Charged particles or ions are inherently unstable and therefore readily interact with other particles to bring about changes in matter within a general context of stability. All charged particles have spin and consequently both magnetic properties and handedness. In stable particles these are equilibrated and appear to cancel one another out. Under certain conditions however, they can be induced to break up into ions and neutral particles of various kinds. K-meson and anti-K-meson are instances of this type.

As with Pasteur's two forms of tartaric acid, there seemed to be two types of K-meson — theta and tau — which decayed differently. Theta decayed into two and tau into three pi-mesons. Research into why this should come about led into the sphere of the weak nuclear interactions which I suggested earlier might have a lot to do with critical thresholds on the frontier between mental and physical matter or on the interface between 3D and 4D space. Parity, mirror symmetry, was found not to be preserved in weak interactions and this turned out to be connected with the magnetic axes in the nucleus. Mme Chien Shiung, Professor of Physics at Columbia University, (23) observed that in beta decay in a radioactive isotope a different number of electrons is emitted from the north and south ends of its magnetic axis, the cause of the two kinds of decay. This differential rate of decay was usually cloaked from observation because, in the normal joggle of particles, nuclei point in all directions. If, however, a powerful magnet is used to induce a field in which all their north ends face the same way, it can quickly be seen that the slower theta decay went on at the north end and the faster tan decay at the south end of the nucleus. This made the nucleus more like a spinning cone than the spinning sphere it had been thought to be. It also upset the idea of space as spherically symmetrical and therefore the same in all directions. Rather there seems to be something like a grain in it; an orientation of some sort with which handedness is associated.

The discovery of the neutrino, a particle with an apparent rest mass of zero and with no charge, was another crucial one for the purpose of this discussion. The fact that Soviet scientists now claim that it has been shown to have a tenuous degree of mass does not lessen its relevance, for its importance is that it is practically disembodied spin with direction and almost nothing else. Neutrinos must be everywhere, passing through everything at the speed of light. They must be capable of interacting with 3D matter or they could not have been in cloud-chamber collisions and so discovered. They differ from all other particles in that they go straight through the earth as if physical matter did not exist. They are like other particles, however, in having both clockwise and anti-clockwise spin. Theories about them suggest that they are connected with weak nuclear forces, right-spinning neutrinos being thrown off with electrons in beta decay and left-spinning ones coming off with anti-electrons in anti-beta decay. Martin Gardner, in his fascinating book *The Ambidextrous Universe*, suggests that neutrinos and anti-neutrinos are the particulate analogues of Pasteur's right- and left-handed tartaric acid molecules. If so they may be on the frontier between life and mind as the molecules are on the frontiers between living and dead matter. The handedness of spins may act like the threads of screw and bolt. According to the way they are turned surfaces can be either joined or separated.

Perhaps we should think of the body-mind relation less in terms of neural switches and electromagnetic currents and more in terms of minute screws being tightened and loosened down there among the elementary particles where demarcation lines between spatial dimensions are almost impossible to draw. Perhaps, with the intuitive aptness of folk imagery, to have a screw loose may be as good a way as any of indicating a certain withdrawal from external reality. A clue may lie in the nature of beta decay.

It is possible that the differential rates of electron emission from the two poles of the nucleus and the left-handed spin of neutrinos thrown off by electrons in beta decay may indicate two distinct types of interdimensional interactions. It is worth considering the possibility that the slower theta decay neutrinos may operate certain screws altering the centre of consciousness but keeping it at a level where the laws of physics still to some extent apply. Something of this sort could perhaps explain its transfer into Monroe's second body in Locale I. This seemed to be one in which 3D and 4D reality tended to overlap. There seems no reason to suppose one has to be in an out-of-the-body condition for this to happen, provided such nuclear mechanisms for interdimensional transactions actually exist. Carrying this idea further, there may be a relation between the faster tau decay and its more rapidly emitted neutrinos and experiences of the kind Monroe had in Locale II. The way in which his second body behaved there is very similar to the way our mind behaves in our dense bodies in daily life. In planning, imagining and remembering we can move as freely in subjective space as Monroe in Locale II. The laws of physics do not govern inner worlds. The images we manipulate, like Monroe's second body, operate in some much freer dimension.

Physicists call the force which governs nuclear decay 'strangeness', and it may be the manner and rate of decay which puts into space the grain mentioned earlier. The grain may get its direction from the left-handedness of the off-spinning neutrinos accompanying electrons which also show an inclination to turn left more often than right. A complementary role may be played by the anti-neutrinos spinning off anti-electrons in anti-matter. If for anti-matter one reads mental substance, one can see that this grain may represent a tendency for physical energy to approach the mental threshold via spirals of a consistent handedness, and for mental energy to approach the physical threshold via spirals of opposite handedness. Assuming this, one can readily imagine that impacts from the outside world reach the mind-matter frontier on a flow of left-spinning material neutrinos in physical Prana, while impacts from the mind would reach it mediated by right-spinning anti-neutrinos and anti-electrons in psychic Prana. The whirling cones which apparently point every which way under normal conditions may operate to spread effects so as to promote diversity and flexibility in the formation of interaction patterns.

What is striking in all this is the apparent primacy of micro-particles over micro-organs in the genesis of behavioural and structural change. The neutrino may be more vital for adaptation and survival than the brain, not least in ensuring that all forms of life are capable of them, amoeba as well as man. The question of origin is more open. Its connection with anti-matter could as easily have preceded as followed its connection with matter, which is certainly not true of the brain. If anti-particles come before particles in the order of generation and mental before physical substance, this would explain more easily than reductionism both the origin of life and the extraordinarily intelligent partnerships between creatures in co-operating with one another to create the environment. From this point of view the brain and nervous system must be regarded primarily as selectors out and only secondarily as selectors in. They have developed like computers. At whatever level it exists neural tissue is programmed to facilitate the interpretation of impacts in terms of needs and ends relative to survival under the peculiar conditions dense matter imposes upon living things. Its job is to put suitably meaningful order into the crude environment. This is done by selecting out all that is irrelevant and confining selecting in to what can be coped with. The development of the brain and nervous system is not a sign of evolution full stop. It is a sign of evolution as a measure of a growing capacity to adjust to an increasingly wide range of variables out of Prakriti's boundless store. Moreover, as technology has now taught us, it is not the size of a computer which is important and there is no evidence that the brain makes adjustments at the micro level less vital.

There is another point which should be stressed before we leave the subject of screws which may possibly control the body's ability to change the level and focus of attention. This is that it is quite an illusion that we spend all our waking hours in the shared external world. Attending to and acting in outer reality is accompanied by continual withdrawals into inner reality to cogitate and decide. The little screws which guard the threshold between mind and matter, between the gross and subtle bodies, are forever on the go, opening and shutting doors to let impacts pass in and out and up and down. Without even being aware of it we may move constantly between ordinary space-time and the space-time of Monroe's Locales I and II in the routine activities of daily living. The value of records like Monroe's and those of a small cohort of astral travellers is that they enable us to become more aware of the implications of such experiences as they describe.

Another fact worth noting is that it is obviously the way an object is interpreted which must set in motion the train of reactions which leads, via the nervous system, molecular dovetailing and nuclear screws, to responses which differ widely from person to person. In other words thought-fields, however primitive, must be involved in all adaptive behaviour. As we have seen, this would be taken for granted by Hindu scholars, assuming as they do that all matter is organised from above downwards. In simpler forms of life, T-fields determining L-fields which, in their turn, activate chemical responses would probably only involve Chitta and Prana. Manas would come in with the capacity, however slight, to convert sensations into perceptions and develop instinctive behaviour patterns. Buddhic T-fields enter with rationality and exert a growing influence in proportion as they are able to mould the body into an adequate vehicle for thought.

Micro-processes of the sort so far described may account for movements of attention, but they cannot explain why memory and identity remain together wherever the centre of consciousness may come to rest. They can be enhanced or weakened, but normally constitute a remarkably stable partnership. According to Tantric doctrine, memory is recorded in Chitta which is a component of the subtle body which survives physical death. Both memory and identity are parts of the enduring personality and become embodied in a different gross body for each separate life-time. Here, most importantly, the physical brain must act as a major selector out. It is becoming abundantly evident through the work of reincarnation researchers like Professor Ian Stevenson of the University of Virginia School of Medicine (82) that some people do indeed carry in them, as their own, memories found to belong to someone already dead. They are, however, exceptional cases. Biologically it is more a liability than an asset to be burdened with two sets of memories, so that it is not surprising to learn that children born with double memories tend to lose those associated with past lives in adapting to the present one.

There is some evidence from hypnosis that strong memories belonging to past incarnations may lie not far under the surface in some people. They are sometimes elicited with therapeutic effect under certain · conditions. Grant and Kelsey claim in *Many Lifetimes* that the catharsis from the recall of a traumatic experience in a past life resembles the relief following an abreaction of one sustained in childhood. Several psychiatrists are working along these lines. Where there are enduring memories of a past life, as for instance in the case of A.J. Stewart (83) and E.W. Ryall, (66) this would be ascribed to some karmic necessity. In the case of yogis the ability to read past lives is said to develop with the purification of the body and the widening of vision.

Attempts are being made to perfect a particle theory of memory, but work on this still remains speculative and is highly complex mathematically. It is based on the soliton, a mathematical object with special properties as a carrier of information. It has a wave character, exceptional stability and consists of a solitary impulse, hence its name. In 1953 a group of scientists (21) examining equations associated with bubble chamber collisions found that some waves retain both speed and shape even after impinging upon other waves. They also found that two such waves could meet without producing interference patterns.

Digital models of soliton processes were developed to illustrate three kinds of physical systems: those which show linearity without dispersion; those which are dispersive but non-linear; and those which are active in generating energy. The soliton was posited to denote a wave which could preserve its form in a variety of interference situations and survive perturbations of often very considerable magnitude. Some solitons move slowly, others fast. They can also exist as standing waves. Above all they can keep their properties as information carriers under all these conditions. As every organism is a generator of electromagnetic fields as well as a recipient of energy generated at other levels and from sources outside itself, one can see the importance for both its continuity and its adaptability of some such stabilising factor as the soliton. On the other hand, if the Hindu scientists were right in assigning memory to Chitta, it is possible that the soliton is only very partially a physical entity. It may, therefore, prove as elusive as the neutrino, possibly even more so.

It has often struck me as a psychologist how extraordinary it is that physicists, and scientists generally, can consider that the key of the universe and the origins of life must lie within some purely physical realm of matter. Clearly innumerable phenomena which, as ordinary mortals, they deal with every day cannot be fully described in the language of science so narrowly conceived. It surely is not surprising that theoretical physics comes up against anti-matter so early in its attempts to analyse the behaviour of elementary particles mathematically. More surprising is the fact that, after subjecting matter to fantastically abnormal conditions in bubble chambers, accelerating and compressing it to degrees not ordinarily found in nature, physicists continue to assume they are observing exclusively physical interactions. Their doing so so readily suggests they must be dealing with some sort of continuum. It also suggests that they are using a technique which is neutral between types of matter so long as they are particulate. I sometimes wonder what Max Planck would say were he living at this hour. The reverence in which contemporary scientists still hold his work, and that of Einstein, derives from the way in which their theories have stood the test of time. Planck's mass and Planck's constant, like Einstein's theory of gravity in which black holes were already implicit, are referred to regularly in the literature. Not the same notice has yet been given to Planck's mentoid particle or Einstein's suspicion that matter would be found finally to resolve into thought. (11) Perhaps Stephen Hawking's (14) brilliant probing mind may presently go exploring in this direction. Some physicists are already advising parents to put their sons into biology, but it is possibly in psychology that the future of physics really lies.

6
Cosmic Kundalini

Kundalini in Hindu cosmology is the Shakti or divine cosmic energy with particular dominion over the matter of the physical world. It is a coiled Shakti, which implies power at rest, energy in a state of equilibrium. It works in close association with physical and psychic Prana, life-forces which are concerned with vitalising and sustaining specific forms for their allotted span. It is also the stabilising agent which holds energies in balance throughout the universe. In other words, all lesser Shaktis are controlled by Kundalini-Shakti as far as the physical world is concerned. It has been called the Logos in bodies and this has to be taken to cover galaxies as embodiments of Brahman as well as bodies in the usual sense of the word. Far from Kundalini-Shakti being a specialised Shakti located at the base of human spines, it is the homeo-static power which enables the physicist to talk of gauge theories, theories which assume that the cosmos is all of a piece, a place where the same energies behave in the same way everywhere. For this reason it may be helpful to speak of Mahakundalini (Great Kundalini) when referring to it as a cosmic force.

As a Shakti, Kundalini is an active stabilising agency and so must be seen, even when coiled, as part of the energetic side of nature and not as something which is acted upon. I spoke earlier of Brahman manifesting in four main ways. One is Atman, which expresses the individualising aspect giving specificity to forms, and here it is important to refer to Brahman as it and not him. This is strictly correct because

Brahman is the neuter form. Brahma and Brahmani, masculine and feminine variants, are polarities within Brahman reflected in the Shiva-Shakti partnership. As this is a discussion about cosmic energy, it may avoid misunderstanding if the basic neutrality of Brahman is stressed. All positives and negatives, all actives and passives, all forces and particles, all forms of awareness and patterns of action, are dualities within Brahman which can manifest through a wide range of interactions and innumerable varieties of partnership. Atman gives separate entities their uniqueness without in any way interfering with these polarities.

The first duality to arise from out of the Oneness of Brahman is the Shiva-Shakti Tattva. Tattva translates roughly as quality. Its Tattva is the characteristic attribute of a thing. As the Atman Tattva gives created things their specificity, so the Shiva Tattva ensures that, throughout the whole cycle of creation and dissolution, the underlying unity of I and That is never lost despite the endless diversity of objects produced by Prakriti and the profusion of conscious states generated by Maya in the Purushas.

In its purest form the Shiva-Shakti Tattva is conceived as a duality still within Parabrahman, the Supreme unmanifested Brahman. Thus in its highest state it eternally transcends the phenomenal world. It arises as part of Parabrahman's will to create and it is this will which causes Shakti to stir and consciousness to centre round Shiva. Power still latent in Parabrahman begins to consolidate till it eventuates as Shabdabrahman, sound Brahman. Shabda or cosmic sound represents significance, the expression of Divine intention. It is what lies behind ideas, the language in which they are expressed and the objects they denote. These rest in Parabrahman as possibilities until such time as Shakti brings all potential objects and all potential modes of experiencing to a point. This point, like that in the midst of the void out of which the physicist imagines the universe to have exploded, is without magnitude but packed with infinite power at rest. The difference is that Shakti's void is Parabrahman and her universe emerges not with a Big Bang but as an exhalation. Nor does she create particles and objects and strew them about at random after the fashion implied in the Big Bang theory. Moreover, the power she gathers to a point is ergo-conscious not purely physical because, for all her apparent independence, she is never separated from the Shiva side of her Tattva. Their partnership is fundamental and indissoluble. Shiva as cosmic consciousness maintains the oneness under-lying phenomenal nature while Shakti adventures forth and with Ishvara, the creative aspect of Brahman, produces a manifold of appearances so varied that its underlying unity is all too readily obscured.

As Prakriti Shakti generates the world of nature, she endows matter with its characteristic Tattvas. First come the Tattvas of mind: Buddhi, Ahangkara, Manas and Chitta. These are followed by the sensory Tattvas, the Indriyas and the Tanmatras. These are the Tattvas associated with the subtle body and are unaffected by physical death. Only after the subtle forms of matter and their Tattvas have come into being does Prakriti as Shabdabrahman give rise to the five Bhutas or states of dense matter and their associated Tattvas or ways of behaving. Once Prakriti has produced the physical plane, she is said to coil up and sleep since no denser uni-verses remain to be generated. From then on the task of keeping the natural world functioning smoothly at this level devolves upon Mahakundalini in the cosmos and Kundalini in lesser bodies. This is why Kundalini-Shakti is called the Shabdabrahman in bodies.

Kundalini, like all manifestations of Parashakti, the Supreme Shakti, is linked to Shiva so that, at deep levels, all nature is in touch with cosmic consciousness, and Brahman-knowledge guides its evolution from within as well as order-ing it from above. In Hinduism all universes are as mentoid as Max Planck's particles. As products of Shabdabrahman (sound Brahman) and Spandabrahman (Brahman as move-ment), they are meaningful processes by definition. This is as true of the physical universe as any preceding it out of the void. That science finds mobile patterns in it and scientists can describe the way it behaves in mathematical equations and make predictions from them only confirms the inherent order which underlies its organisation.

There is, of course, a phenomenological element in all this as both Einstein and Heisenberg were well aware. Tantric cosmologies take this for granted. They acknowledge that any insight we can have into nature is necessarily coloured by the way our embodied minds work. This is what makes Avidya partial knowledge without rendering it false. To know Maya is to know an aspect of reality, its phenomenal aspect, not to be caught in mere illusion. Unfortunately, as we have seen, Shangkara and his followers within classical Hinduism did not share this view, which may be the reason India never developed an empirical science. By contrast Sri Aurobindo's conception of Maya, as something which veils ultimate reality but which can be penetrated by refining our perceptions, both affirms science and also explains why scientists are being perpetually enticed to probe deeper into the hidden mysteries each new discovery reveals.

As Atman divides I from Other and Shiva relates individual to cosmic consciousness, so Shakti, as Prakriti or phenomenal nature, divides things into This and That. She works with Ishvara, the creative principle, using sound and motion to break up Maya for the Purusha into a multiplicity of forms which can be known. The experiencer of these forms is therefore called the Mayapurusha. Only when Maya no longer obscures the vision of the Purusha does the knower become one with Shiva, the Parapurusha. It is then that Avidya becomes Vidya and the truth-seeker becomes the truth-knower.

As we have seen already, the Purusha as the experiencer of nature can be centred at different levels of the personality at different times. Its vision can be obscured by varying degrees of Maya density depending on where it is focused. The true aim of yoga is to free it from the limitations of partial knowledge by union with the Parapurusha, the Shiva within. It is by the proper functioning of Kundalini in embodied spirits that the insights of the Mayapurushas are progressively refined. It plays a vital role in the systematic removal of distortions and the clarifying of perceptions. It is only when it has completed these tasks that it is ready to rise from its resting-place at the base of the spine and move upward through the Chakras to the Sahasrara centre at the crown of the head. The Sahasrara or thousand-petalled lotus is the bodily seat of Shiva, and when consciousness is focused there the Mahayogi can at last view the world from the standpoint of the Parapurusha. Properly this process is an evolutionary one controlled from above and within. That is why it is foolish for the small ego-self to assume it can command the movements of Kundalini or use meditative short-cuts to effect the marriage of Shiva and Shakti in the Sahasrara. The consummation is the evolutionary goal of all human beings as embodied spirits. It is not something human beings can have to order.

Using the Tantric conception of Mahakundalini as the dominant Shakti in the physical universe, it is tempting to explore what this means in terms of the forces known to physics. It implies, for instance, at least three things.

First, as we have seen, the Hindu conceives Brahman as breathing out universes and then breathing them in again. The order of generation is from spiritual universes to dense physical ones. The order of withdrawal is from dense physical to spiritual. The void from which all emerges and into which all returns has no attributes; it is all and nothing; infinite power infinitely at rest. This means that the universe of physics where Mahakundalini acts as regent for Parashakti emerges last in a sequence of universes all interpenetrating one another within the vast field which is the manifested body of Brahman. This field is also space, so that the cosmos is a complex of interpenetrating and interacting spaces exhaled, so to speak, as Brahman breathes out. On the outbreath and inbreath space itself may be thought of as expanding and contracting. As galaxies seem currently to be moving away, we are still presumably in a phase of outbreathing.

Second, the dense physical cosmos is not an isolated creation and the Hindu void is not the void of theoretical physics. The universe we know has, so to say, been precipitated from above or, to use the analogy of space and breath, been developed as a modification of spaces already exhaled. It is also the sphere where Brahman is most thickly veiled in Maya and things seem most sharply separated from one another. Its density may be a function of its remoteness from ultimate reality and its laws relative to the kind of perceptions this distance and density impose upon Purushas in gross bodies.

Third, the creation of the cosmos was presumably the

work of Prakriti as part of a single operation so that we should have a gauge theory, not only for three-dimensional space, but for all conceivable spaces. A single Shakti continuum should also run through the whole multidimensional system from the highest supermental to the lowest gross physical forms of energy. From the Tantric point of view theories about the genesis of the cosmos should properly take account of the fact that what science at present assumes to be the ultimate void may merely be a blank we are as yet unable to fill. It is not necessary to discount the findings of physics in order to rethink the origins of stars and of life along these lines, but it is very necessary to be ready to look at its data again in order to see if they cannot fit more elegantly into some such context.

To do this a first requirement would seem to be to unify energy and consciousness as Maxwell unified electricity, magnetism and light, using some such concept as ergoconsciousness. In doing this it would be essential to distinguish ergoconsciousness from life and mind. Both life and mind are manifestations of ergoconsciousness but of dissimilar kinds. To the extent that they are governed by different laws one must assume they are operating in different spaces. Thus in an extended Shakti spectrum ergoconsciousness might be usefully thought of as having two divisions for the purpose of analysis. There would need to be a division concerned with states of consciousness, kinds of awareness, as co-relatives of matter at different levels of Maya density; and a division concerned with life, patterns of energy which behave differently in forms at different levels of material substance. In such a conception the laws of physics and the laws governing psychological processes would not be any more incompatible than the laws governing the behaviour of solids and those governing the behaviour of gases. Laws are only formulations regarding the general behaviour of classes of phenomena and can be divided into as many subordinate systems as there are categories of phenomena which behave in radically different ways.

In so far as science needs to postulate elementary particles these must be seen as falling within a single Shakti continuum but not necessarily occupying the same spatial universes. In fact there could be a particulate aspect of matter at all levels, in which case it would be axiomatic that some would be supersensible and beyond the reach of current scientific methods of investigation. Those too subtle to be observed by ordinary sense perception may, however, be open to examination by extrasensory perception if the clairvoyants used are gifted in what is beginning to be called micro-psi, the ability to see into the structure and functioning of very minute entities. Otherwise mathematical techniques and computers may prove the only way to discover whether or not particles play a role in higher mental processes. They play an important part in theoretical physics and are already being used to test out the possibility of psychological entities of the soliton type, as we saw in the last chapter. On the other hand, beyond a certain point, wave and field theories may be more useful than particulate ones in exploring higher spaces. In Hinduism and Buddhism, which employ imagery rather than mathematics to supplement their technical terms, this is tacitly implied. Serpentine analogies abound in India and China. So also do discs, spheres, circles and radiations.

The creation and maintenance of the phenomenal universe is, then, the work of Shaktis which are essentially forces. They are ontologically prior to the entities they fashion out of different combinations of matter for specific purposes. These ergoconscious forms, whether simple or complex, are basically responses to needs which in their turn generate forces to meet them. Needs, therefore, give rise to forms and not the other way round. 'Why' and 'how' seem more important than 'what' since the 'what' of a thing depends on why it is created and how it is used. Hence the primacy of Shabda, meaning, since needs are relative to purposes which are themselves dynamic embodiments of meaning.

If it is indeed the forces of Mahakundalini which are responsible for keeping the natural world in working order, understanding their cycles and the role of serpentine formations in maintaining homeostasis and the stability of patterns through change could prove a most fruitful line of research. It also might give us a better idea of how far we may safely go in creating new entities. Until Brahman draws in his breath and the cosmos starts to disappear, Mahakundalini must resist alterations outside the limitations set by Prakriti after she had completed her work in dense matter and come to rest. It might be wise to try to discover what these limits are since their implications should not be ignored by men bent on producing new molecules, experimenting with genetic engineering and building bigger and better particle accelerators. Meditators who have tried to manipulate Kundalini without sufficiently understanding it have paid for their rashness with personal distress. The situation becomes more serious when scientists start tampering with Maha-kundalini, for it is not just individuals but the foundations of the natural order they may be putting at risk. Man is in grave danger of imitating the foolhardiness of Icarus. The fallacy by naming takes a most dangerous form when we think we can safely handle forces which make and break stars merely because we can describe them mathematically and put innocuous names to them, like weak and colour, strangeness and charm. Even gravity and electromagnetism sound mild. Only the strong nuclear force has a sinister ring until we are told that the colour force is even stronger. It is perhaps as well that the men with the bubble chambers are beginning to advise one another to put their sons into biology. Much more and one of their Pandora's boxes might explode, letting loose heaven knows what wildly protesting particles. Mahakundalini in a cosmic rage is no laughing matter if what we are told about her is true. And behind her ultimately is Prakriti herself, multidimensional nature as a whole.

The stupendous power of Mahakundalini lies in its control over the interplay of forces which determine the functioning of all forms with physical aspects and not only the forces of physics, though these would, of course, be included. As we have seen in discussing the soliton, forces involving pre-dominantly psychic Prana can, because operative in gross bodies, come within the scope of Kundalini's overall dominion. Similarly, Shaktis at work in what we regard as inanimate nature are her concern because all matter is ergo-conscious and so cannot be completely inert. It is thus the job of Mahakundalini not only to keep order among the forces of physics but between the forces of physics and those of life and mind as these interact with one another in gross bodies. The degree to which material forms are alive and capable of intelligence differs widely, but because all are expressions of Brahman all share these attributes to some extent. This is as true of particles as of men. Science tacitly recognises this fact. In the language of modern physics particles are said to 'feel' forces and forces between particles to 'become aware' of one another. (14)

At present scientific cosmologies deal very inadequately with the multidimensionality of natural phenomena, failing signally to explain how the universe can be both multi-dimensional and all of a piece. This is largely because our spectrum of forces is not sufficiently wide. As we have seen, it needs to be extended if the search for a force to which all others are sensitive is to be carried forward constructively. Moreover the tendency to reduce life to electromagnetism needs to be counteracted without overlooking the contribution of these important physical forces to the functioning of both life and mind. Holographic theories also hug the ground too closely. They cannot be truly holographic unless they assume that all levels of being are represented at each point of manifestation. It is not only the whole of a body which can, in principle, be discovered in every cell, but the whole of a person.

From the foregoing it is clear that Kundalini must above all be regarded as a stabilising agency. As the energy commissioned to keep the physical universe running smoothly, it is also responsible for its harmonious evolution. As Maha-kundalini in nature, it is responsive to Ishvara as the creative aspect of the Brahmanic impulse and to Atman as the aspect which puts their uniqueness into created things. As Kundalini in humans, it works under the Jivatman, the guiding entelechy at the core of our being. It is in accordance with growth processes activated by this entelechy as a fragment of Brahman that it coils and rests or uncoils and rises. It is only the Jivatman in man which knows Kundalini's proper times and seasons. Our conscious minds can only strive to learn them. It is because they understand this that the Mahayogis who are really of that ilk urge meditators not to interfere with its movements since, though chiefly discussed in connection with spiritual exercises, they are essentially body-conserving activities.

When Tantric science speaks of Prana setting the term to Kundalini's reign, (98) it implies a number of things. For instance, it means Kundalini ceases to operate in forms from which the Pranic life-vehicle has been withdrawn, whether these be plants or animals. It means that its activities are circumscribed when the link between Prana and dense matter is tenuous as in inorganic substances and dead stars. It means that it can disappear from universes being sucked back into the void on the inbreath of Brahman, since gross matter is the first to go. We already know that stars can simply vanish and physicists are speculating whether this is due to their fragmentation or their transposition into another dimension. It is well within the framework of Eastern thought for both these processes to be involved without any contradiction in terms. This is because Kundalini, as Shabdabrahman, only holds the constituents of a form together for its divinely ordained span. Once this is completed the Pranas in its L-fields and T-fields withdraw. Kundalini is freed to work elsewhere as part of the general energy pool of Mahakundalini while its chemical components systematically disintegrate.

Shabda, as we have already seen, is the essence of sound as the distillation of meaning. To act as Shabdabrahman, encapsulating Brahmanic intentions in physical entities, demands powers of great magnitude and intensity. Hence the title Devi Kundalini or the Goddess, given to convey her high divine rank. As custodian of their significance Mahakundalini is responsible for seeing that each fragment of manifested Brahman instinctively knows its place and keeps it, a role which man would be rash to try to usurp.

A coiled Shakti or Shakti at rest should be understood as energy in a state of equilibrium, not a state of inertia. Mahakundalini coiled is therefore the Shakti in the physical world which keeps all lesser Shaktis in balance. It is polarised divine energy holding the universe poised between the forces of generation and destruction, growth and decay, entropy and negentropy. Understood in this way, it is probably the force physicists have been looking for since the time of Einstein. It is as impossible to observe directly as electricity, magnetism, gravity and the nuclear forces. It may be, as the

Tantras imply, equally real and a great deal more basic. It is more basic because postulating it might enable mathematical scientists to bring intelligence and life into their equations since neither differ from the forces of physics in any essential way. Their presence is discovered by essentially the same means. They are similarly elusive in themselves and yet must be inferred from the manner in which things behave. They are every bit as much part of the phenomenal world as the wind. It is only our engrained Western tendency to mind-matter dualism which prevents us from accepting this as readily as they do in the East.

In the Tantras it is stressed that the Chakras and Nadis are centres and channels of force in the subtle body so that it is not surprising they elude instrumental investigation. The Prana circulating through them, as Professor Hasted opined, must therefore be psychic rather than physical. Which means that Kundalini science covers an anatomy and physiology which are supplementary to those taught in our medical schools. Yogis themselves, however, have never been much interested in working out their interrelations. As I suggested earlier, knowledge of the Chakras as energy centres was probably developed by seers with the sort of extended vision rarely found in the West today and even more rarely used in scientific research.

As a result there are at present a great many unexplained phenomena which are either bothering scientists or being ignored by them which the postulation of some such natural force as Kundalini might render easier to deal with. Not least of these are telepathy, so-called spiritual healing and the ancient arts of divination. All these suggest obscure affinities between human beings as receivers and transmitters and also between human beings and the earth. They clearly involve very subtle energy transactions. Doctors are at a loss to explain the mechanics of hand-healings, which are obviously not all cases of spontaneous regression. Attempts to replace dowsers by machines have also proved far from satisfactory in both water- and metal-divining experiments. (9)

In the science of the centres Kundalini and Prana are said to blend in the Muladhara, the root Chakra at the base of the spine. As it is Kundalini's role to adapt all forces for use in gross bodies, this suggests that all Pranas are modified and adjusted to particular bodies in this centre at least as far as man is concerned. It is likely therefore that there is no force operating in the body during life which is unaffected in its action by Kundalini. Indeed this is probably true of all forms everywhere in nature. Each physical entity behaves in a way dictated by its structure which in turn is adapted to the function the structure serves. Moreover, as we have seen, as Shabdabrahman Kundalini uses form and function to express purpose. This would explain why in dowsing, for instance, the same diviner can use the same rod in the same way to dowse for different substances. There is something in the matter of the Earth which responds not to his action so much as to his intention.

As the two Pranas and Kundalini blend in the Muladhara Chakra in man so presumably there must be a blending of forces in the Earth. As all matter is ergoconscious and responsive to formative pressures from above, there must be in our terrestrial context as well as in ourselves centres and channels through which cosmic energies pass and in which they blend. From a Tantric point of view it would be impossible to explain the origin of life on this planet without reference to Mahakundalini and the Earth, Prithivi. All energies at work in bodies become Kundalini forces as soon as they enter dense matter. Similarly all becomes part of the Earth as soon as it manifests within its field of forces.

Cosmic energies are conceived as polarised between spirit as the most refined form of ergoconsciousness and matter as its densest, most solidified state. In Kundalini yoga this polarity is seen reflected in a relation between two centres in the human body, the Sahasrara Chakra or spiritual centre in the head and the Muladhara or Kundalini Chakra at the base of the spine. In terms of life on this planet there is a similar polarity between the centre of the Sun and the centre of the Earth defining a multidimensional field of forces from highest Bodhi-Shakti down to the chemical forces of dense matter. In conformity with this idea, it is not surprising that astronomers are finding space less and less empty.

In addition to being an enormous field of interacting forces, it is packed with fine dust, micro-organisms and an infinity of elementary particles. From the Tantric point of view our scientific knowledge of the Sun, Moon and Earth and, indeed, the solar system in general, is superficial to a degree. Indian cosmologists would never dream of confining the study of it to the denser levels to which Western scientific theories limit themselves. The references in Kundalini yoga to sun, moon and fire as having affinities with the energies flowing through the three major Nadis in the subtle body, for instance, have nothing to do with astronomical or elemental similarities and even less to do with astrology as this is under-stood in the West. The affinities are Tattvic, similarities related to quality and the sharing of attributes.

In *The Lives of a Cell*, to which I have already referred, Lewis Thomas puts vividly the case for regarding the Earth as a living being, a creature which is also a vast community of interdependent lesser creatures in constant communication with one another. From viruses to men these are all signalling their positions and needs to all and sundry in a way which implies a terrestrial organisation as unitary as a human body. He also argues strongly against the view of those who see the world as fundamentally an arrangement of adverse systems with mutually exclusive interests continually at odds with one another. On the contrary he sees the natural order as essentially one of co-operation and symbiosis. This would ultimately derive from what the Hindu would call the Brahmanic Oneness behind the Allness of things. Nature red in tooth and claw is, of course, a characteristic of Prakriti but is relative only to the food-sheath level of her activities where all must eat to live. It is a by-product really of the harshness of living conditions in dense matter where an exuberance of generation is necessary to offset high death rates. With the exception of man, who is a rogue species in this respect, living things struggle with the environment communally and kill one another only for food. The trouble is they seem to need an immense amount to eat, some enormous quantities in comparison with their body weight, and this obscures their highly developed social instincts.

One of the outstanding problems not yet overcome by scientists attempting to solve the problem of the evolution of organisms is how strings of molecules or polymers get themselves organised into specialised membranes, in particular how they learn to replicate each after its own kind. As we saw when discussing handedness, inorganic materials can under certain conditions be converted into organic substances. These conditions were until recently thought to include lightning or ultra-violet radiation as mutant forces. It was assumed also that light was essential for the survival of plants which depend on photosynthesis for much of their nourishment. Now it has been discovered that a whole world of living creatures exists in a plant jungle two miles and more below the surface of the sea. These are far beyond the reach of sunlight, lightning or ultra-violet radiation. More than this it has been found that there are great volcanic ridges and clefts in the ocean floor which are factories where chemical compounds are continuously being manufactured from material thrown up from the Earth's core. It is a place riven by explosions and in its dark depths are to be found all the chemical components necessary to produce bodies. What, in the absence of light, enables the denizens of the submarine jungle to replicate and grow?

The existence of this submarine world at the Kundalini end of the Sun—Earth axis suggests that it may after all be in the depths of the Earth rather than on its surface that organisms were first formed. The emergence of some into sunlit waters and then on to dry land may be instalments two and three and not one and two of the story of the evolution of life on Earth. One of the powers inherent in Mahakundalini may be that which urges all living things up towards the sun as part of the general spiritualising of matter.

Once one starts thinking in terms of life-forces deep within the Earth a whole set of new ideas about their movements opens up. For instance, Mahakundalini must not be thought of as working only at the surface but penetrating the entire substance of the planet. Its hidden activities may be affecting the nature and quality of life in ways of which science is still profoundly ignorant. The ancient Chinese theories about earth currents, dragon lines, the strange artefacts left behind by our neolithic ancestors, the folk wisdom of country people such as dowsers, all lend credence to the possibility that phenomena exist which were once known and understood and are now overlooked or ridiculed.

In so far as there is a cosmic variant of Kundalini and many planets in many galaxies are subject to its overall control, the aim of a Tantric astronomy would presumably be to interpret phenomena by seeking to understand their behaviour and composition in terms of their role in some comprehensive design of evolving ergoconsciousness. In each configuration there would have to be centres to function like root Chakras in human beings, critical areas through which all participating energies must pass and be suitably modified and specialised. To study the Earth as a planet from the stand-point of interior planetary currents and how they function could, if it proved fruitful, give astronomers another tool to explore with. The stars may be sending out waves, like so many signature tunes, giving information about their interior pattern of forces.

In Hinduism a distinction is made between powers in nature which tend to bring about change and diversification and forces directed towards maintaining the status quo. In a sense it is a Shiva-Shakti distinction but one used to distinguish between forces and not between forces of nature and Purushas as experiencers of nature. As we saw earlier, in the pheno-menal world the role of Shiva, as cosmic consciousness, is to represent Brahman knowledge at the heart of the manifested universe, to stabilise it by preserving its identity with Brahman as the One, as True Being. Shakti's divine task is to convert the One into the Many in the phenomenal world of Becoming. She does this in partnership with Shiva so that Being and Becoming are twin aspects of reality never out of harmony with one another. But Shakti also has to be a stabilising force and not only an agent of change. In one role she generates unstable energy patterns; in another she re-establishes the balance of forces in conformity with some fundamental status quo which must not be disturbed. The forces of physics are illustrations of the functional duality within basically stable Shakti partnerships. Magnetism, for instance, tends to maintain constancy while electricity readily becomes unstable. Gravity and the strong nuclear force tend to keep things steady; light, heat and chemical forces facilitate change. In biology hormones and enzymes are agents of change while DNA and RNA molecules act as constants setting limits to what can safely be altered. The analogy can be carried into the mental sphere. Thought is mobile, while attention and intention are selectors-out which keep thought and emotion within the bounds set by need, purpose, character and situation.

The role of Kundalini in all this would be to see that the relations between all the multitudinous Shakti processes going on in the body are held firmly within the patterns set by the Brahmanic purpose for this life which is our destiny, our Dharma or place in the scheme of things. This would apply equally whether that destiny, from the standpoint of the individual, is happy or unhappy, and irrespective of whether he feels it to be just, unjust or merely purposeless.

That intelligence, as a combination of energy and meaning, is inherent in Kundalini as a cosmic force is a basic tenet of Tantric science. The Muladhara Chakra, as Sir John Woodroffe makes clear in *The Serpent Power*, is symbolised by a Mandala or pictured statement in which three divine Shaktis — Kundalini, Prithivi and Dakini — play leading parts. Mandalas are essentially things to ponder over, compact lessons to be contemplated in order to penetrate into the real nature of the thing we are seeking to understand. They were originally circular floor drawings, temple objects of worship depicting aspects of divinity into which the devotee could quite literally step. Later, as paintings, they could be used in private and group meditation. It is as Mandalas that we can learn most from the illustrations of the Chakras to be found in *The Serpent Power*.

The fact that the root Chakra is associated with the Earth is less well known than that it is the resting-place of coiled Kundalini. The joint presence of Prithivi and Kundalini in the main supportive Chakra in the body underlines the fact that Kundalini as a force is inseparably connected with the Earth. What is even less well known is that the presiding Goddess of the Centre is the Devi Dakini. Each centre has such a presiding divinity and collectively they are sometimes called 'The Queens of the Chakras'. Dakini is described in the text as 'the carrier of the revelation of the ever-pure intelligence' and sometimes as the doorkeeper as well as guardian of the centre. Thus we are being told that the forces moving in and out of Kundalini's resting place are controlled by a power that knows the Brahmanic intention for the individual concerned. The same would be true for Dakini's role in nature. The passage of Kundalini in and out of forms in the realm of Prithivi is to be conceived as governed by pure intelligence in the final analysis. This cosmic truth is implied clearly in the Muladhara Mandala. Filling its centre is 'the square region of Prithivi surrounded by eight shining spears', pointing towards the eight points of the compass. This square is not brown as one might expect but a bright yellow and is 'beautiful like lightning'. In other words, it is alight with the pure intelligence manifesting through Dakini Shakti.

This pure intelligence informs all dense matter in both man and nature and is the root (Mula) support (adhara) of bodies, as the name of the Muladhara Chakra implies. Looked at in this way, this Mar.dala, as also the Mandalas of the other Chakras, is correctly interpreted by Jung and others as a subject for meditation. The Muladhara *Mandala* contains a lesson about physical matter. The root centre, the Muladhara *Chakra*, is something else again. It is, as we are clearly told, a force centre in the subtle body, the non-physical body. It is into a Nadi in the subtle body that Kundalini finally rises, not into the physical spinal canal.

The Chakras, being in the subtle body and not in the life-vehicle, are composed of psychic and not physical matter. Kundalini and Dakini are thus forces working on physical matter from above, modifying the physical Prana of the life-vehicle and working on the chemical body or food-sheath at one remove. Mahakundalini would work in essentially the same way in the universe at large. If I am right in thinking there may be tiny spinning particles of psychic and physical Prana acting like screws on the frontier between dense and subtle matter, Dakini, as guardian of this threshold's intelligent behaviour, would presumably be the Tantric name for the force directing their serpentine winding and unwinding in suitably adaptive ways. The Sanskrit word Sir John

Woodroffe translates as pure intelligence is Sadasuddhabuddhi, implying a divine grasp of the true being in things. This is, of course, vital for Mahakundalini's maintenance of the natural order as an integrated manifold.

7
Kundalini as an Earth force

In *Kundalini — Psychosis or Transcendence* Lee Sannella puts forward, on behalf of a group researching a phenomenon they call 'the Kundalini cycle', the concept of physio-kundalini. The term physio-kundalini was suggested by the late Itzak Bentov to denote what he and the rest of the group felt was a specific manifestation of Kundalini energy responsible for a recurring pattern of symptoms found among meditators. Physio-kundalini in this sense is a strictly limited concept covering a particular set of movements of energy within the body, the Kundalini cycle. It does not denote any general aspect of Kundalini as a physical force in nature. It is important for readers interested in the work of the Sannella group to be clear on this, since the term itself is somewhat ambiguous.

The work of the group will be dealt with from a physiological angle later on. Two points only are relevant now. The first is the effect that thought can have on the body. The second is that, although the emphasis is on the cycle from the pelvic area back into the pelvic area, the phenomena first recorded by all subjects were symptoms arising in the feet and legs. In other words events occurring in feet and legs as well as taking thought in a certain way precedes the onset of the cycle.

Later we will consider whether some of the more distressing accompaniments of the Kundalini cycle may not be due to taking the wrong kind of thought. Here it is enough to consider, from the standpoint of Tantric science, what the right kind of thought must entail if it is indeed Kundalini which is involved. It must entail, first and foremost, being in harmony with the proper or cosmically ordained roles of Kundalini in relation to Prithivi and Dakini. Our well-being within a total environment which includes us must in no small measure depend on our understanding and working with all the forces of nature governing entities. Animals and plants do this instinctively, but man has the capacity to think and choose and can use it *contra natura* and all too frequently does. It is important in assessing the findings of the Sannella group to decide whether those experiencing the Kundalini syndrome are doing so as part of the evolutionary development of the central nervous system, as the group suggests, or whether the victims were cases of going *contra natura* and paying for it with pain.

The Mandala of the Muladhara Chakra as a symbolic statement places the Kundalini triangle firmly 'within the square region of Prithivi', as we have seen. This establishes it as an Earth force. As I said earlier, the fact that it is usually discussed in a context of exercises for spiritual advancement tends to obscure the stress in the texts on its primacy as a force at work in dense matter. It can only interact smoothly with the subtler energies of life and mind if its connection with physical nature is not disturbed. In other words it is as essential for the aspirant to keep on good terms with Mother Earth as with pure intelligence, with Prithivi as Dakini. Indeed to go *contra natura* in this sense is to go against the created order of things in physical manifestation, the blueprint for which is safeguarded by Dakini. It follows from this that it might be wise to try to discover how Kundalini operates in the Earth and not only in our bodies to consider Mahakundalini as a geodynamic force.

That the Sannella-Bentov Kundalini cycle starts with sensations in the feet and legs has interesting implications for students of Kundalini science. It suggests that some energies may enter the Chakra at the base of the spine from below, a point not stressed in Tantric texts. Yogic accounts speak of Kundalini as coiled 3½ times round the Linga, the Shiva line of force which enters the body from above. Kundalini itself also enters its resting-place from above, from the causal level of Shabdabrahman to the level of Prithivi. In the Muladhara Mandala the Kundalini triangle is in the centre of the square of Prithivi. Kundalini must therefore be seen as operating within Prithivi. Its place is within the Earth's field of forces. It is not, however, the Earth force itself but a force which plays a central role in preserving the stability of the Earth's force-field. Its position in the centre of the square region of Prithivi stresses this fact, which makes sense since the Earth must precede the entities which arise within its realm; and it is with entities that Kundalini is concerned, not with dense matter as such.

The entrance of Shiva and Kundalini 'from above' requires some elucidation if we are to interpret the Mandala as a bio-logical statement. From above would seem to suggest from subtler into denser configurations of substance. From a biological standpoint what is inherent in the formal organisa-tion of bodies would come 'from above' as the result of patterning by thought-fields and life-fields. What comes 'from below' would be the chemical components which give such patterns their solidity. The building blocks of matter which go to make up the 'food-sheaths' of human beings are pro-vided for us by Prithivi and behave according to its laws. The role of Kundalini as the equilibrating force in the physical world must be related to keeping the forces governing the food-sheath and the forces governing subtle bodies in phase with one another. What triggers off Kundalini cycles could be activities which disrupt this harmony, causing what might be called 'kundalini stress' and consequent physiological disturbances.

The problem of Earth forces raises many questions. There is growing evidence, recently well summarised by Christopher Bird in *Divination*, that there are geodetic currents which physics has under-researched up to now. If such currents exist and are carrying forces as yet unknown to science it is high time we looked into them. Apart from their relevance for scientists and students of yoga, it is possible that a greater knowledge of them might enable us to undo some of the damage we have inadvertently done to ourselves and to our planet by ignorance of terrestrial energy fields of crucial importance for healthy life on Earth. For the purposes of this discussion two valuable books supplementing the researches summarised by Bird are *Patterns of the Past* by Guy Underwood and *The View over Atlantis* by John Michell. The former deals with Earth forces with tendencies to spiral formations and the latter with a network of forces which appear to travel in straight lines.

Underwood was a solicitor interested in archeology. In pursuing his hobby he began to suspect a connection between the siting of Stone Age religious monuments and underground water. He found that this view was shared by the late R.A. Smith, one-time Keeper in Charge of the Department of British and Roman Antiquities at the British Museum and a leading authority on the Stone Age. Smith was unofficially interested in dowsing and suggested Underwood should try his hand at it. The outcome was the series of discoveries he reports in *Patterns of the Past*.

First of all he spent several years experimenting with a variety of divining rods and ways of holding them, trying them out on promising sites. In the course of these activities he did a considerable amount of excavating to check his results and was incidentally the discoverer of a number of prehistoric circles, barrows, mazes and stone-paved tracks since declared authentic finds.

Divining rods locate underground streams by responding to influence lines above them called water veins or stream bands. Underwood's work was particularly valuable because his abilities turned out to extend beyond water-divining. In the course of his explorations he found his rod behaving in three distinct ways. This suggested to him that he must be dowsing at least two other influence lines besides those associated with water. In developing his research he retained the term water line and christened the other two influence lines track lines and aquastats. Because it appeared to him from his archeological surveys that early man had used them to mark out geological and geographical zones, Underwood called the three lines collectively geodetic lines. He found that not all dowsers could respond to all three types of line, and divided them into two classes: positive dowsers who could pick up all three lines and negative dowsers who responded only to water lines. The terms positive and negative were chosen because positive dowsers had a right-handed sensitivity and grasped the rod most firmly in their right hands. Negative dowsers he found to have a left-handed sensitivity and got reactions first in the left hand and arm.

Track lines were so called because Underwood discovered that animals use them and old roads and tracks were aligned along them. Track lines dowsed are seldom straight and can sometimes wind so excessively that animals cannot use them to save distance. They must do so because their bodies move instinctively and therefore more easily along them. This is the likely origin of the saying that the longest way round is often the shortest way home. As Stone Age man covered great distances often negotiating heavy loads, the least fatiguing route would be more useful than the most direct.

Aquastats were so called because they were most frequently found in association with water lines. Aquastats in conjunction with water lines seem to have been regarded as specially sacred in some way. Both, but especially aquastats, were prominent features of all the religious monuments Underwood dowsed. As he progressed he found that aquastats and track lines produced secondary linear effects which governed the way temples were orientated and how they were entered.

These findings suggested some influence generated within the Earth and as yet unidentified by science to which animal organisms respond. The wave-forms associated with it are serpentine curves, coils or spirals which may be why we find the symbols of spiral, snake and dragon in the artefacts of ancient peoples all over the world. Stone Age man may have understood no more than we do what the force was but he seems to have known a great deal more about where to find it and how it works.

Because religious sites were so particularly rich in all three types of line much of Underwood's attention was focused on them. What will be of interest to Freemasons is that medieval architects seemed still to know about them. Underwood extended his researches to include old churches and the great cathedrals, mindful of Pope Gregory's edict that Christian churches be built on the sites of the pagan temples they replaced. He found that not only their location, but their size and arrangement was apparently based on a knowledge of ancient geomantic principles. One of these was that important lines should never be impeded. Another was that every sacred place should be well supplied with aquastats and stand upon a concourse of lines to include at least one spiral indicating the presence of a spring. The more coils the holier the spring.

The siting of a parish church remote from the village it served, the erection of Winchester Cathedral on swampland when higher ground was available, the vast proportions of Westminster Abbey when the congregation of Edward the Confessor's time would not have exceeded a few hundred souls, makes sense only if the builders were taking into account principles we no longer understand. Asymmetries in the placing of pillars and bays were found to be necessary if an important line was not to be broken. In the case of Winchester the customary East-West axis of the building was sacrificed so that the nave and high altar might enclose the longest aquastat Underwood found in any church in England. Why the priests and priestesses of antiquity and the medieval masons found it vital to guard the secrets of the geodetic system we do not know; nor do we know why certain configurations were held to be particularly sacred. The knowledge was presumably lost when the Masonic Orders were systematically suppressed as independent guilds. One does, however, wonder whether it related to the same serpent power the adepts of the East called Kundalini. If so, they may have shared the yogi's belief that its secrets could be dangerous in the hands of the uninitiated. They may also have been aware of its role in the spiritual development of earthlings and treated it as sacred for that reason.

Underwood found that geodetic lines were also positive or negative. He inferred this from the way they affected the body of the dowser. He considered water lines to be negative because they give rise to tensions in the left hand and arm of the diviner. Aquastats and track lines he considered to be positive because the main tensions were in the right hand and arm. The difference in handedness suggests that the autonomic nervous system reacts differently to the two types of influence. Village dowsers tend to be of the negative kind. On the other hand some of them may be crypto-positive dowsers who have never trained themselves, as did Underwood, to pick up track lines and aquastats.

Often sensitivity to water is discovered quite accidentally in childhood. A story is told of Barthelémy Bleton, the famous French dowser. (9) As a child of seven he used to take food to workmen in the grounds of the monastery in Dauphiny. It was noticed that when he sat on a certain stone he invariably became faint. This interested the prior sufficiently for him to have the site under the stone dowsed. Drilling exposed a force of water 'enough to run a mill'. A further interesting point about this story is that the child's bottom, so near the site of the root Chakra, was the sensitive area. When he stood on his feet the faintness lessened. In this may lie a clue as to why the Indian texts, written by holy men given to sitting on the ground and meditating with the soles of their feet upwards, lay so little emphasis on forces which may enter the Chakra via the feet and legs.

Geodetic lines normally wind, but can zigzag, form loops or fold back on themselves in hairpin bends. They usually continue in the same general direction for considerable distances. It is interesting, in view of the possibility that they may be Kundalini-controlled channels, that Underwood found that all three primary lines interweave along their entire length like the serpents on the caduceus. Technically this is called reticulating. All primary lines reticulate even when spiralling through the coils of the springs which divide them into sections.

Two or more primary lines of the same type may run parallel and close together to form multiple lines. Multiples apparently had special religious significance. They are easily missed because dowsers tend to stop after finding the first line. This may be why stones marked with notches are often found at such points on sacred sites, as for instance at Stonehenge. When primary aquastats and water lines run along more or less the same course such places were regarded as holy and some have been so regarded by country people up to quite recent times. All the pilgrim roads examined by Underwood because of their long history as processional ways were found to have all three types of lines running alongside one another. The Ridgeway Path, which goes back

7,000 years, crossing two English counties and passing both
the Dragon Hill at Uffington and the Stone Circle of Avebury,
is especially noteworthy. Its wide track lines were found by
Underwood to be accompanied by no less than six aquastats
and a six-fold multiple water line.

Blind springs, coils in which primary lines terminate, were
regarded as of the highest importance and marked the sites of
all centres of the old religion of pre-Christian Britain. There is
a major one in the eye of the White Horse opposite Dragon
Hill at Uffington. They are plentiful at both Stonehenge and
Avebury. Underwood found that blind springs divide primary
lines into sections. In them lines converge to form many coils
at the centre of which lies the spring. From the spring the
lines re-emerge and travel on. Stones in Britain, as in the Holy
Land, seem often to have been placed above them to mark
them as Beth-els. In Africa, European technicians looking for
water have sometimes been warned off likely locations of
such configurations. They are often regarded by local tribes-
men as the dwelling places of dragons or powerful spirits
which must on no account be disturbed.

Dowsing showed that blind springs underlay not only
ritual centres but barrows and other burial places as if the
dead as well as the living benefited from their proximity.
They are not springs of water, but centres of force found on
all three types of primary line, foci upon which geodetic lines
converge and in which they are given, while passing through,
a spiral course. In other words they are sites at which energy
is given a twist, as we have seen can happen in molecules and
sub-atomic particles. The twists given in primary spirals also
have handedness so that there are both right- and left-handed
blind springs on all influence lines, with left-handed ones
predominating as elsewhere in physical nature. The term
blind spring was used to accentuate the fact that primary
spirals are not necessarily sites at which to dowse for water.
The ancients who regarded them as centres of power did not
dig wells, though natural springs were often venerated.

Underwood discovered that the coils of blind springs can
turn either clockwise or anti-clockwise but that in England
almost all primary spirals turn anti-clockwise as if this came
most naturally. Some important ones turn clockwise,

however, so that the rule is open to exceptions, though the reason for it is unknown. His contention that the anti-clockwise spiral was characteristic in Britain links with the work of a medical contemporary, Dr George Starr White. White notes in his book *The Finer Forces of Nature* that, while climbing plants in the northern hemisphere tend to climb anti-clockwise, those in the southern hemisphere tend to climb clockwise. He attributed this, along with a number of other phenomena, to the polarity of the Earth's magnetic field. Most of White's interest in terrestrial magnetism was related to its effect on the human body and the implications of this for diagnosis. His findings about variations in the behaviour of human force-fields in the two hemispheres might well have relevance here and also be worth reviewing in a number of modern contexts.

That the significance of blind springs was not solely religious can be gathered from Underwood's observations about animals. Farmers have long known that enclosed cattle are liable to break out when about to give birth to young. Studying the sites, often seemingly odd choices, where the birth actually took place, he found them invariably above blind springs. Creatures born in this way also seemed to be naturally healthier than those born under superficially more favourable conditions. If animals have places to which they regularly gravitate when put out to pasture these too are often over primary spirals. It is as if they are centres of physical refreshment, rest and renewal. Earlier farmers placed gates on track-line spirals as animals make for them naturally. Drove roads were often along multiple track lines, as the chances of straying were less. Drovers' resting-places were probably on blind springs for the same reason.

The primary geodetic system appears to be exceedingly stable. Lines still pass between the sacred stones at Stonehenge as they must have done when first set up. Monoliths likewise still stand over the blind springs they must have been placed to mark in Neolithic times. One can only touch on Underwood's topographical account of the devices used by ancient people to indicate to one another sites at which primary lines crossed, looped or spiralled. Once one begins to study dolmens, circles, Stone Age bridges, erect, inclined and recumbent monoliths from this standpoint, however, a sign language does indeed appear to emerge. Our ancestors may well have used mounds, pits, banks, ditches, cairns and sarsen stones much as we erect signposts or print maps for this purpose or that. A similar language seems to have been used universally by Stone Age people as if it were part of a global communication system.

Reginald Smith, in his work on Stone Age monuments for the British Museum, came to the conclusion that the Earth and the Moon played supplementary roles both of the utmost importance to rural communities. As he pointed out, all the civilisations of antiquity except that of Egypt used a calendar based on the lunar month and not the solar year. Control of the calendar was a priestly function right up to the time of Pope Gregory, who amended the Julian calendar in 1582. It was therefore not at all inappropriate that Neolithic temples incorporated references to celestial configurations in their construction. Those referring to the Moon would naturally occur more frequently to ensure that everyone knew where they were in terms of the lunar calendar on which the timing of rural activities and their associated rites and ceremonies were based.

The further he probed into the geodetic system the more convinced Underwood became that he was working in a field more closely related to physics than archeology. He also found his researches overlapping many specialised disciplines as he attempted to discover what his 'Earth force' was and how it worked. In this his experience resembles that of those of us who are trying to fathom the workings of man as a whole person. Like Underwood, we find ourselves ultimately up against the need to postulate a force or forces to which organisms respond but which physics cannot yet explain.

One point about which Underwood was certain was that the dowser's water lines have nothing to do with surface movements of water. Stream bands are influence lines above ground emanating from underground water well below the surface. These influence lines, moreover, did not appear to have any direct connection with electromagnetic currents accompanying the water lines being registered. If this were the case divining rods should respond to all moving water, but this does not happen. On the contrary they appear to react to some force which has affinities with that in track lines and aquastats rather than with electromagnetism or even with water as such. Underwood concluded that there was a primary field distinct from its magnetic field which covered the Earth with a blanket of radiations emanating from its interior. Criss-crossing this was a mesh of geodetic lines which caused discontinuities in the radiating force-field. He conceived the influence lines made by the three spiraline currents as making breaks rather as a wire held against a source of light will break the surrounding light-field to produce a line of shadow. The lines made by such discontinuities are what dowsers can learn to trace.

The energies emerging along geodetic lines seem to be generated within the Earth and to cause wave motions which rise perpendicular to its surface. These reach to a height not yet discovered but could conceivably extend to the rim of Earth's atmosphere. They have great penetrative power and can affect the nerve cells of animals, especially those in reflex arcs. Plants also respond to them. They form spiral and undulatory patterns which appear to follow mathematical laws and to involve particularly the numbers 3 and 7. There is some case for associating the terrestrial blanket of radiations with Prithivi and the serpentine currents with Mahakundalini. The energies associated with 7 seem to relate to the spirals found at blind springs. Underwood found that aquastats and water lines converge on spirals of 7 coils or coils involving multiples of 7. The largest he ever came across himself consisted of 49 coils. Track lines, on the other hand, converge on spirals of 3½ coils or multiples of 3½, which is an intriguing finding suggesting a possible connection with Kundalini at rest in the Muladhara Chakra coiled 3½ times round the Linga.

The number 3 apparently related to the laws governing the formation of the lines themselves. All primary lines were found to consist of triads or finer lines and multiples to be in multiples of such triads. The explanation of these phenomena is quite unknown. Their regular recurrence, however, suggests that mathematical physicists may one day discover their rationale. The reason why all lines reticulate is also obscure. It may one day prove relevant that the most primitive type of nervous system is the nerve net of prevertebrates and that the earliest vertebrate nerves are found in the reticular nervous system only now open to investigation thanks to the invention of the electron microscope.

How far the geodetic influence lines penetrate the Earth's atmosphere is an interesting question from the standpoint of Kundalini science. If Mahakundalini is indeed the Shakti responsible for maintaining the harmonious balance of force-fields within the body of the Earth seen as a living organism, this responsibility must extend to the whole system of inter-acting energy patterns connected with it and not only those which end on its surface. It may well be that the atmosphere is as full of influence lines and blind springs as of gases, viruses, electromagnetic fields and elementary particles. They may interact with life-fields and thought-fields in the energy body of the Earth and not only in the bodies of lesser organisms. There is no reason to doubt that an energy aura surrounds the Earth far more complex than any surrounding the creatures whose multidimensional life-cycles it supports.

Spirals govern the movements of Kundalini in all accounts of its role. Moreover, they are dominant in descriptions of the behaviour of the natural force which is symbolised by the ubiquitous dragons of China. This force is in a sense the dynamic aspect of Tao. Tao is usually translated the Way, though this name gives only the barest indication of the rich inclusiveness of the concepts it is used to cover. There is a sense in which Tao is both Brahman as the One and the All and Parabrahman, the Absolute, Unnameable Void. It is also The Mother who produces 'Heaven and Earth and the Ten Thousand Creatures'. (93, 22) It is the natural order and what works to sustain the natural order. It is the way things are simultaneously both states and processes. All nature thus goes with Tao and is a manifestation of Tao. The Chinese called the geodynamic forces that flow with Tao the dragon currents. They move along lines which the sages studied deeply, for they believed that the wise man adapted his actions to their movements as harmoniously as possible.

The power of the forces of Kundalini and the dragon currents, the great forces of nature which flow through the

Earth and all that is enclosed within its sphere of influence, was greatly feared and deeply venerated throughout the long classical pasts of both India and China as was apparently also the case with our own Neolithic ancestors. Their geomancers considered it was a foolish man who did not study how best to work with these natural currents in order to improve the quality of life without incurring the penalties of going against them. Hence the development in China of the Tai exercises and Kung Fu. We puzzle how ancient peoples could have moved the great blocks of stone used in constructing the Pyramids and Stonehenge without more sophisticated equipment. Anyone who understands the principles of Kung Fu finds it less surprising than do most civil engineers. There is enormous power in natural currents of human and terrestrial energy if used intelligently and one's techniques make positive use of their dynamics.

Physically Tao is conceived as a vast all-embracing terrestrial energy not subject to gravity or eletromagnetism but modifying them as they operate within the Earth's field. How it does this is what we need to find out because, though it must be quietly at work all the time, it seems to be readily overlooked. It may be related to homeostasis in such a way that its strength is negated by our tendency to associate power with perceptible effects of a decisive nature. The geodetic system and dragon currents may operate largely to circumvent, to close doors. They may be negative only in so far as they prevent the wrong things happening.

When I began my researches into the energies associated with subtle bodies one of the things I found most difficult to explain was acupuncture. At first I tried to relate it to neuro-anatomy, but could not discover any correlation between the sites of acupuncture points and nodal points of any significance in the peripheral nervous system. I then moved to the auric field. In an article I wrote for a Theosophical journal in 1976, (77) I got as far as suggesting that it seems likely that 'the superficial application of acupuncture needles can affect deep-seated organs, and even the body as a whole, because they change the polarity of energies at nodal points where auric lines of force and important peripheral nerve paths intersect.' What I could not do was to write off acupuncture altogether. Not only had it survived for centuries to remain a widely used form of therapy in China today, but I had experienced for myself the power of its little needles — sufficiently indeed for me almost to regret playing the guinea pig to my own curiosity since my unfortunate body reacted most unhappily. I got the impression that in my case the needles had been mismanaged. In terms of Underwood's geodetic theory it was as if an energy line had been interfered with which would have been better left alone.

In China the knowledge of Tao in the Earth and in human bodies has managed to survive. Taoism in the Far East appears to have absorbed Buddhism in this respect. Acupuncture, Kung Fu and various forms of art and dancing are practised alongside the yoga systems brought to China by Buddhist missionaries. In India itself the early knowledge of the Hindu sages about Kundalini's connection with terrestrial currents seems to have been largely neglected. The great invasions and centuries of cultural conflict broke the continuity of this part of the Hindu tradition in a way China happily escaped. Yoga methods became more static and escapist. Men turned inward to find release internally from external pressures which must often have been unbearable. When the British first arrived in India they found a multiplicity of warring states subject to religious feuds of the bloodiest sort. One of the reasons they remained so long was the fear of European members of the Indian Civil Service that there would be a bloodbath if their going was not well-timed. My godfather was Acting Governor of the Bombay Presidency for a time and I remember him saying this to me when he retired just before the Second World War. Perhaps it never could have been well-timed. As all the world knows the British withdrawal from India was followed by frightful massacres of Hindus by Moslems and of Moslems by Hindus. Even now, forty years later, India and Pakistan eye each other with deep mistrust. The result of all this turmoil has given to much Indian yoga an other-worldliness which makes its biophysical implications hard to work out.

These historical vicissitudes may be the reason why the two roles of Kundalini, in nature and in enlightened states, tend to become confused. As a natural force Kundalini, as we have seen, sustains bodies. In human beings this is Kundalini coiled 3½ times round the Linga in the root Chakra until it is time for it to rise. The risen form of Kundalini is Kundalini as the energy which, combining with the subtler Shakti forces, permits the enlightened state to be experienced within the body without destroying it. It is a force in nature which can connive at the evolution of the ego and then, in due time, facilitate its transcendence.

The risen form of Kundalini cannot be activated except at the behest of the Jivatman, though its coiled form can be interfered with as we have seen. According to the Rishis neither meditation nor dancing can induce a state of permanent enlightenment. It is both a consummation of evolution devoutly to be wished and a gift of grace. It is not something any Tom, Dick or Harry can achieve 'by breathing exercises and holding the nose'. Or for that matter by Transcendental Meditation, Zen, Subud, prayer, fasting or any other discipline, however helpful these may be as aids along the way.

From this standpoint let us look at Bentov and Sannella's physio-kundalini cycle as a possible reaction involving Kundalini as an Earth force. The cycle begins in the feet; starts from the Earth in fact. The vibrations experienced pass up the legs to the base of the spine. Suppose we think of this process as involving track lines and a coil of 3½ turns which are in-built parts of the human organism. Suppose the blind spring in the root Chakra is a resonator. In such circumstances it could operate as a sense-receptor in the subtle body which keeps us in alignment with the Earth's magnetic field and sensitive to geodetic currents and the flow of Tao in the natural world.

In Taoist performing arts and its painting the unconscious plays a large part. One seeks spontaneously to respond to Tao; to move with it or express how it moves. In Kung Fu the winner is the one whose instincts interact with Tao better than those of his opponent. Because nature is multidimensional, the man who reacts intuitively to the dragon currents tends to be successful. If he is insensitive and impedes their flow, obstacles tend to arise however good his intentions or great his efforts. It is not so much by taking thought as by developing a sort of dowsing instinct that we understand and work best with nature both outwardly in our lives and inwardly in our bodies.

8
Ley lines and telluric emanations

Patterns of the Past deals almost exclusively with field dowsing by what Christopher Bird calls the walk-about method. This form of divination tends to show geodetic lines as taking a mostly winding course, unbroken straight lines covering only relatively short distances. The currents discovered by Underwood in this way were ones which arose within the Earth and the symbols associated with them are universally serpentine. This image he found to be an exact analogy for forces which either undulate or coil.

Though he mentions Feng-Shui, the Chinese system of landscaping in terms of dragon currents, he does not touch on those 'spirit paths' which Chinese lore conceived as passing over the Earth's surface in straight lines. He similarly refers to Alfred Watkins's book *The Old Straight Track* without enlarging on the network of straight ley lines which Watkins saw melding all the Stone Age sites in Britain into a single system. These omissions would seem to be because ley lines and spirit paths are not susceptible to discovery by field dowsing. They also differ from aquastats, track lines and water lines in that they do not appear to arise within the Earth but to pass over its surface.

In ancient times priestly geomancers used a variety of means to find the proper sites for temples and other esoteric centres. There are still innumerable myths and legends surrounding the origins of early Christian churches. Dreams and visions and movements of cattle play a significant role in these stories, which take for granted that the exact spot of ground chosen for sacred purposes was a matter of the utmost importance. Many of these tales show animals interfering with materials put in the wrong places as well as guiding builders to the right ones. It is perhaps relevant in assessing their contributions to note that Underwood was a dowser, while Alfred Watkins first saw the ley system spread out before him in a moment of clairvoyant insight. The Chinese Feng-Shui theory of Earth currents, elaborated over many centuries, was probably the product of several forms of divination. It was developed to so fine an art and practised on so vast a scale that the whole extent of China was a massive exercise in landscaping until quite recent times. Where a dragon current was deemed too strong it would be judiciously modified; where its flow was impeded by some natural obstacle this was either removed or adjusted.

The Chinese recognised two dragon currents as distinct from water veins, a strong and forceful Yang one and the other a gentler Yin one. (22) The former favoured angular mountains and rocky highlands; the latter lower, more rounded hill country. Straight lines were spirit paths of celestial rather than terrestrial significance.

In his work with blind springs and the secondary geospirals, necklaces and haloes connected with them, Underwood found each spring had in addition to its own basic handedness an associated geospiral which changed its handedness with the phases of the Moon. Haloes surrounding blind springs did the same. These operated in pairs. As with geospirals, in the first half of the lunar month one halo could be dowsed readily and the other only with great difficulty. In the second half of the month their roles reversed. Thus there seemed to be a basic function performed by blind springs as primary spirals. This was related to the Earth and demanded a consistent handedness. In addition they appear to have a secondary function performed by geospirals and haloes and subserving some purpose involving a Moon-Earth polarity.

The relations of Earth and Moon are very close, a fact which was obviously recognised by our early ancestors. What is less well known nowadays is that both are really part of a single planetary complex. For instance, it is not strictly true that the Moon revolves around the Earth. Both revolve together about a common centre of mass well below the Earth's surface. Nor does the Moon move on its axis but presents the same face to the Earth at all times so that we never see its far side. Also, contrary to appearances, the Moon is not spherical but has an asymmetric bulge pointing earthward. Its movements are consequently mechanically very complicated, which makes it all the more remarkable that the ancients appear to have been able to calculate them to a nicety. They are primarily influenced by the Earth but also to a lesser degree by the Sun. Its phases are similarly associated with the Earth and the Sun, being based on the positions of these three relative to one another.

The Moon and Earth obviously interact with the Sun more intimately than with any of the other planets. Nevertheless, planetary influences have always been regarded as important. In Feng-Shui five planets, Jupiter, Mars, Venus, Mercury and Saturn, were treated as playing such significant roles that they were given colours and associated with their own characteristic types of landscape. The five 'elements' of wood, fire, metal, water and earth are also regarded as partaking of their influence. Earthworks which form zodiacal patterns and stones relating to planetary azimuths suggest that Western Neolithic man also held these planets to be specially significant.

While students of Feng-Shui and ley lines (45) find constant references to celestial influences in ancient monuments and oriental landscaping, it is noteworthy that Underwood discovered no connection between geodetic lines and either the Sun or these five major planets. The Earth currents he dowsed were influenced solely by the Earth itself and secondarily by the Moon. How then explain why geodetic and ley lines both converge on the same sacred sites?

First perhaps we should look at the ley network in a little more detail since it fits more easily into a Western theory of Earth forces than Feng-Shui. It can also be related to Kundalini science more easily, as I hope to show.

Like Underwood, Alfred Watkins was a lay archeologist. He was a Herefordshire man whose family had lived in that part of England for a long time. His father had moved from the countryside into the town where he set up in business as a miller and brewer. Alfred became a travelling salesman for the brewery and in this capacity rode regularly over a landscape with which he became lovingly familiar. He was interested in local lore and enjoyed listening to tales about the old ruins and giant stones which lay about in abundance wherever he went. He developed into an enthusiastic amateur antiquarian.

One day when riding over the Bredwardine Hills, he stopped on a hilltop to contemplate a wide view over sunlit Herefordshire. Suddenly it seemed to be covered with a network of long straight lines stretching to the horizon. They seemed to run just under the surface of the Earth and to join up all the ancient Stone Age sites in a giant web of sacred but forgotten meaning. The moment of vision passed in a flash but, as with John Aubrey who, after centuries of oblivion, 'saw' the great stones of Avebury reforming themselves into the vast stone circles they had originally been, from then on Watkins viewed the countryside with new eyes. He sought to test his vision by trying to verify the existence of his network of long straight tracks.

His methods were very different from Underwood's. He took 1 inch Ordnance Survey maps and marked the position of the places the lines had seemed to him to link, sacred buildings, ancient earthworks, old crosses and holy wells, stone circles and solitary monoliths. All the sites chosen had long histories about which local legends still clustered. He wanted to see how many of them lay on dead straight lines. He found this true of far more than he had expected, sometimes as many as eight or nine in exact alignment over relatively short distances. He added map to map and found the network carried smoothly over from one map to the next.

In view of what we know of the importance attached to planetary influences in Feng-Shui, it is interesting to note that Watkins found frequent recurrences of place names including corruptions of the names of Celtic, Roman and even Egyptian planetary deities. There were also names incorporating Red, White and Black which were associated in Feng-Shui with Mars, Mercury and Saturn. Ley also appeared surprisingly often and gave its name to Watkins's track system. Watkins thought originally that the tracks might be trade routes so marked that travellers could find their way easily and along the most direct path, but he was never able to make this theory stand up.

The existence of this extraordinarily geometrical network of alignments linking Neolithic sites has been noted by several writers and their astronomical significance has been discussed in some detail by Sir Norman Lockyer in his work, *Stonehenge and Other British Stone Monuments Astronomically Considered*, which actually predated *The Old Straight Track* by thirteen years. Major F.C. Tyler, with the help of a professional surveyor, went over Watkins's material using maps and also following tracks on foot in many places. (85) His book, published in 1939, confirmed the existence of the ley web, if not of actual tracks, of geometrically exact alignments. Some tracks do of course exist, but whether these are the remains of a countrywide network of roads remains very doubtful. Underwood's geodetic lines often run straight overall for considerable distances in the region of important sacred sites and many of Watkins's tracks may have coincided with processional ways based on these.

The dead straightness of the alignments found on maps is very striking and cries out for an explanation, but that there were corresponding straight tracks on the ground all over the country hardly makes sense. Some run over country no traveller would choose to cross even now when so much marshland has been drained and dense forest cleared. It seems far more likely that some geodetic principle of astronomical significance is involved which is not easily grasped by the modern scientific mind. Whatever this may be it links up somewhere with the principles governing the siting of centres where aquastats, water and track lines converge. The common denominators appear to be religious centres and blind springs. The implication therefore seems to be that the sites chosen must both lie in the path of a ley line and bring the line into association with at least one blind spring. This combination would appear to have been a ritual necessity, for what reason no one yet knows. The suggestion is that two distinct sets of forces meet in blind springs, one set associated with intrinsic energies of the Earth-Moon complex and the other related to influences reaching the Earth from the Sun and major planets.

If this is so the phases of the Moon and the lunar year would play an important role in the circulation of the intrinsic energies while solar cycles and planetary movements would determine phases of activity and quiescence along ley lines. The priests and priestesses of the old pre-Christian religion in Britain must have been conversant with all the relevant astronomy, as we can gather from Sir Norman Lockyer's research into the subject. What Underwood and Watkins have enabled us to do is to see a possible connection between geographical mathematics and actual lines of force.

These lines of force do not in either case seem to be connected with energies readily susceptible to investigation by the methods of modern physics. They also need to be distinguished from the influence lines picked up by what might be called physical dowsing, dowsing which can tune in to physical energy patterns such as those of underground water, oil, metals, radioactivity, lost objects or missing persons. If we do this we find that Underwood's three geodetic lines reduce to one capable of being physically dowsed and two that cannot. This in turn suggests that aquastats and track lines may be the two dragon currents of Feng-Shui while ley lines may correspond to its spirit paths.

The Chinese believed that the Earth's underground water channels constituted its chemical cleansing agency. By their means impurities are washed away and healing minerals circulated. I do not get the impression that they were thinking only in terms of the superficial terrestrial plumbing which carries water precipitated from above but also included water distilled within the Earth itself, the 'live' water to which dowsers increasingly refer. They also believed that the solid substance of the Earth lost vitality by being constantly processed through living things. It was these which were revitalised by incursions of energy from the solar system, energy which passed along its spirit paths. From this point of view every blind spring could be an energy vortex in the body of the Earth where Prana and Earth forces blend continuously and phasically, circulating in it as well as in the bodies of the innumerable living things it has spawned.

So far we have been dealing with geodetic forces with little or no physical component and which seem to require the psychic senses of living instruments in order to be detectable. There are, however, other forces of a more material nature giving rise to what researchers in this field call telluric emanations. This is the domain of the physical dowser who picks up such terrestrial influences as those above water lines, oil and other minerals and whose expertise is in increasing demand commercially in spite of the official attitude which tends to regard all dowsing as so much superstitious mumbo-jumbo. This attitude of the establishment towards dowsing applies equally to dowsing by means of autonomic nervous responses and divination involving some form of extrasensory perception. It seems almost impossible for officialdom to think of the human organism as a transceiver of either sort.

In spite of this a considerable amount of research is going on using dowsing techniques in conjunction with medical and engineering skills to investigate not only what lies within the Earth, but the effects of various telluric emanations on living organisms. (9) Some of this work has a direct bearing on our subject and should perhaps be mentioned here.

That some influences from water veins can have adverse effects on health has long been known to country people familiar with rustic forms of divination. Barns are used for crops because animals become sickly when enclosed in them. Houses where people tend to waste and die are said to carry death in families who refuse to leave them. Doctors who have become interested in using pendulums for medical dowsing have begun to look into the possibility that these and other phenomena may be due to telluric forces of a malign nature. For instance, professional dowsers have found that prolonged exposure to emissions from underground water can have an adverse effect on plants as well as animals. These effects are enhanced if they are kept on sites where water lines converge and cross. A French dowser, Abbé Mermet, looking into this, asserted further that harmful radiations could penetrate upwards through houses of several floors and were not only dangerous at ground level. Another dowser found that beds slept in by people who kept falling ill were often over water veins, lesions frequently occurring at the places on the body immediately overlying the vein.

The incidence of cancer in connection with underground

water led French dowsing researchers to elaborate an ionisation theory. As early as the 1930s Pierre Cady carried out a seven-year project at Le Havre checking ion concentrations in houses where people had died of cancer in successive generations. He found there could be as much as ten times higher concentrations of ions immediately over water veins than over places only a few centimetres distant. He found, as Underwood did with his geodetic lines, that telluric emanations rise vertically with no evidence of sideways spread. Cady came to suspect gamma radiations were being emitted at critical areas and used shields to test this out. His findings were so positive that he had them checked by the Duke de Brogli's laboratory which confirmed them. Unfortunately his case for cancer-prone sites, coming as it did from a dowser with no medical qualifications, was not taken seriously by the authorities.

In addition to emissions from underground water there is growing evidence of another source of ill-health emanating from the Earth. This is related to what are called Planetary Magnetic Grids.

These grids were also discovered by dowsing. The first was reported by Dr François Peyre, a French radiobiologist. He had found he had dowsing ability and in the course of prospecting claimed to have uncovered the existence of a regular 4 by 4 metre network of emanations rising from the ground at right angles and orientated towards the magnetic North pole. Later a German dowser called Siegfried Wittman reported a 16 by 16 metre mesh which when superimposed could contain the 4 by 4 metre one reasonably tidily, though his grid seemed orientated towards the geographical rather than magnetic North pole. A German physician, Dr Manfred Curry, Director of the Medical Bioclimatic Institute, reviewing these discoveries, surmised that where these two grids intersect the emanations would probably be as harmful as above intersecting water lines. On the evidence so far this seems likely to be correct.

Yet another grid was discovered by Dr Ernst Hartmann, founder of the German Society for Geobiological Research. Hartmann was particularly interested in the relation between telluric forces and disease. His grid, which he called the global

Netzgitter (usually rather freely translated as the Universal Grid), was thought, like Dr Peyre's, to be orientated to the magnetic North pole. However, unlike the grids of Peyre and Wittman, it did not consist of regular squares. It had a finer mesh with a constant measure of 2 metres on the sides pointing north and south and a variable measurement fluctuating with latitude on the sides pointing east and west.

Dr Zarboj V. Harvalik, when Professor of Physics at the University of Missouri, became interested in this work. He was himself a dowser and had evolved the theory that dowsers respond to gradients relative to changes in the Earth's magnetic field caused by electric currents below ground. Many dowsers recognise that this is one of their sensitivities and certainly those who dowsed these grids must have been able to tune into field-changes of this sort.

Harvalik, examining the European findings, felt something was not quite right with the assumption that the variations in Hartmann's grid were due to changes of latitude in relation to the magnetic North pole. The correlations were not sufficiently exact. Some other magnetic explanation seemed to be required. After comparative studies undertaken in Switzerland, Austria, Denmark, Iceland and Vermont in America, he concluded that the relevant magnetic factor was actually the dip angle between the spot on the Earth's surface where given measurements were taken and the Earth's magnetic core.

It is not yet known what is the significance of these grids, though Hartmann's global network may be found to have some connection with the Moon. The Director of the Eiffel Laboratory in Paris, Louis Romain, has shown that nodes on this grid slow down the movements of torsional pendulums in extremely accurate clocks much as the tidal changes at sea level slow down the Earth's rotation, lengthening the day. As the magnetic centre of the Earth-Moon complex does not coincide with the Earth's own magnetic centre, there may have to be adjustments between the two magnetic fields which Harvalik's grid measurements reflect.

Interesting as these magnetic meshes are, they seem to be different in kind from the asymmetrical networks of the ley-line system. They would seem to present physics with problems more within its present range. The energies emanating from water lines and magnetic grids are physical energies even if the means by which they have been uncovered are not conventionally acceptable scientific ones. This does not seem to be the case with Underwood's track lines and aquastats and Watkins's ley lines. Here we seem to be dealing with forces at work in dense matter but which are not yet included in the energy spectrum of Western physics. They do not have electromagnetic or chemical concomitants as do magnetic grids and water lines. If physical Prana is to be equated with electromagnetism as is increasingly being done, then the Prana coming in along these lines must be a subtler, non-physical type of Prana. This may account for the fact that it cannot be detected by instruments consisting of dense matter alone. If subtle matter and psychic Prana are involved, organic detectors are more likely to register them than inorganic ones. This must be true of all phenomena in which non-physical forces are operative.

If such forces have to be inferred in order adequately to explain the behaviour and environment of living things, the question arises whether or not Western science is prepared to widen its terms of reference to include them. In this regard it is of interest that at the 1977 conference on 'The Frontiers of Physics' in Iceland, the acceptance of mind as falling within the ambience of physics was seriously discussed. (9) The view was also expressed that science had got as far as it could with the exclusive use of non-living instruments as tools with which to explore the mysteries of nature. It begins to look as if both human minds and living tissues are necessary in order to tune in to certain types of force. That this should be the case in investigating energies involved in psychological processes is readily explicable, but that it should be true of Mahakundalini and certain other Prithivi forces is less clear. The answer probably lies in the fact that under normal circumstances all energy fields are mixed when operating within living systems. In addition to this forces as such are never observed directly. They are inferred from the way things behave. The elusiveness of Kundalini and psychic Prana may be largely due to our having so far given too little attention to the phenomena they would help to explain. If Underwood was right in thinking he had strayed into some subtle and obscure field of physics, then what is surely needed is some subtler, progressively less obscure field of physics which will do what was suggested at Reykjavik in 1977, include mind as well as life within the proper ambience of science.

This may become easier as we become more computer-ridden and are forced to learn the hard way the limitations of these labour-saving monsters. Computer errors can make human errors seem small by comparison, and as transceivers they lack both the complexity and flexibility of the human body. The best of them are only extensions of our own skills speeded up and magnified. They remain devoid of the capacity to program themselves or counterfeit our ability to make intuitive judgments about new and unfamiliar data. Nor can they eliminate biases we unconsciously load into their programmes. As mechanisms for exploring multidimensional environments there can be no machine with a potential equal to that of the human body. Nor should we underestimate its value as a transceiver by assuming its range is something science knows already. To do so is equivalent to presuming a complicated computer can only add because that is all we have so far programmed it to do. Dowsing and second sight may be so much mumbo-jumbo, and no dowser or seer worth taking seriously is going to claim infallibility. However, if physics has indeed reached a point where it can go no further with ordinary, non-living instruments, there is surely a case for giving living instruments the same respectful attention which technology gives to non-living ones. It will require a new approach, but if science aims to include mind within the spectrum of energies physics needs to understand, a new approach will be necessary in any event. Either that or scientific cosmologies must remain as limited as ever, abstracting out of the multifarious universe more dimensions than it includes.

It is moreover high time we paid more attention to our parent planet as a psychophysical entity for, at this stage in the proceedings, to go with its Tao is more vital than anything we can learn about the rings of Saturn. It must, for instance, be as complex ergonomically as the most evolved life-forms which have developed within it. Otherwise they could not have come into being in the first place. We have bodies because the Earth provides its chemical constituents. We live because the Earth is an immense repository of organised life-fields within which our own life-fields are contained. Presumably we think because the Earth's Shakti system provides mental energies upon which we can draw. The common unconscious about which Jung wrote may well be the mental body of the Earth out of which our own minds arise and into which they dip in search of inspiration, to dream, or to communicate with one another across space and without words. The whole planet teems with forces from its molten core to the furthest limits of the ionosphere and may well extend beyond its physical envelope in order to accommodate life and mind and the penetrative powers of their associated emanations.

We know far too little about the nature and dynamics of our planet as an integral system. We explode bombs in its depths, dredge oil from its veins, hoist up minerals from its bowels with no thought that we may be doing just what the ancients considered so lethally dangerous — interfering with the equilibrium of complicated power patterns upon whose stability the quality and continuity of life on Earth depend. What we may be doing to it at subtle levels is something to which we pay even less attention, and yet hate, greed and cruelty must be pollutants of the mental atmosphere as harmful and contagious as chemical pollutants and pathogenic viruses are physically.

Here in the materialistic Western world we also know far too little about ourselves. As with the universe, science abstracts out of our totality more dimensions than it includes, while politicians and the media appear constantly to address themselves to humanity's lowest common multiples rather than to its highest common denominators. In such a climate it is not surprising that intelligent laymen tend to become cynical about politics and critical of scientific orthodoxy. Unfortunately the arrogance which so often accompanies power, whether political or scientific, is heightened in societies where those in authority secretly despise those they seek to manipulate. In such circumstances the intelligentsia outside the establishment tend to overvalue unorthodox approaches to almost everything, while those within it tend to be intolerant of anything which smacks, however remotely, of crankiness and quackery. Neither attitude is objective, though both are understandable. They are, moreover, hard to alter and produce difficulties when it comes to expanding the frontiers of science from within. Mixed professional groups like the Medical and Scientific Network in Britain and progressive scientists working in such border areas as parapsychology are helping to break down barriers by staging interdisciplinary conferences open to laymen as well as professionals. However, it is slow work.

A delaying factor is the dismissive attitudes of rational thinkers towards the products of intuitive deduction and symbolic thought. Fortunately this is being to some extent offset by realism in the Soviet Union and pragmatism among entrepreneurs in the United States. As Christopher Bird shows in *Divination*, industrialists are coming to use dowsers increasingly to prospect for water, oil and minerals. They do so for the simple reason that it pays them. Professional dowsers with a sound knowledge of the field score more hits than do surveyors using conventional methods. In business it is success that counts, the rationale is a matter for science.

And there is the rub. The establishment is a stickler for theories and unless new facts can be fitted into an existing framework there is strong resistance to their acceptance. A good example of this is cited by Bird in his section on live water.

Jack Livingston, an American dowser who prospected in the hard rock terrains of the El Dorado and Placer counties of California, had been told that there was plenty of water in this apparently arid country. It was to be found at the tops of hills and mountains and was said to rise up in straight columns from deep underground to form domes which broke up into separate streams to run downwards like the tentacles of a stranded octopus. Like the Chinese geomancers, Livingston came to the conclusion that there were two sources of underground water. He concluded that the water in domes was not the product of precipitation but was distilled within the Earth itself. He claimed in addition that there was evidence that it may once have come up in boiling showers.

The value of live water as a reserve water supply in times of drought was so obvious it seemed likely that water authorities would take up the idea, especially where droughts were a hazard or crops could be enlarged by improved irrigation. This was not the case, however. The US Geological Survey threw out the whole concept of live water as well as dowsing. Livingston's insistence that the water forced itself through deep fractures from sources which did not dry up was not taken seriously. Indeed a brochure was published in 1966 so contemptuous of the use of dowsers that it had to be withdrawn under pressure from the American Society of Dowsers. The resistance continued to affect policy, however, and in a few years the brochure was found once more in circulation.

Meanwhile the reaction of industry was quite different. Wayne Thompson, part-owner of a drilling firm who first shared the official view, was so convinced by results that he began to use dowsers regularly to site his wells. Even the fact that these wells were able to supply water after the municipal reservoirs had run down in the bad drought of 1977 did not influence the experts. They remained unable to accept the possibility of an independent source of water. In their judgment water boards would not be justified in spending large sums of public money on any project based on such a supposition. In other words, the case for live water awaits an acceptable rationale.

If dowsers are still having difficulty in becoming scientifically respectable, astrologers are having rather better luck. Whether or not celestial influences pass along ley lines evidence is coming in from astronomers and geophysicists which suggests that the planets do indeed affect the Earth's field. At first all the forces associated with both fertility and devastation, such as good weather or earthquakes, were assumed to be connected either with the Earth itself or with the Sun. To the chagrin of the more orthodox, a pile of statistics is accumulating confirming the ancient belief that certain planetary configurations are propitious and others the reverse. (24) It has been found, for instance, that the stellar interconnections which astrologers regard as particularly malefic or beneficent, such as the square and the trine, correlate statistically with phases of unusually disturbed or remarkably settled weather conditions.

The scientific explanation of this lies in the way changes of position among planets alter the shape of the solar mass and its whole electromagnetic envelope. Conjunctions and oppositions, when the gravitational pull of two or more planets reinforce one another in dragging the Sun's mass either in the same or opposing directions, coincide with cycles of high explosiveness. The reason they were regarded as grave portents in antiquity may well have been because astrologers had observed how consistently they brought storms, earthquakes, floods and famine in their wake. The square, when the planets pull on the Sun from 90° apart, is another bad weather position and one which astrologers also regard as particularly unfortunate. On the other hand the beneficent trine, when planets form an equilateral triangle in the heavens, seems to be a good configuration weatherwise, presumably because tidal pulls on the Sun are more or less evenly distributed.

I have expatiated on this at some length because it would seem to suggest that, for all their predilection for religious symbolism and the divining arts, the ancients had more practical good sense than scientists tend to give them credit for. The corollary being, of course, that it might do us no harm to re-examine their artefacts from this point of view.

By whatever means our Neolithic ancestors arrived at their knowledge it would be a mistake to assume they were, in the modern sense, a backward people. It is possible that some cultures are more oral than others in transmitting information. Our own society was not particularly literate until comparatively recent times and, with the spread of television, shows signs of reducing its level of literacy once more in favour of oral and pictorial forms of communication. In the Middle Ages much teaching was still done in pictures and 'sermons in stones' were a feature of medieval masonry. Lessons in stone in the nature of things tend to endure, while those on softer materials turn to dust and are lost. Similarly rituals and legends tend to last though temples fall and men die. Here in Britain many stone monuments have survived and rural rituals and legends still remain for archeology to work on. If there are valuable facts to be learnt about Earth forces by this means scientists should set about it quickly. It is becoming increasingly difficult to preserve ancient sites from bulldozers, and global culture is rapidly submerging heritages of local lore.

If Underwood was on to actual forces, however he came by his knowledge, it is worth trying to check his results and evaluate them in terms of as many disciplines as possible. Similarly, if students of telluric emanations have produced theories which may prove valid, we should think twice about building on sites which may ultimately prove to be disease-prone. Entrenched attitudes which work against the common weal should not be encouraged, and it is unreasonable to dismiss the findings of doctors and engineers just because they are also dowsers. Indeed, if they have sensory acuities over and above their professional skills this enhances the scope of their usefulness, as industrialists are finding out. For instance, it is possible that there are arrangements of track-lines which make for road accidents and certain combinations of emanations may contribute to motorway madness, especially when motorists are moving at high speeds. Engineering stress, too, may be exacerbated by patterns of forces underground whose emissions carry their influence upwards. If these exist they would affect not only roads and bridges but also houses, especially high-rise buildings.

9
Kundalini and
the Pranas

From the standpoint of Tantric science the three Shaktis with which biophysics must chiefly concern itself if it wishes to integrate mind into its disciplines are physical and psychic Prana and Kundalini. It is in terms of these that the forces discussed in the last chapter would need to be considered.

As we have seen, all these are cosmic energies with bridging functions linking the dense and subtle levels of matter. The roles of the two Pranas are clearly interdependent since all matter is ergoconscious. They may jointly constitute the screw mechanisms I envisaged as possibly responsible both for holding body and mind together and facilitating the traffic which goes on between them. Such mechanisms must be seen as working not only in lesser entities but also in planetary ones, and indeed in the universe at large.

What is less clear is the role of Kundalini. A clue may lie in Underwood's suggestion that geodetic lines in blind springs are given twists which establish their handedness. Kundalini is unlikely to be the energy undulating through geodetic lines and dragon currents as might be thought at first sight. These seem to carry Earth forces which behave in specific ways and appear to affect organisms differently. They are not forces which co-ordinate all other forces as Kundalini-Shakti is claimed to do. The connection between Kundalini and coils and wave-forms must be explained in some other way.

The answer may be that energies from subtler levels can only enter into dense matter by spiralling through vortices. Kundalini may be the Shakti of handedness. It may maintain stability through change in physical space-time by determining the way the handedness of physical Prana and the opposite handedness of psychic Prana are brought into relation with the handedness of molecules. The term Kundalini is derived from a word which means coiled and may refer to the way physical forces necessarily behave and not, as we tend to think, to the way a particular aspect of it is symbolised in the Muladhara Mandala.

It is interesting to recall in this connection that forces which are thought of as travelling in a single direction have to pass through coils when being harnessed for use. For instance, the Tesla coil may form a blind spring enabling Prana to be stepped down into the molecular world. It would act by reinforcing Kundalini in providing energy with the necessary twist. Straight lines of force may only be found to exist between vortices. The primary spirals dowsed by Underwood were thought to be magnetic centres of some sort and not only convergence sites. This is quite coherent with the physical fact that energy vortices generate magnetic fields. There could well be lines of force joining such magnetic centres. The ley system could be a network of such lines, a kind of Pranic national grid visible to the trained vision of the Stone Age geomancers who, centuries before Watkins, saw them as linking the holy places of Britain. The energy in this grid might well fluctuate with the Earth's magnetic field and be modified by planetary influences. It probably contains 'raw Pranas', unprocessed subtle energies, which may only become assimilable by organic life-forms or be used to revitalise depleted minerals by first passing through blind springs, Kundalini coils.

This is not to say that the Pranas, Chitta, Manas and Buddhi are not generating force-fields at their own levels, only that their energies cannot affect the dense body unless modified by Kundalini. This is why the brain and nervous system are essential to the physical expression of mind and the heart, lungs and blood for the circulation of life through the tissues. The Suksma Sharira and the life-vehicle can be thought of as independent organisations, but during bodily existence on Earth this is not so. The subtle body, the life-vehicle and the food-sheath are, during this period, an indissoluble functional unity. Their patterns of integration may vary so that, in certain dissociated states, this unity may seem to be disrupted. The term out-of-the-body experience, for instance, suggests that the ego has temporarily detached itself in a more total way than is in fact the case. As I said earlier, the repeated references to a cord joining the 'astral traveller' to his body shows that, however tenuous, the mind-body connection is never completely broken. It is an interesting thought that this cord may represent Prana from the life-vehicle whose job it is to maintain the link between the part of it which goes off with the subtle body and the part which remains behind with the gross body of the sleeper. The cord may be analogous to a rope in a sort of tug-of-war between two protagonists cu ntly pulling the force-field in opposing directions, causing a temporary dipolarity of personality.

From this it will be clear that neither the Pranas nor Kundalini should be considered narrowly as Shaktis at work in the body and associated only with the Nadis and Chakras. In the West Prana is most usually thought of as a physical energy absorbed by organisms from the atmosphere and transduced into chemical levels via the Chakras in men and photosynthesis in plants. It is increasingly being equated with the Shaktis of the electromagnetic spectrum. The concept of psychic Prana does not appear to have been taken up, though, as we shall see, its role in mediating psychological states is an essential assumption of Kundalini yoga. The notion of it as a cosmic force has, however, taken root in a way that is not the case with Kundalini. In so far as Kundalini is being treated as a form of energy it tends to be regarded as one generated in the body by the use of certain yoga techniques. It is rare to find a Western text which takes up the oriental conception of it as 'a fire of matter' and as such the concern of physics. Fire in Indian thought is related to power at work.

This is not altogether surprising for, as we have seen, Kundalini appears to be even more elusive than the weak nuclear forces with which it may yet prove to have a close functional relation. The notion of a fire of matter is, moreover, not an easy one to adapt to Western scientific cosmologies since it involves, as does so much translation of Eastern thought into Western language, the simultaneous handling of facts and metaphors. In picking our way through oriental texts it is important to bear in mind that the sages of India and China were symbolic thinkers, as were the alchemists of medieval Europe. They were also far more practical and down-to-earth than is usually assumed. This is especially true of the Chinese. Carl Gustav Jung, (32) who made an intensive study of both Indian and Far Eastern yoga, claimed that they were symbolic psychologists and not, as is commonly presumed, primarily metaphysicians. The very invention of yoga shows this, for the aim of yoga is not a system of knowledge but the actual experience of union with ultimate reality at transcendental levels of oneself. That one enters Samadhi intermittently or has periodic revelations of truth are incidental concomitants of a self-transformation process the goal of which is an enduring state of enlightenment and identification with All-being.

The true yoga-master is, therefore, a very different kind of teacher from the university don whose role is to pass on the products of rational speculation so that they can be applied in a logical way. Oriental science concerns itself with reality not rationality so that it is considered axiomatic that teacher and pupil confront both one another and the universe with the whole of themselves. The guru has to try to convey what he has experienced with the whole of himself in such a way that the Chela can take from it with the whole of himself that which he needs in order to grow.

It is this attempt to maintain an unbroken relation between the individual and total reality which is both the strength and weakness of Eastern science. Its strength lies in keeping all science a unitary life-science. This was found to be so true of the Chinese yogis that Richard Wilhelm, perhaps the Western Sinologist who came closest to understanding the Chinese spirit, wrote in *The Secret of the Golden Flower* that, almost without exception, those who sought the central experience of union through the systematic use of meditation found it. The symbols and paradoxes by means of which knowledge is shared are designed to communicate reality without fragmenting it. A purely rational description of anything presupposes both an abstraction out of the sum-total of its Is-ness and a split between reason and intuition in the searching mind. The weakness of their position from a social point of view is that, unless reason and intuition, subject and object, can be separated and held apart, it is difficult to gain the same degree of technical mastery over the external environment. It is because the East is strong where the West is weak and vice versa that the two brands of science can be mutually enriching. The ability to stand at one another's viewpoints and translate one set of ideas in terms of the other is, however, a necessary precondition of this being successfully accomplished. Any attempt to do so at this stage must inevitably be tentative, especially in dealing with forces as pervasive as Prana and as elusive as Kundalini.

Some oriental writers (98) speak of Prana in a very wide sense, using it to denote the energies specific to each of the various levels of substance. In this usage there can be a whole range of superphysical Pranas and not only the two we have been discussing. This is confusing as it tends to equate Prana and energy, which can be misleading. I therefore propose to confine my use of the word to cover physical and psychic Pranas which step down higher energies through the life-vehicle into the chemical body.

For Prana to enter dense matter there must be enabling forces in matter itself. Nuclear forces must play a part, as we have seen, but not one sufficiently crucial to explain either the appearance of life or the semblance of purpose which characterises the evolutionary process. It is not enough just to say structure is inherent in matter or that purpose is in some way implicit in life. This is, of course, obvious. To come to rest on such conclusions as many scientists tend to do, however, suggests that — in this area at least — science is more concerned to dispose of non-material categories than to find out exactly how patterns get into matter and why they develop increasing mobility and multi-dimensionality within space-time.

There must be some principle of organisation at work the application of which leads to interrelated changes over the whole spectrum of possible energies. Whether this operates in a way which results in a cyclical or linear type of evolution would seem an open question on the present evidence. What is most likely is that it can be analysed in either way dependent upon the data under scrutiny. The principle itself must be a cosmic one since, however practically convenient it may be to concentrate on the properties of matter found on Earth, our planet's cosmic context is proving increasingly germane to our understanding of its nature and origin. The universal aspect of evolution must be similarly relevant if we are to get a picture of it as a total process. Western science, with its bias towards specialisation, tends to overlook the cosmos when studying man and man when studying the cosmos. We need not only a Tao of physics (16) but a Tao of psychobiology as well. The cerebral cortex is a first-class selector out, but can cause grave distortions if the brain is geared to select out too much or, indeed, to select out the wrong things or the right things in the wrong place.

According to Tantric theory the enabling principle is Dakini, 'the carrier of pure intelligence', divine purpose at work in the physical world. Dakini-Shakti is that aspect of Kundalini which gives to evolution not only the semblance of being an ordered progression but ensures that it is one. It works with Prithivi to organise the entry of subtle energies into gross substance. The Shaktis Dakini, Kundalini and Prithivi are thus present in all material objects. So also are the two Pranas. Objects do not vary in this respect but only in the way these forces blend and in the patterns of secondary forces they co-opt in order to achieve the ends dictated by evolutionary necessity.

One of the few experiments undertaken to study Kundalini as a natural force was undertaken by Mayne R. Coe Jnr. (19) He used fasting, breathing exercises and other yoga practices in order to induce bioelectric currents in his own body. He did this in order 'to raise Kundalini' but also — and more importantly in this context — to test its possible connection with moving objects at a distance. Psychokinesis (PK), as its name implies, was first thought by parapsychologists to be a manifestation of psychic energy. The Soviet scientists, with their materialistic bias, questioned this (55) and have since shown that biophysical factors are also involved. Without doubt the phenomenon must include changes in the flow of particles, but whether physical Prana alone can account for the whole occurrence is another matter. From a Tantric point of view it is more likely that PK is a mixed transaction with Mahakundalini enabling psychic energy to combine with physical energy to produce a material reaction. Coe's intuition about a relation between Kundalini and the movement of particles by acts of will may prove well-founded. The feats of metal bending by children (29) probably fall into the same category, their high success rate being due to their youthful freedom from the dis-enabling rationalisations about what they can and cannot do which afflict adults.

In none of these processes would the action of Kundalini be perceptible, but as with electricity, magnetism and gravity something akin to it has to be inferred to account for the co-ordination of forces involved. The solution of Einstein's problem of how to unify gravity and electromagnetism in a single spectrum of energies may be bound up with solving the problem of the co-ordination of forces in multidimensional transactions. Telluric emanations and Underwood's geodetic influences are clearly not gravitational. The considerable penetrative power dowsers claim for them moves in the opposite direction. How high above the ground terrestrial emissions can be registered has not been investigated, as far as I know, nor do I know of any literature which treats of the Chinese dragon currents from this point of view. It is possible they may be instances of a cosmic force which complements gravity, thus holding forces in equilibrium within specific fields whether these be microscopic or macroscopic. If so they would not be in themselves Mahakundalini but Shaktis which, along with other secondary Shaktis, work in dense matter and are co-ordinated by Kundalini Shabdabrahman (causal Kundalini) as the carrier of blueprints for the physical world.

Another approach to PK as involving particles can be worked out in terms of Chinese psychology. The Taoist conceived the Yang and Yin in human nature separating at birth into the conscious and unconscious parts of the personality. With his conscious ego, his Yang side, man relates to, and is conditioned by, his social environment, while his unconscious aspect, his Yin side, remains in unbroken unity with the cosmos. Evolving within Tao was thus seen as a continuous enriching of the whole person by mutual interchanges between the two sides of his being, expressing itself in growing wisdom, good sense and good health. These were above all the marks of 'the superior person'.

From such a standpoint PK, consciously directed, is theoretically quite a possible human ability. It implies, however, not only sensitivity to the Tao of particles which is well within the scope of the Yin aspect, but also skill in directing their flow on the part of a 'superior' Yang aspect. There would need to be harmonious interaction between the conscious self and what Jung called the common unconscious and, a feat much more difficult for a scientist than a yogi, a tacit acceptance of the belief that energy follows thought in a way which can make nonsense of distance. It is the Yin partner, as an inherent part of the physical cosmos, which handles the particles. The role of the conscious ego is confined to manipulating ideas, planning the experiment and appropriately focusing the will. Readers of Max Freedom Long (42, 43) will recognise parallels with Kahuna teaching on multiple selves and their roles in the performance of so-called 'miracles'.

It will now be clear that the sensations reported by meditators and which are usually assumed to be due to movements of Kundalini are not so in any direct sense. The action of Kundalini is very subtle and pervasive. It operates normally far below the threshold of consciousness, organising mind-body teamwork from the particulate level upwards through molecules and tissues into conscious levels of awareness, not vice versa. We do not control its movements but it ours. What we control are thoughts about Kundalini, not Kundalini itself. It is important to bear this in mind when evaluating such experimental work as that of Coe and Sannella.

If we accept the oriental conception of the primacy of intelligence in the generation of substance, we have also to accept that thought can induce matter to conform to its patterns. This is what happens in genuine instances of PK and metal bending. In the case of Coe's experiments the clearly defined intention was to raise Kundalini and then use it. A mental concept of Kundalini and its localisation at the base of the spine was employed and the conscious assumption made that certain practices could cause it to rise. There was the further presupposition that, by raising it, bioelectric currents could be induced in the body. In other words the mind of the experimenter was creating a situation round a concept of Kundalini and then concluding that the bodily responses were Kundalini responses. In the event what he was really proving was that energy follows thought and that thought can engender changes which modify physical events.

The experiment could not have worked at all unless Kundalini existed as a mind-body co-ordinator in the Tantric sense. To this extent Kundalini must necessarily have been involved. However, the experiment assumes rather than proves that the sensation of a force rising from the basal Chakra into the spinal canal was in fact a discrete form of Kundalini actually performing this manoeuvre. The projection of well-defined thought-forms into the body in a concentrated way cannot but influence its multidimensional field from mental levels downwards. To modify its behaviour in the area concentrated on in a manner which conforms to the thought-form is therefore more likely than not. The modification may remain at the level of the Indriyas and Tanmatras and the induced symptoms remain purely psychological. Alternatively the gross Bhutas of the dense body may also be involved causing actual changes in physiological function. In the case of meditators trying to raise Kundalini both kinds of reaction have been reported.

We will go into the raising of Kundalini as a psychophysical happening in enlightened states in a later chapter, since it is something which is well documented in the Tantras. It is, however, a special case involving transformation well beyond the scope of ordinary individuals. The so-called 'Kundalini cycle' would seem to be a phenomenon of a different order. There are obviously definite energy patterns associated with it which occur sufficiently often to merit investigation. To call them manifestations of Kundalini may be both to oversimplify and also, at this stage, to generalise far in advance of our data.

10
The Sahasrara-Muladhara axis

Paramount stress is laid in Kundalini science on the central Nadis in the subtle body and the seven major Chakras which modify behaviour in specific ways. As well as these main energy pathways and force centres in the vital and mental counterparts of the gross body, there are innumerable subsidiary paths and lesser Chakras. These form an energy network which is actually a mesh of superimposed networks since each level of substance in the Jivatman as an embodied spirit is a distinct energy system in motion.

Both major and minor force centres transduce energy from one level to another so that the entire corporeal field operates as a functional whole. This is a role similar to that Underwood thought primary spirals must play in the body of the Earth. He was, of course, speculating in terms of physical energies, but if we assume the Earth to be a multidimensional organism, the mechanism must have a range which also includes those of life and mind. The Tantric conception of the Earth's Shakti spectrum would be compatible with this since it is much nearer that of Teilhard de Chardin (18) than that presently current in orthodox physics. Chardin's biosphere and noosphere and the Tantric vital and mental aspects of terrestrial being are two ways of embodying the same idea.

The superimposition of Shakti systems within the spatial area of each individual's total field and the equipotentiality of Chakras as transducers and adapters are valuable models to bear in mind. Doing this prevents our breaking up the integrity of the Jivatman conceptually into a body, mind and spirit as separate entities existing on different planes which lie one on top of the other like so many geological strata. What makes the major Chakras distinctive is that they are force centres through which the whole gamut of energies pass on their way down towards the chemical levels of the food-sheath and up which they must rise in order to mediate conscious processes. Lesser force centres will exercise more limited functions and many of them will be concerned with Shakti processes below the threshold of awareness.

This whole energy organisation is polarised between the two elements of the Shiva-Shakti Tattva. In the human body the Shiva centre is in the head and the Shakti centre at the base of the spine. The crown and basal Chakras are par excellence the centres of spirit and matter and all the forces which subserve existence in the physical body operate within the magnetic field generated between them. Shiva and Shakti thus influence all lesser Shaktis and Purushas and every structure and function through which experience is gained. This is true of objective as well as subjective experience. Shakti when physically embodied is of course Kundalini-Shakti.

The Sahasrara or crown centre is often called the abode of Shiva. It is also the goal of Kundalini when, as Shakti, she rises to reunite with the Shiva side of her Tattva. This union is the result of the spiritualising of matter by the gradual modification of energy wave-lengths and of the modalities of conscious states until the Purusha is more at home in the Bodhi body than in those levels of his nature dominated by the food-sheath with its material needs or the mental body with its more psychological demands. It is the Tantric view, as also that of Teilhard de Chardin, that it is through man that matter is spiritualised. Indeed, there are many points of similarity between Hindu theories and the Christian evolutionary cosmology of de Chardin. For instance, the role of the Brahman self and the Omega are identical in that they are both conceived, humanly speaking, as radiating centres at the core of our being, preserving its true essence and directing our development. It is not something imprisoned in space-time but is that which holds it steady for the duration of our need to experience it. It is that which both transcends the world and simultaneously directs evolution from within. To reach the Omega point at which the little I is transcended and the Christ self achieved is also to enter the Brahman self in which I and Other are unified in the All. In Tantric yoga the Brahman self is attained through the reunion of Shiva and Shakti in the Sahasrara.

There is a sense in which Shiva and Shakti are never parted. As eternal aspects of the Brahman self they remain inseparable from one another and from Brahman. But when the Brahman self decides to gain experience in the realms of substance it is Shakti who must provide the necessary bodies. To do this she has to accept exile for part of herself. She becomes first Prakriti, the formative Shakti of universal nature, and then Kundalini, the Shakti of the physical world.

Meanwhile Shiva's task is to ensure that his active partner, busy in the realm of Becoming, retains through him unbroken contact with true being at the Omega level of things. When his symbol, the Linga, appears in the Mandalas of three of the major Chakras this is the point that is being made. In each case it is set within the Trikona or three-sided symbol of Shakti.

In the body the vital energy path linking the Sahasrara and the Muladhara Chakras is the Sushumna, the central Nadi along which the intermediate Chakras are spaced. It is important to note that neither of these centres arises from the Sushumna as is sometimes thought. On the contrary the Muladhara Chakra is below it and is that on which it rests, the Sahasrara Chakra is above it, overshadowing and crowning it.

In dealing with the structures of the Kundalini system I will be making free use of the texts quoted by Sir John Woodroffe in *The Serpent Power*. Sir John, writing as Arthur Avalon, translates and comments in this book on two Tantric texts. The first, *Shat-Chakra-Nirupana*, deals chiefly with the main Nadis and six lower Chakras which Kundalini passes through on the way to the Sahasrara. The second, *Paduka-Panchaka*, deals with a less well-known but important twelve-petalled lotus or Chakra which lies just below the Sahasrara and in a way forms part of it. It is at this Chakra that the

Sushumna terminates. In his scholarly introductory chapters to the translated texts references are made, in addition, to a wide range of Tantras and Upanishads. The book is, therefore, a composite account of the Kundalini system which goes far beyond what can be derived from the two translated texts alone. It is this which makes *The Serpent Power* so valuable as a source book for Western students.

The book, however, is not easy reading, as Sir John tends to assume that the reader is familiar with, or has ready access to, his other works. As a result he uses Sanskrit terms with which the reader may be unfamiliar. Another smaller problem arises because of alternative forms which can be used in converting Sanskrit words into English. The two scripts are, of course, entirely different. Some writers use English spelling in a way which makes for better pronunciation; others try to transcribe more literally. Differing results can be seen in the way I have consistently spelt Chakra. This is most nearly how the word is pronounced. Others, however, prefer to spell it Cakra. Similarly, the word I spell as Sushumna may appear as Susumna. Chitta can be spelt Citta. Shangkara, the Hindu philosopher, sometimes appears as Sankara or Samkara; Ahangkara can be spelt Ahankara or Ahamkara and so on. Sir John makes life just that bit more difficult for his admirers by using one set of spellings in his original book and the other in his last revised edition.

As far as possible I am using the phonetic spelling, since this will make it easier for readers to pronounce the terms reasonably correctly. One can never succeed entirely with pronunciation without some oral lessons for, even when one gets the sounds right, the stress can be wrongly placed. An example of this is the word Mandala with which we have become familiar not only from yoga writings but also from those of Carl Gustav Jung. Properly this is pronounced with the stress on the first syllable and not, as can easily be done by readers who have never heard the word pronounced, on the second syllable. The thing is not to mind getting the word wrong but to try to find an Indian friend who can set one right. Or, of course, we can go ahead and anglicise the terms we adopt as we have done with innumerable words we have borrowed from other languages both alive and dead.

Apart from these difficulties there was one which I found myself unable to overcome. This was in adapting the concept of consciousness as used by Sri Aurobindo and Woodroffe for use in the sort of bridge-building on which I am engaged. The Sanskrit word they translate as consciousness is Chit.

In both Sri Aurobindo's teaching and Sir John Woodroffe's commentaries ultimate reality is described in terms of pure consciousness and assumed to be spiritual. Spirit (Atma) and consciousness (Chit) are often treated as synonymous. For instance, in the introduction to the two texts translated in *The Serpent Power*, Woodroffe writes, 'The ultimate or irreducible reality is "Spirit" in the sense of Pure Consciousness (Chit).' Sri Aurobindo, in the glossary of *The Life Divine*, defines Tantra as 'a yogic system based on the principle of Consciousness-power . . . as Supreme Reality.' Consciousness-power here is Chit-Shakti.

As Chit plays a crucial part in Kundalini yoga, we come across the word a good deal and it is important to resolve any difficulties caused by identifying it with consciousness as early as possible. This is all the more necessary in the light of the identification of consciousness and ultimate reality. The trouble is that making Chit synonymous with consciousness and relating both to ultimate reality brings Chit into conflict with other English usages once one tries to translate it consistently. The attempt produces confusions and ambiguities which cannot be avoided. Since Eastern ideas are exercising a growing influence, the sooner such semantic problems are tackled the less misunderstandings already in existence are likely to be compounded.

There are two tendencies at work in the West favouring the adoption of consciousness as a term applicable to ultimate reality which have nothing to do with oriental influence, and these also need to be taken into account. The first is the development within science itself of a growing belief that some form of intelligence is implicit in matter. The second is the desire among scientists to keep their terminology free from religious implications when considering this possibility. Earlier generations could speak of ultimate reality as the Divine or the Absolute and what writers now call consciousness they called spirit. This will no longer do. Thus the polarity between spirit and matter, once common to both East and West, has now become in the West one between mind and matter, at least in academic circles. The presence of these newer usages will no doubt have influenced the way in which some Sanskrit terms have been translated into English.

The Eastern conception of Chit-Shakti as cause and matter as effect has not as yet had much influence on Western academic thinking. It is being brought round to some such idea, however, under growing pressures developing in physics, depth psychology and psychosomatic medicine. Whereas it was once taken for granted that mental events were secondary to bodily processes, an increasing volume of data is quietly undermining this view. In any problem situation it is very much less clear which is the cart and which the horse, subjective needs or objective factors. This dilemma is not confined to medicine and psychology. To a growing extent it is being shared by science in general and must be faced by Western philosophy in particular. The causal relation between mind and matter has to be worked out quite independently of whether we find we need to postulate another spiritual category or not. Nevertheless the possibility that we may have to exists, and it is then that the identification of Chit and consciousness will lead us into our worst semantic difficulties.

As a psychologist I have come to associate the terms conscious and unconscious with mental states in which there is either awareness or lack of it; where a focus of attention is either present or absent. In other words my vocabulary in respect of them has a thoroughly mental flavour. Various usages support me in this. The words unconscious and sub-conscious imply that consciousness is not something which is always present and, when it is, can vary in amount. Moreover, being conscious or unconscious is a distinction made in relation to the ego as the centre of awareness. As we normally use the word, consciousness is equivalent to awareness by the ego of what it is experiencing. To be conscious is to be awake and aware; to be unconscious is to be either asleep or unaware. Thus to speak of consciousness as ultimate reality does not readily make sense to the ordinary person. Before it can do so consciousness must be so radically redefined that we would have to introduce a completely new set of usages. In this context it would be simpler to find an alternative and more apt translation of Chit. The advantages of doing this came home to me forcibly while wrestling with Sri Aurobindo, Woodroffe and other commentators on, and elaborators of, Indian thought in this area.

In the East there is no doubt about the primacy of mind over matter or, indeed, of spirit over both. If one were able to read Sanskrit fluently, the terms used in discussing reality might yield up alternative renderings which could be handled more easily in exercises of this sort. As it is, consciousness seems to be used by translators as a sort of 'Brahman word', as a One which is also an All. This makes it very confusing for those of us accustomed to think of it in the everyday sense of that which enables us to know what is going on. For instance, in many contexts Chit has no connection with either the mind or the conscious self. In itself it is essentially ego-transcendent and supramental. Being a fundamental aspect of Brahman, it is inherent in all reality and not only in those parts of it which we would normally call conscious. Chit can be thought of as underlying both material transactions and psychological processes. Indeed, by definition it underlies everything and is inherent in all forms at all levels of mani-festation. Consciousness can only be said to do this if we use the term in a very special sense and when we do this we have difficulties with its derivative words, such as conscious, unconscious and subconscious. Sri Aurobindo shows this when he finds himself having to coin terms such as inconscient, conscient and superconscient in order to avoid confusion.

Another problem arises in connection with the unchanging nature of Chit, and its presence in all things equally. Atma is similarly changeless and indivisible. As with spirit (Atma), Chit in itself is without states, degrees or kinds. These — so characteristic of consciousness — are the products not of changes in Chit but of the activities of the Shaktis at work in forms. To arrive at some idea of what the Hindu means by ultimate reality we do better, I have found, to go back to the composite Sanskrit word Satchitananda which denotes, not consciousness, but ultimate reality in its fullness. Sat has to do with Being, Chit with knowing and Ananda with enjoying.

The triune word is usually translated Being-Consciousness-Bliss, which is where the trouble starts.

Consciousness here is only one aspect of reality and not identical with it as is so often implied. In manifestation Chit is that element in creation which is responsible for its grand design. In his translations of the texts themselves in *The Serpent Power*, Woodroffe calls the Chit-Shaktis 'carriers of the Pure Intelligence' and it is this usage, far more than the consciousness usage, which best conveys to me the true character of Chit. Pure intelligence as implicit in all created things is moreover a notion which does not lead us into such contradictions in terms as unconscious consciousness. There is no such contradiction in speaking of unconscious or implicit intelligence, and the concept of intelligence also carries with it the notions of purpose and pattern, design and adaptability which consciousness does not.

If we replace consciousness by intelligence, Satchitananda can be conceived as a state of Being in which infinite possibilities of intelligent creation are joyously contained. This state can be maintained as Being or burst forth joyfully to manifest as cycles of Becoming. The bliss inherent in ultimate reality is due to the rightness of things whether at rest or in motion. This rightness is ensured by Chit as pure intelligence. In the realm of the unmanifest all three are one in Being (Sat), but in the order of creation the initiative lies with Chit and Chit-Shakti, which is why everywhere in nature forms are inseparable from the purposes they serve. Even in the construction of the most elementary of elementary particles intelligence comes first. The reason for its being precedes the structure through which it functions. We cannot make, in English, meaningful statements about the consciousness of atoms, though some psychics claim to be able to enter into their states of awareness. We can, however, be in no doubt about the intelligence implicit in their activities. In fact it is because of the unfailing coherence of its design that we can envisage science as eventually encompassing the entire universe irrespective of what part of it we explore first or include last.

When we are told of the close relation between Chit and Atma and of the embodiment of Atma in human beings as the Jivatman, it is easy to see the Jivatman as the carrier of the pure intelligence within our individual selves. If Chit in itself is the carrier of the grand design of Satchitananda, then it is the Chit in the Jivatman which ensures that each separate Jiva is the right self in the right place, doing the right thing at the right time. From this standpoint free will at the lower end of the manifested order must necessarily be limited. The freedom to deviate may be one that no one wants to exercise at the level of the Chit-Atma within. At that level there may be only joyful knowledge of and participation in the grand design and its fulfilment. This certainly is the yogic view. Unhappiness and the desire to deviate are seen as due to Avidya caused by separation of the small ego from the true self. Humankind's tendency to self-will is a sort of protest against the limitations of physical incarnation, an accompaniment of a growth process often far from comfortable for souls deeply embedded in matter. Unhappiness is essentially homesickness for we know not what. Its cure is yoga, an attempt to link up with the Chit aspect in the true self and, with its help, find our way home. In Tantric yoga this means so refining the material aspects of ourselves that Chit-Shiva and Chit-Shakti (pure intelligence and applied intelligence) may be reunited. The raising of Kundalini is the process whereby the bodily Shaktis are transformed so that all become carriers of the pure intelligence. Unhappiness and homesickness end with the reunion of Shiva and Shakti in the thousand-petalled lotus, for then, according to yoga, the Sadhaka can experience the Satchitananda state which is both enlightenment and the true 'bliss of Brahman'.

Because Chit and Atma, like Brahman, cannot be divided but are always and everywhere the same, our separateness from one another and the miseries we experience are connected, not with spirit or intelligence, but with the forms in which they are currently manifesting. Both our being and our intelligence are, as it were, on loan from ultimate reality for the term of our bodily existence. They are qualified by the ways our bodies are made and how they interact. What we call consciousness is, therefore, qualified Chit, not Chit itself. It is in a very real sense a function of our bodies, not our physical ones only but the mental and causal ones as well.

It is the need to distinguish between Chit and qualified Chit that has led me to make this distinction between intelligence and consciousness. In actual experience it is easily seen that states of consciousness are closely related to states of bodies both in terms of awareness and centres of attention. They can be modified merely by the transference of attention either vertically or horizontally. We can become objective and examine the outside world horizontally. Alternatively we can become subjective and move the centre of attention vertically into the subtle body to explore our feelings or analyse ideas. Our intelligence is an attribute of greater constancy. It is an expression of our basic constitution and how we have been predisposed to use it. It is not something we can readily alter by bringing our attention to bear in one way rather than another.

This difference between intelligence and consciousness seems an important one to stress in dealing with the role of the Chakras and Nadis as organs through which we adjust to ourselves and to events in the process of living as well as in the practice of yoga.

The carriers of pure intelligence work with Kundalini to produce, maintain and destroy bodily structures. It is they who determine the cubits of our stature at every level and in every sense. Really good aptitude tests are trying to discover the individual's range and limits in terms of this kind of intelligence. It is of interest that it is easier to arrive at these objectively than it is to be objective about states of consciousness. Also the methods involved are essentially the same as those used to uncover the intelligence implicit in a crystal lattice or an enzyme.

We will need to look out for the way in which carriers of pure intelligence work with other forces in the Chakras because it is clear from the texts that the major Chakras play a vital part in our experience of consciousness and its changing states. The interplay of intelligence and consciousness in man is really the central study of Kundalini science, and the chief concern of the gurus who practise its yoga. Our first step must be to recognise that they are, once Chit has entered into manifestation and divided into Chit-Shiva and Chit-Shakti, two distinguishably different sets of energies.

Consciousness, intelligent awareness, is a Purusha energy, receptive of experience. Adaptive behaviour uses Prakriti energy, applied intelligence structuring creation. Their inter-actions are ultimately controlled by the Jivatman and proxi-mally by Kundalini-Shakti. Kundalini is sometimes called Devi Tripura, the Threefold Goddess, and one set of her attributes is cognition, volition and action. Consciousness may or may not be present in all these processes, but Chit-Shakti, intelligence at work in human behaviour, is neces-sarily so and gives each its characteristic significance.

In terms of the Sahasrara-Muladhara axis the union of the risen Kundalini-Shakti (Chit as active intelligence) with Shiva (Chit as passive intelligence) is a precondition of achieving the experience of Satchitananda while in the body. While Chit-Shiva remains polarised in the head and Chit-Shakti at the base of the spine, consciousness is always partial and variable in emotional tone. It can never express itself in its pure form. In preparation for Kundalini's entry into the Sahasrara, therefore, changes in the Chakras and Nadis have to be effected both in relation to our Purusha side, the experiencer aspect, and the bodily side through which experience is gained. This preparation is both a prolonged and an evolutionary process which the various Tantric Sadhanas are designed to facilitate. Kundalini yoga is only the last of these Sadhanas, not a preparation sufficient in itself. Before one can embark on it one must be competent (Adhikari) in terms of both character and abilities. Body and mind must have developed the required aptitudes and Chakras and Nadis undergone the requisite changes.

There are two main Nadi systems which link the head centres with the root Chakra at the base of the spine. The one with which Western readers will be most familiar is that comprising the Sushumna, Ida and Pingala. The Sushumna is a straight Nadi running within the spinal column from the Muladhara to the small twelve-petalled 'lotus' which lies just under the Sahasrara and forms part of its field. The Ida and Pingala also take their rise from the Muladhara but lie outside the spinal column. In most Western writings they are described as taking a winding course, spiralling from left to right and from right to left round the Chakras. Woodroffe, however, points out that there are accounts of the Ida and Pingala which deviate from this, suggesting that there is a certain flexibility in their movements. All commentators seem to agree that the Ida moves to the left side of the spine on leaving the Muladhara and the Pingala to the right and that each ends up at the nostril on the opposite side, but between these points their routes can vary. For instance there is a well-authenticated account of their forming, not a caduceus pattern, but an arrangement suggestive of two bows standing away from the spine and reaching the Ajna Chakra by way of the shoulders. The Ida and Pingala rejoin the Sushumna briefly, forming a threefold knot in the region of the Ajna centre before passing to the nostrils.

There appears to be a functional energy connection between the spinal axis of the central nervous system and the Sushumna and between the Ida and Pingala and the ganglionic nerves of the autonomic nervous system which lie on either side of the spinal column. What the two accounts given by Woodroffe may be reflecting are two types of energy interaction at subtle levels, one in which the Ida and Pingala are drawn together so that they appear to form a helix, the other in which they draw apart. The Ajna Chakra with which they are connected may also be involved with autonomic functioning, since it encompasses the site of the pituitary gland which, in the gross body, controls the hormonal balance to a major extent. The fact that they terminate at the nostrils is also interesting since breathing, as the importance given to Pranayama indicates, plays an essential part in the body's utilisation of Prana. It is therefore possible that Ida, Pingala and Sushumna form a trinity which transduces and adapts higher energies primarily for use of the autonomic nervous system in its mediation of physiological processes which are largely unconscious. The control of nasal breathing, regarded as so important in yoga, may be a means of steadying the mind by quietening the vegetative activities of the body through the influence of the Ajna centre on the pituitary gland.

The other system linking the head and the Muladhara is that within the Sushumna itself. This system is less well known in the West. It consists of three Nadis all enclosed within the spinal column and surrounding the space up which Kundalini finally rises. The outer Nadi is the Sushumna. Inside this is the Vajra and inside this again the Chitrini. It is the Chitrini which is closest to the inner space which will become the Brahmanadi when Kundalini enters it. Nadi comes from the root word 'nad' which means motion, so that this inner space is not strictly the Brahmanadi until Kundalini starts to move in it. It should also be noted that a Nadi is not a channel which acts, like a vein, as a container. It is a channel in the maritime sense of a stream or current.

This Sushumna group is termed Triguna because of the three distinct Gunas or qualities which distinguish the separate Nadis. The Sushumna itself has the quality of Tamas, its energy tending towards inertia and unconsciousness. The quality of the Vajra is Rajas and its energy is active and tends to forcefulness. The energy of the Chitrini is Sattvic. Sattva is an equilibrating energy which counteracts the inertia of Tamas and the hyperactivity of Rajas. It stimulates the development of consciousness. It is upon the Chitrini that the five intermediate Chakras between the Muladhara and the Sahasrara are strung like jewels on a thread.

Unlike the Ida and Pingala, the Sushumna is said to cling to the inside of the spine. Its place of origin is an enormously important energy 'knot' in the subtle body called the Kanda, from which all the 72,000 Nadis are said to spring. 72,000 here is not to be interpreted as an exact number but as implying a very great many. In fact in some Tantras the number is given as 300,000 and in others as 350,000. What is being indicated is that, in spite of their vast numbers, all Nadis emanate from the same place in the subtle body close to where Kundalini lies coiled. The Kundalini centre at the base of the spine is not only a blind spring which modifies energies passing through it; it is a fountain of formidable and diversified streams of power. Mula means root and Adhara support. The Muladhara is both the root of all the Nadis and the support of all the Chakras. The Nadi network of fine streams represents the energy circulation of the subtle bodies, the Chakras acting as junction boxes or transducers according to circumstances.

The Chitrini is par excellence the Nadi of Chit as its name

implies. It is particularly concerned with feeding forces connected with intelligence into the Chakras spaced along it and so into nerves and glands which subserve adaptive behaviour. The Chitrini-Sushumna circulation can thus be thought of as supplying the brain and voluntary nerves with energies from the higher levels of mental matter while the Ida-Pingala-Sushumna circulation feeds less subtle energies into the involuntary nerves which control instinctive and reflex behaviour. The degree and quality of the consciousness mediated by Chitrini and the Chakras will depend on the balance of Tamas, Rajas and Sattva in the system as a whole. The more Tamas the less alert and aware the individual; the more Rajas the more active and forceful. These qualities generated by the energies in the Nadis will affect the Chakras. The tendency will be for them to react over-slowly if there is too much Tamas predisposing them to inertia; to react over-fast if there is too much Rajas predisposing them to hyperactivity. Chitrini energy is Sattvic, as we have seen. It tends to have a stimulating effect on Tamas and a quietening effect on Rajas. Chit is therefore a stabilising Shakti which plays an important part in assisting Kundalini to maintain the balance of forces within physical forms. As it mediates intelligence the Nadis associated with it work in close association with Dakini, who is the carrier of the revelation of the ever-pure intelligence in the Muladhara, and also with the Shakti who presides over the Mula of Mantras, the Shabda centre in the head.

From this it will be seen that the evolution of the nervous and glandular systems in the direction of enlightenment is not just a matter of Kundalini rising into the Brahmanadi, but also of the energy in Chakras and the two Sushumna circulations becoming more Sattvic. Embodied consciousness must become capable of handling the forces of pure intelligence and this means that the Chitrini pathway must be able to deal with it without Tamas darkening it or Rajas disturbing it. Chit-Shakti, like Dakini-Shakti, is a 'carrier' of pure intelligence but the expression of it necessitates bringing the energy-field as a whole into an enabling condition. This is the purpose of yoga seen as a dynamic process.

Chitrini energies are apparently not confined within the

Nadi but spread over the 'petals' of the Chakral 'lotuses'. The energies of the Vajra and Sushumna must also do this to some extent. The Chakras have been described as funnel-shaped and are said to taper into the Chitrini from the surface of the auric field, where they appear as a series of rotating discs one above the other in the front of the body. All the energies in their vortices spiral in and out from the Chitrini, moving at different rates and in changing directions depending on what is going on in the individual at any given time.

The nectar and ambrosia said to drip from Chitrini and also into the Chitrini from Chit centres in the head are not meant to be understood literally, but denote forms of joy associated with the exercise of intelligence. They are present in states of consciousness where there is a mixture of Jnana (knowledge) and Ananda (bliss). Swami Sivananda Radha, in *Kundalini Yoga for the West*, identifies them with inspiration and intuition and the happiness which accompanies activities involving them. They are closely related to creativity, as is, of course, Chit itself. Nectar is also associated with the Ida Nadi of the other Sushumna trinity and both Ida and Chitrini are likened to the moon which shines with reflected light. They must both be understood as receptive Nadis in some way connected with stepping down forces of 'pure intelligence' from the Sahasrara Chakra which also has a moon-like aspect and is said to be filled with nectar. If I am right in thinking the Ida and Chitrini are Nadis whose energies relate to the autonomic and spinal nervous systems respectively, they must support one another in mediating intuition and inspiration. Both these arrive in the conscious mind fully fledged. Our ego-selves fashion neither, only embellish them or try to rationalise them away.

The bliss associated with true enlightenment is a very special form of Samadhi and innumerable commentators on this yoga point out the dangers of misinterpreting experiences because they are productive of ecstatic states or sensations suggestive of actual nectar, sweet tastes, smells or sounds. The bliss of Brahman is Satchitananda and must contain elements which relate to Sat and Chit as well as Ananda. There must in other words be a sense of being Brahman, of knowing as Brahman as well as experiencing the bliss of Brahman. This is why true enlightenment necessarily involves transcendence of the ego in Indian thought.

The two sets of Nadis are not only qualified by the three Gunas, Tamas, Rajas and Sattva, but also by three Bindus symbolised as sun, moon and fire. The references to sun, moon and fire are frequent but also difficult to interpret. By and large the moon represents aspects which produce nectar and diffuse a cool, white radiance; its forces nourish and build up. The sun gives out a ruddier light and is associated with poison since its forces tend to break down and destroy. Fire seems to stand for power, creative energy as such; its forces are intrinsically neutral. Interestingly the sun, though destructive, is also positive while the moon, though constructive, is negative. This throws a revealing light on the oriental attitude to disintegration and death. Kundalini yoga is sometimes called Laya yoga. Laya means dissolution. The aim of yoga is to seek the end of all that Westerners regard as making life most worth living. The search is for a state of the body which will terminate the need to live in one again. The end of life on earth is not sought as a death wish, however. Behind the pursuit of dissolution of our gross natures is a philosophy which assumes that when human beings have sanctified the matter with which they have been associated, they move into a state which is in every sense their spiritual home. The Indian's attitude towards life in the body is similar to his attitude to life in society. The Sadhaka does his duty by them and then is free to renounce both. The moon shows the way by shedding the light of wisdom upon his path, and when the goal is reached the sun destroys all that is no longer required. Fire presumably fuels him upon his way. Which may be why Kundalini is sometimes called the serpent fire. Its role ends when the goal is reached.

It is important to distinguish between Kundalini coiled in the Muladhara and Kundalini Devi Tripura whose threefold energies are wherever force is involved with form at the physical level. In his commentary on the second text in *The Serpent Power*, Woodroffe cites a number of authors who stress the triple nature of all Shaktis and their omnipresence. The Trikona, the triangular Shakti symbol, is found in all but one of the Mandalas of the major Chakras.

The threefoldness of all the Shaktis, and of Kundalini as the Shakti controlling the body, is an essential corollary of the threefoldness of the modes of Brahmanic manifestation. The powers of Kundalini must be able to handle the energies of the three Bindus (creative growing points) of sun, moon and fire; of Gunas, Sattva, Rajas and Tamas. They must be able to encompass the three basic activities of will, action and cognition and sustain the three levels of the body, the physical, vital and mental. In all the Chakras where it appears, the Shakti Trikona points downwards. This indicates that the energy flow is from above downwards because the Jivatman is in an earthly body which spiritual forces must enter into. The threefold Kundalini is responsible for seeing that they are suitably adapted for entry into physical manifestation.

In three Chakras the Trikona contains the Linga, symbol of Shiva. They are therefore sometimes called the Linga Chakras. They are the Ajna, between the eyebrows; the Anahata in the heart region; and the Muladhara at the base of the spine. In each of these the threefold Kundalini works in distinctive ways in relation to consciousness (Shiva). In the Ajna it operates as a mental energy enabling the Purusha to become progressively more aware. In the Anahata it is the psychic Pranas operating subconsciously in the mind of the Purusha. In the Muladhara it is physical Pranas putting intelligence into bodily processes. The Pranas of the heart centre tend towards the subtle body while those of the Muladhara tend down towards the food-sheath so that life is maintained by a sort of disciplined tug-of-war between the two sets of Pranas. Kundalini 'dwells' in each of these three sets of forces, diversifying experience through them to produce the three basic states of consciousness with which psychologists are familiar, consciousness, subconsciousness and unconsciousness.

In each and all Chakras Kundalini operates differently, modifying life and mind in specific ways, but in the three Linga Chakras the Shiva-Shakti Tattva has a particularly strong hold. In them the Linga is shown enclosed in the Trikona representing Kundalini in the fullness of its threefold powers. Shiva in these centres is thus brought into relation with Kundalini at its most dynamic. The Linga Chakras are pre-eminently places in which the forces of consciousness and nature modify one another most potently within a field bounded by Kundalini's controlling influence as Shabdabrahman.

It will be recalled that Kundalini is called Shabdabrahman in bodies and here we must note another polarity between the head and the base of the spine. As the Muladhara is the root (Mula) of all the Nadis, a twelve-petalled lotus associated with the Sahasrara is termed the Mula of Mantras. This is because it is the centre in the head from which, at subtle levels, emanate all significant sounds (Shabda) through which the Jivatman is embodied and lives as a spiritual being in the physical world. There would thus be a range of reciprocal interactions between Kundalini as Shabdabrahman in the Mula of Mantras and Kundalini as the *fons et origo* of the energy upsurge from the Mula of Nadis at the base of the spine.

This idea of the primacy of sound over movement in the order of creation is the Hindu equivalent of the Christian teaching summed up in the opening verses of St John's gospel, 'In the beginning was the Word.' Like 'The Word' in the gospel, 'sound' here is not to be interpreted in a literal sense but as that which is the source of all meaningful creative activity. Round the conception of Kundalini as Shabdabrahman lies the whole Indian science of Mantra Vidya. Mantras are a topic so misunderstood and over simplified by us in the West that an attempt to clarify at least some of the more relevant aspects of this difficult subject would seem to be mandatory since the role of Kundalini as Shabdabrahman is a crucial one.

11
Kundalini as Shabdabrahman

To understand the science of Mantra we must first be clear about what Mantra in fact means. The general impression is that a Mantra is a kind of prayer with or without words. The best known is the OM or AUM. It is thought that if this single syllable is intoned in a sustained way, it is a form of invocation and a source of power. If asked, most Westerners would say that a science of Mantra would be concerned with the vocalisation of sounds in a ritual way to bring about spiritual changes in meditators or to mediate help to others. Mantras, in other words, are sounds which in some mysterious way have evocative powers. Sound would be understood in the ordinary sense of orally produced spoken or sung syllables which can be carried over the air and heard by others.

This is not at all what yogis understand by Mantra nor would a Hindu think of Shabda as sound in the generally accepted sense. Mantra is derived from the root word 'man' which means to think. The same root word gives its name to mankind. Knowledge of Mantra, Mantra Vidya, is therefore about thought as a force — Mantra-Shakti. To use Mantra properly it is first necessary to be able to control and manipulate thought. Mantra Vidya is the science of thought-power, its range and possible applications. As such it is a science that is morally neutral. Its use in religion is only one way in which it can be applied. For example, black magic is so called because it is the use of Mantra to achieve evil ends. In parapsychology experiments in telepathy and telekinesis would involve the exercise of Mantra. Spontaneous thought-transference is an involuntary Mantric phenomenon. In other words, an effective Mantra is a dynamic process whereby a thought-form or mental energy pattern is projected either with or without intent. It can be accompanied by uttered sounds but these are aids to concentration and the direction of thought. They are not essential. If a thought is well formed and properly directed it can be projected just as effectively in silence.

What constitutes a proper state of mind in the meditator is an interesting question to which one can sometimes receive surprising answers. I spoke earlier of being switched off and of my youthful discovery that conventional ways of meditating did not seem open to me. As I was not similarly switched off where other spiritual activities were concerned, I never understood what, if anything, went on in me in lieu of meditation until many years later.

A friend of mine was a keen member of an occult group which took meditation and healing very seriously. Its members held meetings at which they 'Sent out the Light' regularly to parts of the world where there was war, famine or great distress of any kind. They also held a very beautiful carol service every year to which my friend once invited me. It was when it was time to send out the light that I learnt what may have been going on in me in place of meditation in the ordinary sense.

I was, of course, more than willing to send any help I could to the trouble spot chosen which was, as so often, the Near East. I put myself in an appropriate inner attitude with my will prepared to co-operate and my attention directed towards Israel and the surrounding countries. On these occasions I do not fill my mind with contents. My feeling is that, when it is impossible to know exactly how best to assist a person or improve a situation, it is wisest to invoke what Sri Aurobindo calls the 'supermind'. Such levels of oneself, I tend to assume, are in a better position to direct operations and to send down intuitive guidance as to what needs to be done. So as usual I merely asked that I might be used as it thought best in this matter of sending out the light. I then sat with my conscious mind empty and my body relaxed, prepared to be with the meditators but not myself meditating.

On this occasion, however, a curious thing happened. It was as if something quietly displaced me so that my conscious self became a quiescent element somewhere on the periphery of my conscious being. It was not ousted. I was entirely myself in that my ego was fully awake and remained part of the whole, but it was not the part that was active. I had asked that I might help and I was aware that my request was being answered but how I had no idea. I was also aware for the first time how one can be filled to the brim from above so that one knows (not merely believes) that one's ordinary self is part of a wider self which is also a higher one.

The term 'higher self' is much current among occultists and mystics but the perceptual accuracy of the adjective had never before been so clear to me. The energy — and I did not experience it as a separate person — which displaced my ego and banished it to the fringe of my inner being is actually experienced as coming down into one from somewhere above one's head and then spreading outwards. It is not only the body which is filled but an area some distance round it. Whatever we call this aspect of ourselves it is certainly a greater self and its entry point appears to be not in one's head but slightly above it. W. Brugh Joy's transpersonal point, illustrated in Fig. 7.1 of *Joy's Way*, could well indicate the area from which I felt the process of displacement to originate.

Since this experience it has always seemed to me that enlightenment must begin by descending forces entering us in just such gentle ways and small amounts. Similarly real spirituality seems more likely to be something which is wrought in us rather than something we produce by taking thought, doing good and praying hard. As the prayer book suggests, it is 'What Thou hast wrought in us, not what we deserve'. At least not as we measure deserts.

Until recently I could not fit this experience of a descending force into the yogic teaching of Kundalini as an ascending one. As a result I did not study Kundalini yoga beyond exploring the Chakras as possible psychosomatic force centres. However, in 1977 I was sent a copy of the journal of the Human Dimensions Institute which was devoted exclusively to the subject of Kundalini. It included an excerpt from the writings of Sri Aurobindo which introduced me for the first time to his conception of Kundalini as a descending energy. Sri Aurobindo writes:

> The awakening of the kundalini power is felt as a descending and an ascending current. There are two main nerve-channels for the currents, one on each side of the central channel in the spine. The descending current is the energy from above coming down to touch the sleeping power in the lowest nerve-centre at the bottom of the spine; the ascending current is the release of the energy going up from the awakened kundalini.

And again:

> In our yoga there is no willed opening of the chakras; they open of themselves by the descent of the force. In the tantric discipline they open from down upwards, the muladhara first; in our yoga they open from up downward. But the ascent of the force from the muladhara does take place.
>
> The ascension and descent of the force in this yoga accomplishes itself in its own way without any necessary reproduction of the details laid down in the tantric books.

This excerpt appealed to me, not only because it reflected my own experience of a descending force, but also because it confirmed for me my instinctive feeling that if one lived appropriately the Chakras would open of themselves. It also strengthened my conviction that they were actual energy centres and not just Mandalas upon which to meditate.

It is probable that spiritual fulfilment is achieved through stages subject to a wide range of individual differences. It is in the highest degree unlikely that there is an infallible method which requires only that we can assess the state of our Chakras. Moreover, if spirituality is wrought in us by the Jivatman, it is impossible for us to discover where we stand by probing ourselves introspectively or by allowing ourselves to be judged by others in terms of our personal characteristics and outward behaviour. We simply cannot know, with the conscious segment of ourselves, what is going on in the depths of our being, far less what is going on in the souls of others. Judge not that ye be not judged is, however, good advice we seldom take. As a result we far too often and too easily condemn both ourselves and one another for all the wrong reasons. As I learnt when practising as a psychologist, the borderline between pathologisms and growing pains is hard to draw, as is that between the illnesses caused by germs and faulty life-styles and those due to attempts by the body to relieve pressures in the psyche.

Descending forces seem to imply activities of Kundalini as Shabdabrahman. They may well be indications that the sleeping form of Kundalini in the Muladhara is being roused. The head, as we have seen, is the Shiva or conscious pole of the Shiva-Shakti axis. It is therefore feasible to assume one should be more readily aware of descending than ascending forces. It is even more possible that to be aware of ascending forces and unaware of descending ones is abnormal and a warning sign from a health point of view. Also, if I am interpreting Sri Aurobindo correctly, there should be an interplay between ascending and descending forces in the central Nadis for a considerable time before the most deeply embodied aspect of Kundalini is ready for the final ascent into the Sahasrara. The Nadis and Chakras have to be rendered fit and this must be a gradual process. Meanwhile, as the meditation experience just described suggests, Shabda-Shakti may be operating in silence through Mantras of which we may be totally unaware. To understand better how this may be so it is necessary to go into the Indian conception of Shabda in some detail.

Shabdabrahman only becomes Kundalini when it reaches the physical plane and starts to create forms in dense matter. Shabda itself is a primordial aspect of Brahman present from the first impulse towards manifestation until the withdrawal of the creation back into the void. It is the Shakti above all of Brahman as Ishvara; the force behind creation. It is the Hindu equivalent of the Word that is with God and also is God. Both the God of Genesis and Ishvara are the Divine in the role of creator.

We have already dealt with the creation of matter as that out of which both gross and subtle forms are fashioned. The Shabda side of creation is responsible for forms being as they are and not otherwise. It is that which patterns things in terms of divine intention. It is sound in a very special sense indeed. It originates with the first uprising of the will to create. At this stage it is motionless within the darkness and silence of the void. It then begins to stir and from then on is inseparable from movement (Spanda) since creation involves change. Being, one and unchangeable, has to become many and diverse; darkness must give way to light; silence to sound.

The Indian theory of perception derives from this conception of the genesis of the universe. (98) It is a curious one in that it uses the letters of the Sanskrit alphabet to symbolise first, that which denotes or names things, Shabda, and second, the things denoted, Artha. Thus Shabda is divided into lettered and unlettered sound. Unlettered sound is perceived and so is a form of Shabda. It is the sound of things striking one another. It is not Shabda in the full sense, because it is meaningless. Lettered sound is sound infused with significance. It can be represented by letters, words or sentences each of which has its own meaning. Something corresponds to it, either an object or a percept or a concept. Each has a specific energy pattern in the mind. Speech in this theory is essentially a mental activity, a silent language. It is also a universal language in which everyone thinks. Uttered speech is not similarly shared. From a Tantric point of view linguistic problems in telepathy are easily overcome. All people sharing common experiences think through a common set of images and concepts. In telepathy these do not have to be translated into spoken words and so can cross language barriers. It would be equally easy to explain telepathic communications with immigrants from outer space provided there were sufficient common experiences and familiar objects to produce shared mental images. It is as universal symbols representing meaningful categories that letters are placed at the centre and in the petals of the Chakral lotuses.

It is Shabda in association with Spanda (movement) that organises matter into forms which first become mental images and then physical objects. As such it is the dynamic aspect of creative intelligence, Ishvara-Shakti or Ishvari. The Tantric distinction between Shabda and Artha is thus that between the organiser of meaningful gestalts and the gestalts it manufactures.

Artha are of two kinds, Suksma Artha (subtle objects or mental images) and Sthula Artha (the gross objects of the physical world). In an ultimate sense all Artha are shared by us in common because all are objects created by Ishvara-Shakti. The objective world, in other words, derives its universality from the fact that all its contents are images in the consciousness of Ishvara. Similarly, we all see them in much the same way because we are all percipients perceiving from within this consciousness. This is an interesting phenomenological theory of perception because it manages to avoid solipsism. To do this is easier in the East than in the West where mind tends to be regarded as a by-product of bodily activity instead of the other way round.

Mantra is thought conceived as Shabda at work in mental matter, as the creative forces of mind. Mantra Vidya is knowledge of these forces and how to manipulate them as aids to yoga. It has always been treated in India as an occult science kept secret because Mantra is immensely powerful but morally neutral. It can be used as effectively to do harm as to do good. Its power in the hands of a skilled practitioner is such that it is said that the saintliness of a great guru can be transferred by a touch of his hand, while a clever villain can kill without trace. Telekinesis and metal bending would be evidence of Mantra in genuine cases. Many stories are told about people exercising such powers without it being generally recognised that they refer to instances of Mantra. Conversely many meditators who think they are using Mantra effectively by vocalising sacred syllables may be effecting nothing at all. It is only when sound is used to carry thought that uttered sound operates as a force. Otherwise it is just the sort of unlettered sound referred to earlier. It may break a glass but not by the exercise of Mantra. By contrast a skilled Mantrist could bring about a similar result in silence and without moving. Woodroffe quotes a good story told by a veteran of the Indian Mutiny who once saw a holy man kill a scorpion in this way. It shrivelled up before the soldier's eyes while the yogi just looked at it in silence.

The conjuring arts are to a large extent exhibitions of Mantra. They utilise projection and suggestion to manipulate the minds of others, creating images without objective reality and obscuring the percepts which might otherwise have filled them. Much witch-doctoring is based on Mantra. It can be highly effective when used to dispel fears and disperse the negative attitudes which underlie much illness. Belief in the creative power of images and the value of manipulating them therapeutically is a very ancient one based on long experience of the human condition as it actually is and is not to be lightly dismissed.

Mantra yoga is so closely associated with Kundalini yoga that the two are sometimes confused. This is because of the prominent part played by meditation on the letters found in Chakral Mandalas, particularly the central letter. This letter is called the Bija or seed mantra of the Chakra. It is supposed to represent the lettered sound characteristic of the Chakra and its role. It is also said by some to resemble the subtle sound which accompanies the movements of energy through it. To understand the meaning of the Chakra is to be able to handle its Mantra effectively. Meditating on the Muladhara, for instance, is not aimed at placing one's consciousness in a particular part of the body, but at understanding a Mandala with a view to grasping the significance of the Chakra's place in the life of the Jivatman. It is part of learning how best to manage the body as the vehicle of the spirit.

The embodied spirit 'wears' the Chakras and Nadis in order to gain experience of a world that its Jiva, as an ordinary human being, does not always find pleasant. The gurus say reality is not only Sat (Being) and Chit (Consciousness) but also Ananda (Bliss). Therefore it seems only sensible that the Sadhaka should try to understand more about the garments of the Jivatman in order that he may share not only the garments but also the bliss. Mantra in Kundalini yoga is thus the use of thought to discover the working of the Chakras and so reduce the conflict between our lesser selves and our Brahman nature. From the point of view of the ego this means putting ourselves into a state of receptivity towards Shabdabrahman in the Bodhi body so that we are open to its promptings from above. At the same time we should use our minds to co-operate intelligently with Kundalini at work in our bodies and in the physical world, since it is the physical world which the Jivatman is currently exploring.

The more we open ourselves to the true self the greater its power to change us from within as a descending force. In the imagery of the Tantras this means more nectar and ambrosia drips into the Chitrini Nadi from the Sahasrara and circulates throughout the subtle body, predisposing the mind to inspiration from above. This enlarges the scope of Mantra. It brings in intuitive sources of knowledge to reinforce rational intelligence in diagnosing problems, defining ends and selecting means.

The working of lettered Shabda is discussed by Woodroffe at considerable length in *The Serpent Power*. It is not an easy subject and it is probably unnecessary to go into it in great detail here. It cannot be dismissed, however, because letters figure prominently in the Mandalas of all the Chakras. Every Mandala has a different letter on each of its petals and at its centre. No letter appears more than once except in the thousand-petalled lotus at the crown of the head. There are fifty letters in all, each representing a letter in the Sanskrit alphabet. The Sahasrara has fifty times twenty which is why it is called the thousand-petalled lotus. The presence of the entire alphabet would seem to imply that the complete range of powers made possible by Shabda can be exercised through, and fulfilled in, the body, and to a vastly greater extent when the Sahasrara comes into play. This may be all that the use of the alphabet is meant to imply.

An interesting point which emerges is that the bodily site of Shabdabrahman is said to be the Muladhara and not, as one might have expected, at the Mula of Mantras. In the Mula of Mantras, it works more specifically in the mind. In the Muladhara it works with Ishvara and Kundalini to create, maintain and when necessary destroy at the physical level. As part of the Shiva-Shakti Tattva there is a sense in which Shabdabrahman is inseparable from Shiva whose bodily site is in the head. There is another sense in which Shabdabrahman, being Brahman, is in the body everywhere. How then do we explain what it is doing as a causal agent in the Muladhara? This placing of the focal point of the impulse to create bodies at the base of the spine and not the head or heart is extremely interesting from a biological point of view. It fits into embryology in a most apposite way, as we shall see.

It will be remembered that it is from the Muladhara that all the Nadis arise and that it forms the base of the Sushumna column which supports the Chakras. According to Tantric theory it is also the point of impingement of Shabda which first influences the root Chakra and then those above it. It does this in stages, operating formatively with Kundalini to fashion suitable structures for the expression of consciousness in physical matter. In the Muladhara Shabda is associated with a dim state of consciousness in which there is little or no differentiation. It is only as the bodily organs are made ready that Shabda can move upward through the Chakras and initiate further developments in consciousness. The ability to particularise, to distinguish objects, does not emerge until Shabda-Shakti reaches the heart and the life-principle becomes anchored firmly there and psychic Prana can circulate freely. Shabda is said not to function much above this level in animals. The ability to think, to separate subject from object and manipulate images, is peculiar to man and becomes possible only when Shabda forces reach the Ajna Chakra between the eyebrows. Only then do the human powers of Mantra begin to open up.

This is a theory about the evolution of consciousness in relation to perception. It is, however, a theory developed as part of an account of creation to which perception is treated as a formative force. It is the power of cosmic thought controlled by causal Shabdabrahman from above which generates the physical world and gives its externality. At the physical level the generation of new kinds of forms becomes limited by the fact that Prakriti ceases to produce other types of matter. From then on creation becomes a process of releasing latent powers inherent in nature by virtue of work already done by Shabdabrahman in bodies. Kundalini, as Shabdabrahman as far as the physical universe is concerned, is therefore responsible for creation upwards as well as downwards in terms of consciousness. First the emphasis is on producing dense organs and then on making them capable of mediating consciousness in ever more subtle ways. This is the process which is referred to as the spiritualisation of matter. In the individual human being it works by Shabdabrahman first entering the Muladhara and moving up gradually into the Ajna, implanting powers in the matter of the various bodies as it goes. These are the ascending forces and the powers are the Siddhis or capacities associated with the various Chakras. When the Ajna is reached, the Mula of Mantras becomes active and the descending forces in the Sahasrara become stimulated. Kundalini as Shabdabrahman is now 'awake' at both ends of the Sushumna. Kundalini as Chit-Shakti is able to release more of its latent insights into the consciousness of the Purusha. Only coiled Kundalini remains 'asleep', thereby seeing that the body remains able to sustain all the demands this inward and upward evolutionary urge places upon it. What is interesting is how growth of the embryo in the dense body follows a course which parallels that of ascending Shabdabrahman. (27)

When the ovum is first fertilised it grows simply by cell division. All the cells are totipotential. Each cell is capable of becoming any sort of tissue that may be needed in order to produce a human foetus, nourishing it and keeping it safe in the womb. There is no differentiation until there are twelve of these totipotential cells. Then, by some means still unknown, the bulk of cells separate off to produce a protective and nutrient environment for the embryo, only a small group retaining their totipotentiality. In the early stages of pregnancy the environmental cells divide and multiply far more rapidly than the formative cells. They become a variety of tissues and develop the capacity to dissolve maternal cells so that the growing mass of the foetus is gradually embedded in the wall of the uterus in close contact with the mother's blood vessels. They are called trophoblasts to distinguish them from the cells of the embryo.

The cells of the formative mass also lose their totipotentiality in stages as tissues differentiate. They first become pluripotential, capable of developing into a variety of cell types but only within a given range. Some, for instance, are earmarked for the nervous system, others to form the internal organs, and yet others to become skin and the other superficial organs derived from skin cells. Progressive differentiation within the embryo leads to progressive loss of pluripotentiality until finally each tissue comes to have its own cells and to replicate in an exclusive way. Totipotentiality, however, gives ground to pluripotentiality and pluripotentiality to specificity in a completely ordered progression. The whole foetal development is in fact a miracle of orderliness, but what is responsible for the process remains a mystery biologists are still unable to solve. Obviously hormones and the nucleic acids, DNA and RNA, are present in great numbers. Millions upon millions of mitochondria ensure a metabolic rate consistent with the enormous amount of cellular activity involved. But how the body is enabled to marshall all these forces is not known. Nor is it known why development takes the course it does.

What fits in so well with the presence of causal Shabda-Shakti in the basal Chakra is the fact that the centre of totipotentiality in the embryo is at the caudal end of the developmental axis. The growing-point of the foetus lies at the base of what will later be the spine. The body also emerges before the head or limbs and, in the body, the spinal column and its associated nerves are adumbrated first. Pluripotentiality is retained in this growing-point after it has been lost elsewhere. The head develops only after the formation of the body is well advanced. From this it will be seen that the growth of the embryo follows just such a course as is suggested by the Shabda theory which postulates the movement of creative forces up the spine, energies becoming progressively more differentiated as they advance. The Brahmanadi, the space in the centre of the Sushumna up which Kundalini is ultimately said to rise, has its analogue in the neural groove which gives rise to the central nervous system and which in the foetus closes round the spinal cord to form the neural tube. It is also of interest that the area of exceptional growth at the caudal end of the embryo is called the primitive knot. This could be the gross body equivalent of the Granthi or knot from which the Sushumna and 72,000 Nadis are said to arise in the subtle body's energy system.

From this Shabda could be seen as a Shakti which operates creatively over the entire range of bodies clothing the Jivatman. Mantra can then be understood as thought acting as a formative force capable of influencing the movement of energies at grosser levels. The Tantricist would regard the ultimate organiser of the embryo as the Jivatman, the Brahman self in the causal body. The proximal organiser would be Kundalini as Shabdabrahman in the subtle body. The uterine development of the human being would be a logical corollary of the way multidimensional Shakti systems work as integral parts of a coherent whole. There would seem to be some grounds for believing this to be the case. One needs, however, to go to embryology rather than adult physiology to see this most clearly.

Ultimately Shabdabrahman is the formative force underlying natural law. It is the agent of pure intelligence at the causal level, ensuring that divine intentions are suitably clothed in matter on all planes and at all times. The meanings it enshrines must be conceived as patterns and processes. As Kundalini, it is responsible for the unfolding of the design implicit in physical nature. And since Kundalini is an aspect of Shabdabrahman this unfolding is necessarily in phase with events going on at other, non-physical levels of reality.

Shabda, as meaning, becomes threefold in manifestation, as we have seen. It has been associated variously with sound, light and movement, each of which is regarded as in some sense inherent in matter. What exactly these elements become when translated into non-physical matter cannot be exactly determined. Attempts to describe psychic and mystical experiences, however, constantly make use of them as the nearest analogues of what is inwardly perceived. It is also worth noting that ultrasonics and invisible light frequencies are being used increasingly in industry and medicine. In a very real sense matter seems to be made up of these three aspects of energy in ways which are consistent with the Tantric view that they are inherent in Kundalini as a formative force in nature. That both light and sound can be extremely powerful agents of change is evidenced by the capacity of a laser beam to cut through metal and ultrasonic vibrations to vaporise liquids.

Light is so often used as a synonym for understanding that one is drawn to speculate whether this aspect of matter is not related to its conscious component, its responsiveness to stimulation. Sound as Logos or the Word is said to precede it in the order of generation, which suggests that it stands for something causally prior to light as well as movement. In Tantra Shabdabrahman is the causal precursor of both, arising as it does out of the original Brahmanic will to create. As Devi Tripura, the Threefold Goddess, Kundalini could thus be said to 'wear' sound, light and movement in the same sense as she 'wears' volition, cognition and action. If taken seriously this has curious implications for physics. It means that sound, light and motion must be conceived as being more than mechanical movements and electromagnetic energies. They must also be seen as Kundalini forces in terms of which other forces can be classified. On this basis it is interesting to work out how the three might interrelate in, for example, giving the neutrino its spin. To begin with it implies that the neutrinal spin can never be dissociated from what the spin is meant to be doing. Nor can it be fully described without knowing what effect the spin has upon the responsiveness of what it is spinning in.

The closer we look into it the more clearly Kundalini is seen to be an integrative force which influences the operations of all other forces at work in physical nature. To accommodate it adequately it is necessary both to widen the scope of physics and set it in a multidimensional context, one in which particles and their meaning become as inseparable as the perceiver and the object perceived. This raises a relativity problem which can only be solved by placing both within a single reality. The holographic model which is developing in physics is already a step in the right direction. It demonstrates that light can be so split that what is apparently a three-dimensional object outside the observer is in fact an image projected within the perceiving mind. It is only necessary to assume that consciousness can be similarly divided, an assumption made readily in the East where the essentially psychological nature of experienced reality is taken for granted by many more scholars than is the case in the West. The greatest stumbling block to the acceptance of this view by Western scientists is the corollary: that what gives the external world the same objectivity for us all is the fact that the universe is a system of images in a cosmic mind which includes us — a variant of the bushman's 'There is a dream dreaming me'. (87)

As an integrative power inherent in the operations of all forces and responsible for maintaining objects within a gauge theory which covers all spaces, times and universes, Kundalini is a Shakti of a unique kind. Unlike light, sound and velocity, it is elusive when it comes to direct quantitative analysis. It is possible that it can only be handled mathematically in terms of the way in which it determines proportions and preserves ergonomic balances in force fields. This is no doubt why Tantric texts place it everywhere in the body while at the same time differentiating it according to structures and associating it with innumerable other forces.

Kundalini Devi is above all the promoter of design, the organiser of fields as elements within a whole in which nothing is isolated from anything else and nothing is meaningless. Apparent isolation and apparent meaninglessness are the result of seeing only bits of a mosaic and not being able to envisage the pattern which makes sense of them. Any scientific accounts of natural law which leave out classes of phenomena fall into this error. The very concept of supernature is evidence of an inadequate gauge theory of the universe. We do not have to be gullible to cast the net of our assumptions wider than we do. It is rather a matter of starting out with the idea that all is possible and then allowing ourselves to discover the laws which limit what can be achieved by physical bodies in a physical world. In other words, to discover the bounds set by Shabdabrahman as Kundalini instead of imposing upon ourselves, in the name of reality, those set by the methodologies of scientific disciplines.

12
Tantric and
Western psychobiology

Before dealing with the role of the various Chakras, about which there is considerable divergence of view, it might be helpful to set them in some comparable contexts.

As we have seen, they are not physical energy centres, yet they are treated as real entities affecting physical existence by Indian yogis and the Tantric Buddhist lamas of Tibet. Clairvoyants in the West have claimed to see them, and Western healers in increasing numbers claim to be able to feel their emanations. There is, however, a considerable number of individual differences in accounts of their structure, function and distribution.

From the Tantric standpoint they are multidimensional entities through which formative forces generated at causal levels move through the three bodies of manifestation, the mental and physical bodies and the life-vehicle, under the overall control of the Brahman self. The dynamic processes involved are the responsibility, for the period of physical existence, of Shabdabrahman working through Kundalini. Under ideal conditions there would be a smooth movement of energies through the Chakras and Nadis of the various bodies and harmonious interaction between the Brahman within individual human beings and the Brahman in all surrounding entities both human and otherwise. There would in fact be a state of universal Satchitananda, and no need for either change or effort. All men would be part of nature, already in a blissful state of yoga. There would be a creation but no creative process, no sense of separation, no feeling of stress; above all there would be no ego-awareness as we understand it.

So where does the need for evolution, for healing, for peace, for love, for fulfilment come from? The answer must lie in the nature of the Fall. Somewhere along the line of involution into matter division must have arisen. The possibility of deviation and resistance must have been injected into the system, introducing alternatives and widening the scope of experience by extending the range of available responses. The unfortunate choices which lead to suffering and death can be variously attributed to original sin or the misleading influence of Maya, but without them there would be neither evolution nor learning. However much we may kick against the pricks, this fact seems obvious. It also means that what we experience as suffering is simultaneously an 'act of God' and 'our own most grievous fault'. In so far as God's will can be known one could say He must have intended these experiences when He willed the creation of man in His own image. In order to create out of ourselves we must first be divided into the part which creates and the part which is created; that which fashions and that which is wrought. It is the business of working on ourselves or being worked on from within which is so uncomfortable. It involves a continuous process of seeing in new ways. In particular seeing suffering in new ways. The suffering which comes to us from outside is only suffering if we see it as such and fight it as something forced upon us against our will. We fight our angels as if they were Apollyons.

Why do we do this?

In Tantric terms the best answer is probably that of Sri Aurobindo. (1, 79) He does not, as most Westerners do, identify soul with spirit and the ego or conscious self with the mind. He assumes that at all levels of our bodies we are dual. There is our surface self which is subject to conditioning and a subliminal self which remains always in touch with cosmic Being and which cannot be distorted either by events or by the way the ego makes decisions. From first to last it stands fast at the core of our personalities accepting instructions only from the Brahman within. Sri Aurobindo calls this stable subliminal self the 'real soul'. The real soul enters into the world and influences us from within. At various times in the spiritual life differences of direction can be felt. The real soul is task-orientated and ensures that, however far from the purpose of our lives the ego tries to drag us, the surface or desire-soul can only succeed within limits. It is the tug-of-war between that part of our natures which responds to the real soul and the part responsive to ego-pressures which causes suffering. The conflict is not between spirit and body, but between our essential nature and the ego. Many spiritual psychologists and healers will confirm this. It is at mental levels that the disruptive influences come in. The fault, however, is not in the mind as such, only in that part of it which gets caught up in ego-distortions, errors of judgment made by the conscious self about the nature of things.

The ego is a much more difficult construct to understand than we tend to suppose. And a construct is what it is. It is a complex of images and attitudes which gather round our idea of ourselves. It is really our self-portrait and is far from being the consistent whole we feel ourselves to be. It is the product of our conditioning and of our reactions to the opinions and judgments of others about the sort of people we are. It can deviate widely from the people we really are both in the direction of self-inflation and self-depreciation. Different segments of it come into play in different situations some of which lead us to behave in logically quite incompatible ways without our recognising our own inconsistencies. While it owes its existence to Ahangkara, the I-making principle in the Antahkarana or mental body, it is not the same thing. Ahangkara is merely that which separates self from other, I as a subject from the world as object.

It is nevertheless with the emergence of Ahangkara that the split in consciousness arises which divides the surface self from the real soul. The subliminal self 'sees true' at all times since it is part of the Brahman self. The surface self is what can be misled by appearances and fall into Maya-traps through ignorance. Neither the gross body, which is a passive principle, nor the Jivatman in the causal body, which is beyond the reach of Maya, are the causes of suffering. The one is above it in a constant state of Satchitananda. The other is subjected to it willy-nilly because we include it in our self-portraits, involve it in our misunderstandings. Thus we can be said to cause our own ill-health of mind and body out of ignorance of our subliminal selves and how to live in tune with them. This is to go *contra natura* in its proper sense.

Our immunity from suffering is a function of the closeness of our ego-view of reality and reality as it is and as our subliminal selves know it to be. In my experience, coming to see people and situations as they really are involves a progressive depotentiating of ego-reinforcing attitudes until, finally, the ego becomes little more than a lens focusing being and awareness on the world of space-time. Essentially the ego is not a complex but a point of impingement. We fabricate the complex out of ideas about ourselves and then identify with it. It is in this sense that the Indians say 'The mind is the slayer of the real.'

Our self-portraits are images partly self-generated, partly the result of our reactions to the judgments of others. The ego which acts in any given situation may differ widely from the one we imagine to be there. Moreover, as we all know, our ideas about ourselves can be very different from those other people have about us and even from those we have about ourselves at different times and in different moods. In such circumstances it is surprising that we so confidently feel ourselves to be all of a piece with consistent and stable characters. From the standpoint of yoga preoccupation with this essentially artificial structure is counter-productive. Excessive introspection, in however good a cause, tends only to strengthen the thought-forms in it. What is needed is not ego-refinement but ego-transcendence. This means a progressive dissolution of the surface self and the emergence of the subliminal organisation it has been obscuring.

The first step in this movement is to reduce the importance of conscious behaviour, of logical reasoning and of planning in terms of ego-determined ends. The aim is to have our lives directed increasingly from the real soul and not the conditioned one. The 'subliminals' are those aspects of our various bodies which know how to respond to guidance from this level. Consequently the conscious mind must extend its boundaries to include much it previously suppressed, undervalued and ignored. There needs to be a relaxing of the conscious mind into a wider one with benign reaches both above and below the threshold of awareness. Not all infiltrators from the unconscious are enemy aliens.

It is not by deliberately placing thought here and there among the Chakras that their psychosomatic activities are best regulated. Our surface minds do not know enough about either how they work or what would constitute an improvement in their behaviour. As Krishnamurti frequently points out, one cannot heal the conditioned mind with the conditioned mind and, as Buber says in another context, the teacher should always enter the classroom from above. Since the subliminals are essential parts of the real soul it follows that anything wrong with the working of the Chakras will have been caused by the surface self interfering with subliminal control mechanisms. In other words, Chakral malfunction and consequent psychosomatic disorders are due to divergence between ego-directives and the needs of the real soul of which we are all too ignorant. To will health and then let nature take its course is probably far wiser than using our minds and possibly visualising the wrong things. It also reduces the risk of the ego developing an inflated idea of its role.

Sometimes knowing what needs to be done in regard to the real soul and the subliminals is easier than getting the ego to agree to being demoted. Attitudes reinforcing our self-portraits and tendencies to react in terms of ego-desires and values are not readily overcome, which is why character retraining and psychotherapy can often take a long time. Moreover, it is hard for us in the West to recognise that much of what we see 'out there' is our own work. Freud and Jung have helped by stressing the role of the projection outwards of our fears and prejudices in creating problems in personal relationships. Psychologists researching perception have also assisted by making us more aware of how much of what we see and hear are mental additions to what the senses actually record. Recognising projections and realising how we elaborate sensations makes us more conscious of the way the ego can modify and even wildly distort the real state of affairs. One of the functions of a guru or a spiritual director is to support the novice when his confidence in his ego is faltering and his belief in his real self has not yet taken firm root. The psycho-therapist plays a similar role in psychoanalysis, where the problem is often a weak ego and no sustaining framework of belief. That the ego projects fears instead of intolerances does not make its distortions any less damaging. It is as hampering to be guilt-laden as it is to be conceited and critical.

The absence of religious belief in materialistic societies tends to make for another kind of handicap in replacing the ego by the real soul. The whole idea of a spiritual order of reality has first to be absorbed. This can be made more diffi-cult if the notion of psychic reality has been made frighten-ing by tales of the supernatural getting mixed up with half-remembered childish nightmares. Moreover, no one can help people through to the discovery of the true self within who does not believe that such a thing is really there to be dis-covered. Much psychotherapy fails for this reason. This is because — more often than is generally realised — neurosis can be a sign of spiritual stress arising because the time for the ego to transfer control is imminent. The strength of the transference on to an analyst is often a measure of the intensity of the need to find some Other on which the patient can rely as he can no longer rely upon his ego-self. For the analyst to accept the role thus foisted upon him instead of recognising what is happening is perhaps the greatest disservice a healer can do to a person in this situa-tion. Too often a spiritual need is diagnosed purely as a hang-up from childhood when this is not so. Moreover, the less religiously aware the analyst the less likely he is to see the necessity for redirecting the transference to the patient's own inner healer. It is also harder for him to resolve the trans-ference neurosis which will free him from the patient's excessive dependence on him.

Sri Aurobindo, in his treatment of our divided natures, makes use of the Hindu categories of mind, life and matter, associating them with Buddhi, Manas, Chitta, Ahangkara and Prana in the conventional way. He also accepts Antahkarana as a collective name for the mind as a whole. The I-making principle is thus seen as part of the Antahkarana and not part of a separate ego structure as in the West. In her work with the Tibetan, Alice Bailey refers to the Antahkarana a good deal and always as something which has to be worked on by all seeking spiritual goals. As the term crops up in sections on the Chakras to which we will be referring later it is worth trying to understand exactly how she is using it. Something has to be worked on to produce the Bailey Antahkarana. The question is what.

As the Tantric Antahkarana is a term applied to the cosmic as well as to the human mind perhaps the clue lies here. In her Tibetan books the prevalent notion Alice Bailey conveys is that the disciple must build a bridge. Building the Antahkarana as a spiritual endeavour may be another way of saying we must work at our minds until they cease to be an impediment between us and cosmic consciousness. For a long time I thought Antahkarana actually meant bridge, an error only corrected by research into actual Tantric texts. Reconverted into Tantric terms the Tibetan lama's teaching would now seem to me to be that we should work at removing the barrier between the ego-limited mind and subliminal mind which is part of the Brahman self or Sri Aurobindo's real soul. It is not, therefore, the subliminal Antahkarana which has to be built but ego-distortions in the surface self which must be removed. This is something which can only be done by our own conscious efforts. This means pulling in our projections and seeing our suffering as something to which we contribute to a far greater extent than we realise. It also means being willing to be a junior partner in a larger firm.

The hardest part is pulling in the projections, especially accepting that our harshest criticisms of others are about the faults we tend to share but dislike too much to acknowledge even to ourselves. Many of us need help at this stage because ego-confidence is a positive value only to be replaced by confidence in the Self with a capital S. We need someone to believe in us during the period when self-doubt and self-disgust can be crippling. The tendency to judge others and blame life, when transformed into self-criticism and shame, can be difficult to bear alone. Many neurotics are in one or other of these phases, which is why I said that many psycho-somatic disorders are symptoms of spiritual stress. If there is no other help available distress may be pushed into the body. To see our poor sick selves with the eyes of compassion is hard as the projections are pulled in. And yet this is what is required of us for we, in our true selves, are not either the ego we thought we were before nor the sorry mess we feel ourselves to be now. Both are equally artificial constructs and may be far from the mark as assessments of our real characters and potentialities. The efforts demanded by the Tibetan would seem to be largely essays in removal, removal of veils of Maya by recognising them for what they are. There are also acts of faith which have to be made. Intuitions, often tenuous, that there is indeed a wiser self within need to be hung on to until they can form a nucleus round which other similar intuitions can cluster. This opens the way for the emergence of the true self as a guiding influence of which we become progressively more aware. This self is not worked at: it is discovered.

Once this self becomes a working partner and we can accept its presence, if not fulfil all its demands, the descending forces of which Sri Aurobindo speaks begin to be experienced. We become conscious of being inspired as well as aspiring. There also begins to arise a sense of sometimes being several sizes larger than our physical bodies and of there being an area, somewhere above our heads, from which some of our impressions come. There is little in Tantric texts about a centre higher than the Sahasrara. Nevertheless the assertion that the Mahayogi passes through the Brahmarandhra, (98) the cleft at the crown of the head in the subtle body, in order to enter an enduring state of Satchitananda, implies something of the sort. It is also noteworthy that the stalk of the thousand-petalled lotus is always shown rising into the air above the head. It must presumably be rooted somewhere. That the somewhere is not delineated is consistent with its being the abode of Parabrahman and therefore transcendent and unimaginable. It is then the Mahayogi reaches Nirvana, for Nirvana means nothingness. What becomes nothing is the I that experiences separation. Nirvana is a much more final state than Moksha. To be touched by Parabrahman is one thing: to enter the lotus that has no form is something else again.

The site of the centre from which descending inspiration seems to come may be what Dr Brugh Joy (31) calls the 'transpersonal point'. He claims that such a point exists about eighteen inches above the head and can be seen by some sensitives. It may also be represented by the dove seen hovering over the head in paintings depicting the descent of the Holy Spirit. In this connection it is important to distinguish being influenced from this point and entering into it. Accounts of mystical experiences from both East and West confirm the presence of an area above one into which consciousness appears to rise and where there is no sense of separation or any formal boundaries. There are parallel descriptions of something entering into one's being and expanding consciousness from within. Behind these experiences presumably lie Sri Aurobindo's ascending and descending forces.

According to his teaching the Pingala Nadi carries the ascending forces and the Ida the descending ones. As we have seen, these Nadis are qualified by different principles, the Ida being Sattvic and so predisposing to consciousness and the Pingala Rajasic and so stimulating activity in the various bodies. This is an interesting notion and suggests that their energy connections with ganglia on either side of the spine is a loose and flexible one. The idea also fits in well with existence of a polarity between the Sahasrara Chakra at the crown of the head and the Muladhara at the base of the spine, and the way their interaction keeps the development of consciousness and the structures mediating it in phase with one another.

The Tibetan speaks of magnetism being associated with the Chakras, which fits in with the description of them as vortices. As energy vortices they would have spins which could go clockwise or anti-clockwise, not only at different levels, but at the same level at different times. Indeed, in my own healing work I used rotary movements in both senses and in patterns of considerable complexity. Chakras are also said to 'awaken'. By this is meant that they evolve from small, relatively sluggish centres of activity to become increasingly more energetically rotating fields. At the outset they are chiefly concerned with transducing energy to various parts of the physical body. Higher mental energies would not at first be much involved, so that the consciousness Nadis, Ida and

Chitrini, would be relatively inactive. The forces in circulation in the Chakras would tend to be either Rajasic or Tamasic, tending, on the one hand, to activity in the bodies and on the other to inertia. This means that, in the less evolved person, Kundalini's role in maintaining the balance of forces is mainly one of seeing that physical and psychic Pranas are available for physiological needs and the basic mental processes. The sympathetic and parasympathetic nerves and their subtle body counterparts and back-up systems would be dominant over the cerebral cortex and cortical back-up systems. This suggests that the centre between the eyebrows chiefly passes energy to the pituitary gland at this stage and only becomes a transducer of higher mental energies later.

Neither Sri Aurobindo (1) nor the Tibetan (3) make much of Vajra and Chitrini, the two Nadis within the Sushumna, though these should act upon the Chakras far more directly than either the Ida or Pingala. The Chakras, it will be recalled, are said to be strung on the Chitrini like a necklace of jewels. This relates them primarily to the development of Chit or Consciousness-Intelligence and it is with states of consciousness the yogis most associated them. Since Chitrini, like Ida, is a recipient of those drops of nectar which always fall from above, it not only carries a descending force but must also feed it to the Chakras along its length. Both Ida and Chitrini must be channels of downward-flowing energies from the head. Similarly Pingala and Vajra must be carriers of the active Pranic currents rising from below. They must together constitute the major ascending channels. This leaves the Sushumna itself. This is a doubly Tamasic channel, being a common element of both the central Nadi systems. It appears mainly to mediate those stabilising energies which keep activities in balance and prevent the too-rapid emergence of consciousness relative to the body's ability to meet its demands.

This last is an important evolutionary function of Kundalini which is sometimes overlooked in theories of creation from above. It is responsible for timing the integration of forces from higher levels into physical forms. Earth forces must present spiritual forces with resistance in order that the forms created can generate sufficient power to master the problems associated with existence in dense matter. Creative agencies have had to move slowly through geological time in order to arrive at human beings capable of achieving yoga. That they now can suggests that all the necessary structures have been built into our physical bodies. The caution advocated by the teachers of yoga is tied up with timing and problems of latency as a factor in all growth, spiritual as well as physical. It is this which leads them to tell us, 'When the pupil is ready, the master appears.'

The discretion needed is relative to the handling of subtle energy systems and not to the physical body as such. Psychological hazards arise out of the division of the mind just described, which was necessary in order to make self-conscious awareness possible, but which carries its own difficulties with it. It produces two potentially conflicting force-fields which we have to learn to cope with. It is in the direction of an increasing ability to manage this split in our internal environment that evolution now seems to be moving. No more species are likely to arise in a contracting physical environment. The great evolutionary challenges today are human ones. They are to be found within us and between us and to date we are not meeting them very well. We persist in concentrating on material things when it is our social world which presents the chief threat to our survival as a species. If we cannot learn to live with one another there is no technological miracle which can save us. To learn to live together requires, odd as it may seem, first learning to live more harmoniously and wisely with ourselves; to see the split within and bend all our considerable ingenuity to the task of discovering how best to heal it.

Clues may lie in more knowledge about how to diagnose what is going on in the Chakras seen as evolving structures. The Tibetan's teaching through Alice Bailey makes the most detailed contribution I know of in this field. The ancient Tantrika were not much concerned with the Chakras as psychological entities, but what the Tibetan says (4, 6) about the illnesses which can accompany inner growth processes fits into classical Tantra quite readily.

Briefly what he says is that to begin with the Chakras are

sluggish and more active below than above the diaphragm. As higher energies are released into the body from above during development, the Chakras brighten, rotate more rapidly and begin to enlarge. Moreover there are other polarities among them than that between the crown Chakra and the Muladhara. There is one between the sacral centre, the first Chitrini Chakra just above the Muladhara, and the centre at the throat. These are both creative centres, the one feeding energy into the physical reproductive system and the other energising all the parts involved in cultural and social creativity. There is another between the solar plexus centre and the heart centre. These are the lower and higher Chakras mediating emotional responses. As our characters and abilities evolve, lower centres which were positive become increasingly negative while their higher partners become increasingly positive. Some sort of magnetic force is exerted by the positive pole which draws energy towards it. This causes a constant up and down traffic of forces as Chakras change their polarities in the business of living. There is, however, an overall upward tendency so that, seen clairvoyantly, the less-developed person tends to be more alight below the diaphragm than above and the more evolved person brighter above than below. In the intellectually advanced person the brow centre rotates faster and is brighter and larger than in a person who lives emotionally. The selfish person is a solar plexus person. The saint can have a literally shining heart.

As evolution proceeds the Chakras must develop. The real soul, acting as an entelechy quickening growth from within, ensures this. The changes of polarity cannot always be effected without stress, however, because of the resistances put up by the surface self and also by the inertia inherent in dense matter. Thus physical disorders can occur in areas where there is critical Chakral activity going on. These are primarily energy disturbances in the subtle body which have spilled over into the physical one. This is why we need to know more about the Chakras and Nadis as fields and streams affecting health. Some disorders, for instance, are best left untreated medically. In such cases the aim should be to discover what transfers of control are taking place within the personality as a whole. These can then be explained and aid given with a view to assisting inner growth rather than removing symptoms by medical means. One of the reasons why psychotherapy and unorthodox healing techniques can sometimes cure where conventional medicine has failed is because they may disperse blocks to the smooth passage of forces by removing psychological stresses. These, in cases of evolutionary disorders, can often be better handled by the promotion of insights into what is happening than by working away at symptoms.

The difficulty about this approach from a scientific point of view is that we can only learn about the Chakras by processes not regarded as methodologically sound. Thus, if we are to get more information on them, science must not only accept mind into physics but psychics, sensitives and intuitives onto its advisory panels and into its laboratories.

13
Kundalini and physio-kundalini

I referred earlier to the work of Itzak Bentov, Lee Sannella and their associates eventuating in the concept of physio-kundalini. (70) This seems an appropriate point at which to deal with this valuable attempt to give a physiological dimension to the yogic teaching.

It will now be apparent that the rise of Kundalini from the basal Chakra to the crown of the head must be regarded as a special case of the action of Kundalini and not the only activity of Kundalini in the body. This is true whether we approach the problem of Kundalini from the standpoint of classical Hinduism or from that of Western science. The Sannella group recognised this when it decided to call the clinical entity it was studying physio-kundalini and treat the physio-kundalini cycle as only one aspect of a wider phenomenon. That they from time to time make assumptions about the nature of Kundalini outside their own terms of reference is not surprising. As we have seen, Kundalini is a wide-ranging, subtle and elusive force.

Two strands came together in the work of this group. One was connected with the increasing incidence among meditators of what appeared to be experiences of Kundalini arousal. This came to the attention of psychologists and psychiatrists interested in differentiating between stresses in spiritual development and cases of psychotic disturbance. This seemed to them a diagnostic necessity if they were to give adequate help, since great distress could arise among meditators if misdiagnosed and consequently mistreated. The other strand was growing interest in the energy systems responsible for processes and structures postulated by yogis and sensitives but discounted by scientists unable to find any objective evidence of their existence. Chakras, Nadis and Kundalini all came into this category. Bentov, like Motoyama, was engaged in trying to find instrumental ways of verifying their existence. When I had the good fortune to spend a few days with him and his wife in 1974 we were both still hoping the energies involved might lie within the electromagnetic spectrum. I was also much interested in the physiological theory he was evolving to account for the experiences described by meditators, and was deeply saddened to learn of his tragic death in the Chicago air crash of 1979. I would have enjoyed discussing my present work with him, for the theory he was then elaborating is the one adopted by the Sannella group to explain the physio-kundalini cycle. It is an ingenious one and well reasoned and makes out a good case for a definite physiological mechanism. Whether this mechanism or the cycle have any direct connection with Kundalini as this Shakti is understood in Tantra is, however, far from clear, as I shall hope to show.

While the physio-kundalini cycle described by Bentov can be activated during meditation, it can also start up spontaneously or be induced by exposing the head to electromagnetic or sound waves. Bentov demonstrated this experimentally. Reactions in such cases were monitored by the application of modified ballisto-cardiographs while subjects were asked to change their state of consciousness in a meditative direction. In a deep meditative state Bentov found a pattern of rhythmic sine waves. This he attributed to a standing wave in the aorta which is reflected in minute wave-like body movements. The heart-aorta complex was seen as constituting the primary resonating oscillator driving four associated micro-oscillators. When locked into the heart-aorta resonating system the combined operation of these resonating oscillators generates a fluctuating magnetic field around the head.

The standing wave in the aorta is caused by a complex of movements. The gush of blood from the left cardiac ventricle into the aorta when the heart empties forces the elastic walls of the aorta to bulge. The resulting pressure pulse passes down it until it reaches the iliac bifurcation where the vessel divides. Part of the pulse is stopped there and rebounds, generating a reflected pressure pulse. The standing wave is the result of these two pulses — the one going down and the other coming back — either coinciding or being in phase. This wave, approximately 7 Hz, causes the body to move up and down and sets up micro-oscillations in the skeleton including the skull. Bentov assumed there must also be a feedback loop between the iliac fork and the heart which relates to breathing and heart rates.

Because the head is a dense, tight structure, acoustic plane waves generated by oscillations in the body subject the brain to mild rhythmic up and down impacts. Since the brain tissue acts like a piezoelectric gel, these mechanical vibrations can be converted into electrical impulses and vice versa. This has a stimulating effect which is further enhanced by vibrations reflected off the skull. When the spread of acoustic waves through the skeleton reach the skull they can go no further and are reflected inwards. This focuses them on the third and lateral ventricles at the centre of the brain. These are cavities filled with cerebro-spinal fluid and are continuous with the cavity running down the middle of the spinal cord. The impact of the acoustic plane waves on the cerebro-spinal fluid sets it oscillating, producing a second standing wave, this time in the head.

It is these standing waves in the cerebral ventricles which trigger off the circular movement of nerve impulses in the sensory areas of the cortex which are thought to be responsible for the physio-kundalini cycle. They do this because the ventricles underlie the median fissure which divides the cortex into two hemispheres and along the invaginated sides of which the sensory areas associated with the feet and legs are distributed. The ventricles are only separated from the base of this fissure by the corpus callosum, a narrow band of brain tissue which joins the two halves of the brain. Mechanical vibrations in the corpus callosum and the sensory nerve tissue above it, converted into electrical impulses, generate waves of stimulation in the two hemispheres simultaneously, one wave of impulses going clockwise from the midline and the other anti-clockwise. Each of these, running from the ventricles back to the ventricles, forms a closed circuit. These circuits generate fluctuating magnetic fields with opposing polarities. The stimulated areas involved in these circular movements include two at least of the pleasure centres in the brain, a fact which Bentov felt could account for the tranquillity and happiness reported by meditators. The sounds heard would be secondary results of standing waves in the cerebral ventricles activating structures in the middle ear and producing 'inner sounds'.

The collection of data relative to psychosomatic events which can be studied as discrete clinical entities, and the relation of such events to specific physiological mechanisms, are invaluable research techniques. The work of Bentov and Sannella are important attempts to develop our knowledge of mind-body interaction and should be esteemed as such. Their findings do, however, make a great many assumptions. There are also gaps in the theoretical framework which lay the data open to alternative explanations.

I have stressed the semantic problems with which all Kundalini research must contend and the need to be wary in assuming we understand what terms borrowed from the East mean in their original contexts. Even oriental students of the Tantras get muddled between subtle and gross bodies when discussing the physiology of the Chakras and Nadis, as Woodroffe makes abundantly clear in *The Serpent Power*. A lot of modern theorising by Indian no less than Western writers relates these subtle energy structures far more directly to anatomical systems than can be justified upon close examination of the classical source material. I have tried to show that, not only in the Tantras, but in Hindu literature generally, there is explicit reference to Kundalini as primarily a universal force. It is unambiguously identified with that aspect of cosmic nature which comes to rest at the physical level because the creative impulse goes no further down into matter than this. Prakriti-Shakti, we are told, on reaching the realm of Prithivi (Earth), coils up and sleeps. At this point she becomes Kundalini-Shakti in her coiled form. The coiled form of Kundalini thus represents nature at rest, nature as the end-product of the involutionary descent into matter. As such it is that aspect of the physical world about which we can formulate laws of permanent and universal application. The coiled form of Kundalini in bodies is similarly the basis of the stability of individual entities and that which makes it possible to frame physical and biological laws regarding their behaviour. Coiled Kundalini is Kundalini-Prakriti not Kundalini-Shabdabrahman. This distinction is important. Shabdabrahman is operative at all levels of matter; Kundalini is a limiting power which confines the activities of Shabdabrahman within physical limits.

Kundalini as Shabdabrahman is the representative of Ishvara, the creative principle at work. It is that which governs the development of entities within the bounds set by Kundalini as Prakriti, the Kundalini represented as coiled. Shabdabrahman is an aspect of Kundalini which is not symbolised as coiled because it never sleeps so long as a form is in physical manifestation. The image associated with it is a flame. It is active in all the mechanisms through which the creation unfolds in the material world of nature. It is coiled Kundalini's dynamic partner and as such 'dwells' in every structure and 'lives' in every process through which evolving Brahman expresses itself in dense matter. It is Kundalini as a causal agency within Kundalini as a limiting factor.

The departure of coiled Kundalini from the Muladhara is something which should only happen when Kundalini as Shabdabrahman has brought its work in a particular form to fruition, whether that fruition be the end of the earthly life of a sinner or the liberation from Samskara of a saint. While there is a gross body, its continuance depends on coiled Kundalini staying firmly in the Muladhara. Otherwise Prakriti has no anchorage point in the physical body. Also there would be no proper centre in which Prana can be modified for use at chemical levels, for we are told that Prana and Kundalini blend in the Muladhara Chakra before passing into the 72,000 Nadis for general distribution.

On this view any Kundalini activity involved in the cycles described by Bentov and Sannella cannot be due to coiled Kundalini rising out of the root Chakra since all the fifteen subjects researched are alive and well and do not claim to have attained Moksha. Nor is there any evidence that, as meditators, they have interfered with the working of the Muladhara by concentrating on it in any way. They were reported as using either Zen or Transcendental Meditation or as following practices prescribed by Swami Muktananda. In other words what happened to them was only a Kundalini phenomenon in the general sense that all bodily processes are Kundalini processes. There is no reason to doubt that the cycles themselves occur. It is only their identification with an upsurge of coiled Kundalini which is being called in question here.

If what occurs in these cycles is not connected with the uncoiling of Kundalini what other explanation can one offer in terms of the dynamics of the subtle and physical bodies? That the cycle is not directly connected with spiritual developments is demonstrated by the fact that it can be artificially induced by the application of electromagnetic fields as Bentov has shown. Even its ultimately beneficial effects may derive from other causes than meditation, though the cases studied were meditators. For instance, if the locked-in state and comparable brain-waves were found to be related to deep relaxation rather than spiritual orientation, its function as a purificatory process would need to be re-evaluated. This could be done by mounting an experiment subjecting two groups to induced fields, one group using meditation to reach the locked-in state and the other using only relaxation techniques with no spiritual objective in view. Transcendental Meditation is itself largely an exercise of the latter sort, its spiritual dimension being derived from the general orientation of the meditator rather than the content of the meditation, which involves the inner repetition of syllables that have been given no specific meaning.

Deep relaxation has been found by many therapists to produce a wide range of stress-relieving patterns en route for a condition of enhanced creativity and peace of mind. The same is also true of psychotherapy. A comparative study to explore the incidence of pseudo-kundalini experiences in phases of stress-relief might be well worth undertaking. Clearly the body is capable of producing mechanisms to promote states of tranquillity or they could not be artificially induced. It is possible that disturbances of physiological harmonics are related to conflicts between natural rhythms and interference patterns generated by the ego-attitudes and misconceptions discussed earlier. What we are examining may not be evidence for evolutionary developments in the nervous system so much as evidence of functional discrepancies between the surface and subliminal levels of the self. The removal of these discrepancies, whether by meditation, psychotherapy or any other means, would inevitably be both liberating and healing and, therefore, spiritualising in a broad sense.

While we are still in the phase of trying to discover our true selves, these are necessarily in varying degrees depotentiated by the ego, which is reluctant to give up the centre of the stage. The correlation between stress and self-centredness is well known. What is less well known is that attention focuses automatically on the personal self when the personal self is a problem, just as pain focuses attention on the body when the body is a problem. Nevertheless self-absorption is a social nuisance and a great handicap. It also pinpoints a need to understand ourselves as a precondition of a more harmonious state of affairs within the individual as a whole. This is why a theory of personality which takes account of all its reaches is so necessary. As Sannella and Bentov both insist, the times are urgent. Our failure to recognise and live up to our full potential as essentially spiritual beings is creating increasing distress and frustration in society, especially among the young. There are too many psychological theories which amputate human nature at all its growing points; too many social attitudes in high places which maximise weakness and fail to set sufficiently challenging goals for the spiritually adventurous and the idealistic to aim at. By putting too material a value on ourselves and imposing unjustifiable constraints on nature, we unconsciously take power from the true elite and place it in the hands of those whose reach most grievously fails to exceed its grasp. The crying need of the time is not just for more meditation. One wishes it were that simple. It is for a view of ourselves which will allow us room to stretch to our full height and which will take quite matter-of-factly that we are all as much members one of another as the mitochondria on which our lives depend are parts of us.

If the cycle researched by Bentov and Sannella is not a phenomenon associated with the arousal of coiled Kundalini, what is it? How do we account for it in terms of the interactions of the gross and subtle bodies and Sri Aurobindo's distinction between the surface and subliminal selves? Certainly it appears to indicate sensitivity to energy movements of which we are normally unconscious. What causes this is less clear.

Bentov points out the neural connections between the cerebral cortex and the various parts of the body in which the energy movements are felt. His theory, however, implies that a cortical circuit must be set up before the cycle can be experienced and this means prior entrainment of five series-linked harmonic oscillators. The end-product of this entrainment, according to his theory, are two magnetic fields around the head of opposing polarities. This conjoint field, radiating from the head, acts as an antenna. It interacts with other fields in the environment, making the head simultaneously a receiver and transmitter tuned to resonant frequencies in the brain. Environmental fields, fed back into the brain, modulate its resonant frequencies in ways which are translated into information.

Stated like this, Bentov's theory seems only indirectly associated with the physio-kundalini cycle described by Sannella. In its own right it would seem to be a theory about physiological mechanisms which make for effective inter-communication between individual and environmental fields and the translation of those interactions into impulses which convey useful knowledge to the organism. The induction experiments suggest that the experiences of Sannella's subjects can be products of the entrainment process, but there seem to be no grounds for assuming them to be necessarily present. Indeed, the finding that as the subjects became more tranquil and creative, the symptoms departed and did not recur indicates the incidental nature of the Sannella cycle. In other words, it appears to be due to interferences with the smooth operation of physiological mechanisms which some persons register while others do not. There may also be predisposing conditions associated with stress which heighten the body's responsiveness to aberrations. The fact that the symptoms reported by meditators included motor as well as sensory reactions enhances this possibility.

Though in his account of the stimulation patterns set up in the brain Bentov confines his exposition to the circulation of impulses generated in the sensory cortex of the two hemispheres, the adjacent motor cortex must have been equally involved. There is no reason to suppose a parallel circulation in the motor areas would not be engendered and contribute its quota to the fluctuating magnetic fields he postulates. The roof of the lateral ventricles and the corpus callosum underlie both these regions. Indeed the lateral ventricles form a large and spreading cavity and, in addition to abutting on the corpus callosum, their hornlike branches extend into the visual and auditory projection areas in the occipital and temporal lobes. The pituitary gland lies at the tip of one of its narrower extensions and the pineal body rests immediately against one of its walls. It tapers down into the smaller third ventricle. This in turn connects with the fourth ventricle which lies below it and forms the junction, at the level of the cerebellum and brain stem, between the cerebral cavities and the spinal canal. Standing waves in the cerebro-spinal fluid must thus set up very widespread patterns of stimulation and, together with the mechanical impacts reflected back from the cranial vault, must be a major factor governing the evolution of the brain, accelerating by continuous micro-motions the overall responsiveness of its tissues. By feedback this must similarly accelerate nerve systems in the body, increasing their responsiveness to stimulation from the cortex and ductless glands. The channelling of stimuli towards the ventricles and the spine is reflected in the structure of the corona radiata, an arrangement of brain tissue which spreads like a fan from the centre of the brain outwards.

This extension of Bentov's theory fits in with Sri Aurobindo's contention that the up and down movement of subtle forces through the Sushumna, Ida and Pingala are responsible for the development of consciousness. As we have seen, the Ida and Chitrini Nadis mediate descending Sattvic energies while ascending energies use the two Rajasic Nadis, the Pingala and Vajra, and the Tamasic Sushumna. What Bentov appears to have found are the physiological analogues of the activities of Chit mechanisms in the subtle body under bipolar stimulation from the two ends of the Shiva-Shakti axis. The texts imply that Shiva in the Sahasrara exerts a magnetic attraction, drawing the centre of consciousness and all the forces associated with it towards ever more spiritual goals. In the imagery of the Tantras this is seen as a desire in Shiva for reunion with his lost Shakti. It is also the description of an evolutionary urge.

The idea of magnetic fields around the head should not be allowed to obscure the fact that the body is an integral field to which many somatic as well as cerebral fields contribute. It is not only the head which is a receiver and transmitter in Bentov's sense. It is often overlooked that the primary sense organ is actually the skin. In the most primitive organisms there is no nervous system and, indeed, no head, until a considerable distance up the evolutionary ladder. Nerve nets developed as refinements of epidermal cells. Touch, moreover, is essentially a matter of interchanges of atoms at micro-levels between overlapping magnetic fields. The amount of this interchange which we perceive is a minute segment of the changes actually involved. What we are visually aware of is similarly a very small part of the spectrum of waves actually impinging on the eye. It is only a step from there to the realisation that consciousness as we understand it is only a narrow band in the range of awareness potentially open to us.

What Bentov's theory suggests is that the physical body is already in possession of a mechanism which can mediate greater powers of conscious awareness than we are currently able to exercise. Sannella's contention that there are blockages of energy flow underlying the physio-kundalini syndrome is an interesting one in this connection. It suggests that the essential problem is one of discovering what prevents us from being creative, tranquil and enlightened since the necessary physiological machinery appears already to exist. The answer seems to lie in discrepancies between the objectives of surface and subliminal selves which cannot be avoided while these two vital personality structures remain unaligned.

What seems likely is that, in the course of development, a

stage is reached when the relation between the ego and the true self must be sorted out at all levels. Deviations between the way the surface self is using its mechanisms and the way the subliminal self wants them used will then set up a new kind of stress situation which may well not be recognised for what it is. It will no longer be simply a matter of tensions between the surface self and its social environment. These will now be complicated by tensions between the surface self and its subliminal opposite number. The inner environment of the ego will no longer be under pressure solely from society and material hazards; it will also be under pressure from an emergent subliminal organisation geared to removing the ego from the centre of the stage and replacing it by the true self.

From the standpoint of the bodies which have to mediate all the processes involved in this change of orientation, this must be a phase of greatly heightened activity. Energies have to be re-routed with orders coming at them from two centres of control. Kundalini, both in its coiled form and as Shabdabrahman, has its work cut out. The one must hold the bodies steady and firmly anchored at the physical level; the other must marshall all the relevant forces and re-allocate energies to work in new ways. All this must be done without too great disruption in the developing organism. Suicide under these conditions can be seen as a failure of coiled Kundalini to anchor the bodies sufficiently firmly in the Earth. Intractable psychotic disturbances indicate comparable breakdowns in the realm of Chit-Shakti. In between lie the whole range of psychosomatic difficulties dealt with at length by Alice Bailey's Tibetan teacher in *Esoteric Healing* and *Esoteric Psychology*.

One of the things the kinaesthetically sensitive will be likely to experience at such times will be energy movements in the two subtle bodies, the life-vehicle and the Antahkarana. So much going on must mean extra energy coming in as well as energy having to be redistributed via changing polarities within the subtle energy fields. This must involve a lot of activity at the Kanda, the 'knot' at the root of the Sushumna from which all the Nadis take their rise. With all the Nadis springing from that one region and spreading from there all over the body, it is surprising we are all so little aware of it as an energy source. It is only when the back tires or is injured in this area that we realise how pervasive is the well-being associated with it. It is, I suspect, the influx of force into this Nadi plexus which triggers off the physio-kundalini syndrome reported by Sannella's subjects and others experiencing similar symptoms. It must be an active phase for all subtle structures and one involving a good deal of transitional stress. It would be no time for coiled Kundalini to leave 'the square region of Prithivi', but rather one in which to hold on there firmly so that the basic integrity of the body be disrupted as little as possible.

The Muladhara Mandala, it will be recalled, showed arrows leaving the square c Prithivi (Earth) in all directions and the relation between Kundalini in the body and Kundalini in the Earth is shown to be quite central. It must be maintained at all costs if the physical body is to remain in one piece during the spiritualisation process. It does not seem to me in the least surprising, therefore, that some people register an uprising of energy from the Earth into the feet and legs at such times. It would be a natural corollary of the admission of additional Prana into the Nadis at the Kanda. Kundalini reinforcements must come from somewhere and Prithivi is their most obvious source. I myself have never experienced the Sannella cycle. I have, however, had a period when I was very aware of movements in various Chakral areas in the front of the body and ant-like creeping sensations at the top of my head which still occasionally recur. These sensations cannot be explained physiologically, but they do appear to resemble those which sweep up and over the body in the physio-kundalini cycles described by Sannella. A sensory threshold is probably crossed in these cases. Such experiences suggest an extension of one's awareness into subtler levels of one's total field rather than some reflection into the body of cortical transactions at the physiological level.

Like Dr Brugh Joy, (31) I found the theories offered by the Tibetan master the most satisfactory I have so far come across to account for my own personal experience of transition phases in myself and other people. These, however, relate more to changes of polarity in the Chakras than to movements of energy through the Nadis and for that reason will be dealt with more fully later.

It should be noted that the blockages in energy flow assumed by Sannella to be responsible for physio-kundalini symptoms are not the same as the Granthi or knots which risen Kundalini has to 'pierce' on its way to the Sahasrara. These Granthi are natural stopping places, representing phases in spiritual development not log-jams caused by interference with the proper circulation of forces in the subtler bodies.

According to the Tantras dealing with this subject quoted by Sir John Woodroffe, (98) Kundalini has to manoeuvre fourteen Granthi. These are the two other Lingas in the Anahata and Ajna Chakras; the six Chakras strung along Chitrini and the six Devas or aspects of the Parapurusha in these six Chakras. The Lingas and Devas are all elements in the Chakras representing Shiva and therefore connected with conscious awareness. The Granthis are thus places at which Shiva and Shakti have to achieve lesser unions preparatory to their final marriage as Parashiva and Parashakti in the Sahasrara. This suggests that, under natural conditions, the rising of coiled Kundalini is a progression during which there are expansions not only of consciousness but also of character and ability. These would be consequent upon the merging of Kundalini with the Purusha aspects in the various Chakras giving the individual deeper insights and wider powers. The need to remove blockages in the Nadi system which interfere with the surfacing of the subliminal self is a necessary part of spiritual development. Doing this may coincide with the uprising of Kundalini, but the two phenomena are quite distinct.

The resolution of disturbances in Nadi systems is a continuing necessity throughout human evolution. It is a necessary factor in any successful healing process. The presence of Kundalini in the Brahmanadi is not, however, a *sine qua non* of such resolutions. As the Tibetan master points out, there are symptoms which afflict the spiritually advanced which must be diagnosed differently from the way in which the same symptoms would be interpreted in more ordinary mortals. How to distinguish the one group from the other is an art still in its infancy. It is an art which involves highly developed intuition, for those who appear the most saintly are often laggards behind some who, caught in a plethora of misfortunes, look and feel more like spiritual wrecks than Jacobs wrestling with their angels. All too many healers who consider themselves competent to judge overlook this possibility. Having some unusual gift is often taken as a sign of grace entitling its possessor to pronounce on people's spiritual standing. It is not only doctors and psychiatrists who misdiagnose those who come to them for help. Where the full nature of man is concerned, both as researchers and healers, we have still a very long way to go. Nothing becomes us better than humility before our ignorance and a proper anxiety not to pontificate upon the spiritual status of the unfortunate.

14
The Linga Chakras

I have already pointed out the distinction between the Chakra as an energy vortex in the subtle body and the Chakra Mandala as a symbolic representation of the various forces which contribute to the working of particular centres. In this chapter I am going to try to elucidate the meaning of the Mandalas of the three most important of the Chitrini Chakras. The Sahasrara is above and unattached to the Chitrini chain which runs only from the Muladhara to the Ajna. It belongs in a separate group. Hence its omission here.

As has already been stressed, while one can discuss the Shaktis as if they were independent forces, they are in fact co-relatives of Shivas. Both are always and everywhere manifestations of the Shiva-Shakti Tattva. As Woodroffe puts it, all powers imply a power-holder and, conversely, all power-holders imply power held. (98) Shiva represents consciousness, the container, while Shakti represents dynamism, the fashioner of a universe in which nothing exists which is not in some measure both alive and conscious. Differences are only in the degree of dominance of one side over the other in any interplay of forces.

Shiva is the Purusha that is aware and Shakti is the Ishvari, the creator of that of which the Purusha becomes aware. There is a sense, therefore, in which there is no activity in the body where there is not a Shiva element just as there is no Shakti in the body which is not also an aspect of Kundalini. The Tantras and the Upanishadic commentaries on Kundalini yoga are in agreement on this point. Thus it is not only where one finds the Linga that one must assume the presence of Shiva any more than we should assume that Kundalini resides only where we find coiled serpents. When a Linga is found in a Mandala, however, the presence of Shiva is being especially stressed and in the three Mandalas under discussion here it is centrally placed.

The three Linga Chakras are the Muladhara, the Anahata and the Ajna, respectively at the base of the spine, in the heart region and between the eyebrows. It is said that yogis find the forces in these areas particularly difficult to deal with because of the density of Maya. It is also said that the gross body is anchored in the Muladhara, the life-vehicle in the Anahata and the mental body or Antahkarana in the Ajna. They are thus centres where the Shiva-Shakti Tattva must be present in strength. This is confirmed by their Mandalas each of which contains both a Linga and a Trikona, the downward-pointing triangle of threefold Kundalini-Shakti. The force of Maya at these three points is no doubt due to the need to keep the spirit securely in its three bodies and their energies directed towards life on Earth. It is of the essence of Kundalini yoga to achieve enlightenment and bliss while still in this world and for the Mahayogi to be able not only to raise Kundalini, but also bring it safely back into the Muladhara.

In view of the necessity that Kundalini stay coiled in the root Chakra in order to anchor the Jivatman in the physical body, this raises the question of how Kundalini can remain in the Muladhara and also pass up and down the Sushumna at the will of the Mahayogi at one and the same time. The answer seems to lie in the nature of the Trikona in which the Shiva-Linga is set. Kundalini must always be thought of as threefold. So far we have dealt with only two of its aspects, coiled Kundalini which does not move and Shabdabrahman which operates causally in terms of functional significance. It must be the third which moves through processes and which it requires the skill of the Mahayogi to manipulate up and down when it passes directly into the Sushumna. Since it is responsive to the pull of Shiva as consciousness, the missing Kundalini force must be an aspect of Chit.

We have already discussed the problems which arise when

Chit is translated as consciousness. When speaking of it in relation to Shiva, however, the usage is appropriate, for Shiva is conscious intelligence. The Shiva side of the Shiva-Shakti Tattva represents the experiencer, the Purusha. Chit-Shakti is the intelligence which informs the creations of Prakriti, the intelligence implicit in natural phenomena. At the physical level Chit-Shakti becomes the third constituent Shakti of the triangle of Kundalini forces symbolised by the Trikona. It is the Kundalini the Mahayogi can learn to work with once he is an Adhikari (one who is competent) in Kundalini yoga. His relations with the other two Kundalinis will be more passive. Since he is functioning in a physical body he must respect the right of coiled Kundalini to remain in the Muladhara. This means attending to diet and making use of the correct postures and breathing exercises. He must be in tune with the Shabdabrahman aspect of Kundalini, matching his spiritual endeavours and his Dharma. His efforts must be geared to the fulfilment of his own particular role in the scheme of things and it is a necessary part of his competence that he should know what this is.

There are two quite distinct energy patterns when forces are circulating normally through the Nadis and when Kundalini energies are passing directly from the root Chakra into the Sushumna. In the ordinary way the Nadis and the nerves and blood vessels of the physical body co-operate in maintaining a constant state of warmth throughout the tissues. When energy is withdrawn and concentrated in the Sushumna the entire body goes cold, leaving only an area of warmth at the crown of the head. This latter state of affairs can be accidentally induced, which suggests that physical mechanisms associated with energy distribution can trigger off pseudo-kundalini phenomena of this sort as well as of the sort described by Sannella. In *The Serpent Power* Woodroffe tells the story of an Indian who was parodying the postures of a Hatha yogi when suddenly 'sleep' came on him. He was found on the ground unconscious and stonecold except for a small warm patch at the top of his head. He was resuscitated by massage until warmth returned. In Woodroffe's account this came back slowly at first until the neck was reached and then it spread with a rush over the rest of the body. Unlike the Mahayogi who can handle these energy transactions with full awareness, this man would have remained unconscious without help from outside. The force and rapidity with which subtle forces can surge through the body are a measure of the power with which Kundalini yogis must learn to deal. Unconsciousness is only one hazard of mishandling it. Others are imbalances in any or all bodily systems due to the disturbance of natural processes in one way or another. Kundalini-Tripura needs to be understood along all her three dimensions. To will her rising is not enough. One must be able to act out of knowledge that this is her proper time to do so. As Sri Aurobindo points out, (1) in practice this usually means doing nothing.

The importance of the Linga Chakras is that they are vital meeting places of Shiva (Linga) and Shakti (Trikona) forces, and are mechanisms for enhancing the scope of their interactions in the spheres of body (Muladhara), life (Anahata) and mind (Ajna). How they do this is symbolically described in the Chakra Tantras we shall be discussing here and in the Mandalas Woodroffe uses to supplement them. The texts are full of imagery which needs elucidating. To attempt this is necessary but far from easy. The outcome must be judged as the tentative offering of a student, not the exegesis of an authority.

The Muladhara Chakra (verses 4-13)

Verse 4 of the text tells us that the Muladhara is attached to the Sushumna and has four crimson petals each adorned with a letter of the Sanskrit alphabet. The head of the lotus hangs down. The flower analogy of stalk, pericarp and petals enables us to envisage the structure of the centre as roughly funnel-shaped but with functionally distinguishable levels. It is conceivable that there are transduction mechanisms operative at the interfaces between petals and pericarp and between pericarp and stem. As indicated when discussing the role of the letters, the petals represent force-streams with their own distinctive parts to play within the total economy of the body. By saying the head of the lotus hangs down, verse 4 is telling us that these streams are normally directed towards the ground. The Chakra's opening faces the Earth, a point I have not found generally stressed though it is of the greatest significance in the light of Underwood's contention that organisms interact with geodetic forces.

From verse 5 we learn that the pericarp of the Muladhara lotus contains the yellow square region of Prithivi with its eight spears directed towards all points of the compass. This is very much the Chakra of the Earth. Within the square is the Bija of Earth or the letter which represents its characteristic sound. This is said to typify its essence and to be made up of a synthesis of the sounds of all the forces at work in the Chakra. This Bija is 'mounted on the King of Elephants' and is associated with 'the child Creator'. The elephant symbolises the enduring strength of the Earth and the child Creator, a Shiva aspect, indicates the relative immaturity of consciousness at this level. The Muladhara is reputed to govern the skeleton, the densest material component of the body, and the feet with which it meets the ground. The sense connected with it is smell, the dominant sense in animals and the one which determines their mode of consciousness.

The Shakti who companions the child Creator is the mature Devi Dakini, 'the carrier of the revelation of the ever-pure intelligence' (verse 7) to whom I have referred before. Called in some Tantras the doorkeeper and in others the Queen of the Chakra, Dakini is presumably the guardian of the opening through which forces pass in and out of the centre through the petals. The door into the Brahmanadi, at the mouth of the Sushumna, would only be her indirect concern as the presiding divinity of the Chakra as a whole since this door is normally blocked by the head of coiled Kundalini. It is not used by forces from below until Kundalini wakes and moves her head. The energies from below pass into the Ida and Pingala and the 72,000 other Nadis from the Kanda, the 'knot' at which all these innumerable streams meet and separate. All will be modified by the various forces within the Chakra with which they interact on their way up through the pericarp and by the Shabda influences represented by the letters on the four petals.

The Kanda lies within the Trikona which is beneath the

square of Prithivi. Purnananda, the author of this Tantra, calls this the Tripura triangle, confirming it as symbolic of the threefold Devi Kundalini. All the trinities of Kundalini qualities therefore contribute to what goes on here. He says the triangle is filled with a Vayu which is characterised by desire. Vayu means breath or life-principle and is often used as a synonym for Prana. Vayu in the Muladhara, however, is a form of life-energy with a downward urge towards physical manifestation. The desire element in it ensures the fulfilment of material needs. Life-energy with a downward pull is called Apana-Vayu and in the basal Chakra it counters an opposing pull from Prana-Vayu in the heart centre. I have introduced the term Vayu not only because it helps us to distinguish between the various Pranas but also because it is used consistently throughout the texts in *The Serpent Power* to which readers may want to refer.

Verse 8 tells us that the Trikona is full of Apana-Vayu and, since the forces of Prana and Kundalini are said to blend in the Muladhara, this must be the place at which they mingle since the great stream of Nadis from the Kanda passes through it. From the Trikona the modified energy surges into the Prithivi square and from there goes to all points of the compass. Before this, however, some Nadis separate off to proceed to the petals, the others dividing up and spreading out over the body. The streams passing over the petals will be further qualified by their letters before going their separate ways. Qualification here, of course, means being functionally adjusted to the purposes for which their specialised energies are intended. Apana-Vayu is the only force mentioned as filling the triangle so that it is presumably a form of Prana modified by Kundalini. The Kundalini factor is no doubt responsible for its earthward pull.

In the midst of this Apana-Vayu, which is 'always and everywhere' in the Trikona, is the Linga complex. This is not simply the phallic symbol with a serpent coiled 3½ times round it as is usually thought. The imagery is a great deal more complicated. Understanding it is crucial to our discovering how Kundalini can both rise and remain coiled; how one can reach Moksha (liberation) and experience Samadhi (ecstasy) while still in a physical body.

Inside the Tripura triangle, we are told in verse 9, the Linga has his head downwards. In the Mandala illustrated the phallus is erect, which seems to contradict the text. What Purnananda may have been trying to convey by this image is that in this Chakra the Shiva element (consciousness) is oriented towards life on Earth, whereas in the Sahasrara it is directed up towards the completely disembodied state. This would be in keeping with many other texts. For instance we are told that in the Muladhara Shiva 'resides happily'. The Linga here thus represents Shiva as the partner of coiled Kundalini quite content to remain within the play of Maya in the physical world. He is not pulling against Apana, urging consciousness towards liberation before its time. His presence in the root Chakra underlines the fact that knowledge and the body evolve together.

At the top of the Linga is a depression containing a small opening. These are overlaid by the head of the coiled Kundalini serpent. This Kundalini, verse 10 informs us, is 'the world-bewilderer gently covering the mouth of the Brahma-dvara (Brahman-door into the Sushumna) with her own'. She is also the same whose 'shining snake-like form goes three and a half times round Shiva'. Coiled Kundalini not only sur-rounds Shiva, she also seals the aperture of the Linga and the door into the Brahmanadi. In these ways she appears as a constraining influence, ensuring the Jivatman's physically embodied state. It is this Kundalini who, by lifting and dropping her head, controls the comings and goings of the Kundalini who rises from and returns to the Muladhara. The two Kundalinis must therefore be distinct.

In the verses on the Shiva-Linga relation to Kundalini (9-11) Purnananda does not touch on the willingness of Shiva to accept the constraints placed upon him by the coiled Kundalini, but the fact is stressed in other texts quoted by Woodroffe in his commentary on this verse. In one Shastra Shiva is made to say, 'This Maya is dear to me by which the world is bewildered,' and in another he says, 'This Supreme Shakti is in me and is Brahman itself.' So it is man and not Shiva who wants Kundalini to uncoil and tries to force the pace of spiritual growth. Shiva is content to wait upon the times and seasons of each individual Jivatman which, deep

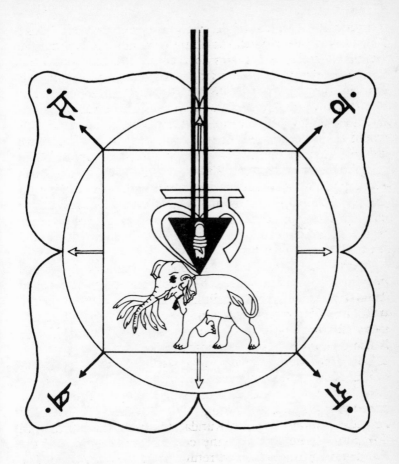

Figure 1
Muladhara Chakra   1st Linga Chakra   Base of spine
Presiding divinities   *Devi*: Dakini; *Deva*: Child Brahma
Tattva   Earth (Prithivi)
Associated sense   Smell
Petals   Crimson with golden letters
Pericarp   Shining yellow square of Prithivi with
   (1)   Bija of Indra (Earth) of same shining yellow
   (2)   White elephant - divine strength and solidity
Trikona   Lustrous deep red Shakti triangle with
   (1)   Linga of molten gold
   (2)   Coiled Kundalini of lustre 'like young strong lightning'

Figure 2
Anahata Chakra   2nd Linga Chakra   Heart region
Presiding divinities   Devi: Kakini; *Deva*: Isha
Tattva   Air (Vayu)
Associated sense   Touch
Petals   Petals and letters both a shining vermilion
Pericarp   Interlaced triangles the colour of smoke with
   (1)   Bija 'grey as a mass of smoke'
   (2)   Antelope representing swift movement of Vayu
Trikona   Shakti triangle 'like to million flashes of lightning'
           Shiva linga 'like shining gold'

within our subliminal selves, Kundalini and Dakini know as we in our superficial conscious selves cannot.

Within the Linga round which Kundalini is coiled, and the dominant element there, is a Shakti of which one seldom hears, 'The Awakener of Eternal Knowledge'. Into this 'dominant Para' flows a continuous stream of ambrosia from Eternal Bliss. She is its receptacle in the Muladhara. Though so seldom spoken of, this, I suspect, is the third Kundalini aspect.

In the Muladhara Mandala Para is represented by a shaft of flame the tip of which lies just below the aperture of the Linga and points straight towards the entrance of the Brahmanadi. Para is Shabda at the causal level, sound as a formative force shaping matter for specific purposes. As such it is an aspect of the Jivatman operating at the very core of the Chakra through which are filtered all the energy streams which fuel the bodies in which the Brahman self is clothed. This is the causal growing point, the subtle analogue of the formative mass of totipotential cells in the physical embryo. It carries the individual's multidimensional blueprint and ensures its precipitation into matter level by level. It is thus a hologram in time as well as space, a fragment of Brahman linking an apparently isolated piece of mosaic and the universal design into which it fits.

While Shabdabrahman represents the aspect of Kundalini-Shakti which carries the causal hologram, it does not appear to be the one which enters the Brahmanadi like a serpent of fire. This Kundalini operates in denser matter than Bodhi or we would never be conscious of its activities. It works with consciousness and only rises into the Brahmanadi when consciousness has developed to a certain point. It is called Chit-Kala in the commentary on verse 12 and is expressly identified with Kundalini. The flame in the Linga is power geared to destroy the Maya that coiled Kundalini is geared to maintain and this can only be done with the help of consciousness. Shiva in the gross body, symbolised by the Linga, is thus constrained by the one and freed by the other while Kundalini-Shabdabrahman controls their interplay. When the time arrives for the door into the Brahmanadi to be opened it will be set by these three Kundalinis acting together as

Devi Tripura, the Threefold Goddess. The evolutionary design of Shabdabrahman must have sufficiently unfolded, coiled Kundalini must uncover the apertures and Chit-Kundalini must rise through them. During the period of preparation for our final release from 'the wheel of birth and death', the rising and sinking of Chit-Kundalini should become increasingly frequent. This is because more and more of the eternal knowledge inherent in Chit gradually 'awakens' and becomes able to express itself through the human body. The capacity of consciousness to rise develops in phase with the capacity of the glandular and nervous systems to adjust. The timing of both is controlled by Shabdabrahman.

The final verse about the Muladhara in Purnananda's account deals with meditation, not as something directed towards either coiled Kundalini or the Chakra in general, but towards Chit-Kundalini-Shakti. It involves contemplating a Divinity within who can awaken in us that wisdom which derives from our true selves, a knowledge of reality which is also a source of joy. The reward of this sort of meditation is all that flows from being able ultimately to function from this level of ourselves.

The Anahata and Ananda-Kanda Chakras (verses 22-7)

Just as the Chit aspect of Kundalini in the Muladhara tends to be overlooked so does a centre called the Anandakanda. It lies just below the Anahata and is essentially a functional part of the heart complex. It is a small golden lotus with eight rose-red petals in which are depicted an altar and a tree. The tree is the Kalpa tree. It is sometimes called the 'wishing tree' because it is said to grant wishes generously even before they are framed. The jewelled altar is the proper place to offer up prayers and praise. It is the Chakra of the devotee whereat to worship and ask for nothing, aware that Brahman already knows what should be asked. This little centre is of greater spiritual than biological significance.

The same, of course, cannot be said of the Anahata or major heart Chakra which is important on both counts. Spiritually it is where the desire for Moksha (liberation) originates. It is here too that the inner meaning of things can be grasped or, more picturesquely, 'where the sound of Shabdabrahman is heard, that Shabda or sound which issues without the striking of any two things together' (verse 22, commentary). It is also said to be the dwelling-place of the Purusha aspect of the Jivatman. This means that the Anahata is the main consciousness centre in the individual as the Muladhara is the chief form centre. In the Muladhara the downward flowing energies create significant forms; in the Anahata these forms yield up their meanings, their Shabda, to the Purusha who then 'knows' the form for what it is intended to be.

In verse 22 we are told that this lotus is 'the Region of Vayu' symbolised by the hexagon at the centre of two interlaced triangles which fill the pericarp. This contains the Vayu Bija and the image of an antelope which signifies the swiftness with which Vayu moves. The element associated with the heart Chakra is air. Vayu here must therefore be thought of as air as well as Prana-Vayu. Prana-Vayu, it will be recalled, pulls against the Apana-Vayu in the Muladhara. This double use of Vayu can be confusing.

Verses 23 and 24 tell us about the presiding divinities found, each in its own circle, at the top right of the Mandala. The male deity is Isha, a compassionate variant of Shiva, seated in 'the Abode of Mercy'. The goddess is Kakini seated, as are all the 'Queens of the Chakras', in a small lotus of her own. Being Dakini's opposite number, she presumably supervises what goes on at the petal end of the centre, influencing the thresholds of the various energies passing in and out of the Anahata via the twelve streams represented by the twelve, lettered petals. She is described as a very happy goddess, 'three-eyed and the benefactress of all'. Shiva is always depicted with three eyes, so her affinity with the Shiva aspects in the Anahata is here being stressed. In the Muladhara Dakini was the mature carrier of the revelation of the ever-pure intelligence while her male partner was only a child. Here both the divinities are adult so that the forces of consciousness and form are in relative equilibrium. Kakini, we are told, has a heart 'softened by the drinking of nectar' so that she is another of the receptacles of well-being flowing down from 'the font of Eternal Bliss' in the thousand-petalled lotus. In her this takes the form of exhilaration. This well-being of the root Chakra gives strength, that of the Anahata a light heart.

Verse 25 takes us down the pericarp to the level of the Trikona and Linga. The Trikona is the usual downward-pointing triangle found in all the Linga Chakras. Both the Linga and the interior of the Trikona are golden. At the head of the Linga is a small crescent moon and immediately above it a minute orifice. The Shiva-Linga here is called 'the resplendent abode of Lakshmi'. Lakshmi is an oriental equivalent of Aphrodite and symbolises beauty so great one cannot but desire to possess it. Here is the place where the desire for Samadhi takes its rise, not so much the Samadhi of complete liberation from the round of births and deaths as the Samadhi of the union of Shiva and Shakti-Kundalini in the Sahasrara. Below the Linga within the Trikona is a small flame. It is not a shaft of fire as is the flame in the Muladhara triangle but like 'the steady tapering flame of a lamp in a windless place' (verse 26). This is Hangsa or Hamsa which is one of the many names for the Jivatman in its consciousness aspect of Purusha. In the basal Chakra the emphasis is on the Jivatman as the occupant of a physical body. Here the emphasis is on the awareness of the occupant rather than on the body occupied.

Verse 26 is rather obscure in its reference to the wishing-tree Chakra but in the commentary on verse 25 we get a clue as to its importance as part of the heart centre energy system. It suggests that Anandakanda falls within the magnetic field of the Trikona in such a way that the Linga element in the Anahata is in contact with the altar element in the Anandakanda. It is to this central complex that the yogi directs his meditation as a form of worship, for here is 'the seat of the Ishta-deva', one's personal divinity, who should be meditated upon 'according to the ritual of the worshipper'. It is the presence of Shiva-Linga upon the altar of the heart which ensures that what one needs is already known and so does not have to be explicitly asked for.

The polarity between the Anahata and the Muladhara is not only between Shiva as Purusha and Shakti as coiled Kundalini but, as was indicated earlier, also one between

Prana-Vayu and Apana-Vayu. As the commentary has it, 'the two Vayus, Prana and Apana, go different ways, pulling at one another; and neither of them therefore can leave the body, but when the two are in accord — that is go in the same direction — they leave the body.' In other words during life there is pull and counter-pull between them. It is only at death they move together out of the body. Their mutual antagonism is thus vital to life in the same sense that the antagonism between flexor and extensor muscles is vital to movement.

In Pranayama exercises efforts are made to transfer Prana from its centre in the heart down into the basal Chakra. The idea is to get it to join forces with Apana in a concerted attempt to force the Brahman door and enter the Sushumna. This sort of practice is very risky and is strongly counter-indicated except under the most expert guidance. It is unfortunate that Woodroffe goes into such detail about the various Mudras and Pranayamas associated with Kundalini yoga. It is true that, like all responsible writers and teachers, he stresses the importance of being taught by a qualified guru and the need for a great deal of prior character training, but there are always the foolhardy and the spiritually presumptuous who think warnings do not apply to them. Sometimes, as we have seen, postures adopted accidentally or playfully can bring about spontaneous reactions of the physio-kundalini type. Certain meditational practices which aim at calming the mind can also precipitate part of the syndrome as a result of particular interactions between the autonomic nervous system and the Prana-Apana mechanisms of the subtle body. This may especially be the case when there are blockages in areas where physical and subtle energy fields are in functionally close relation to one another. According to the Yoga-Tattva-Upanishad, human beings oscillate up and down under the influence of Prana and Apana and are never at rest. This has obvious parallels with the oscillations in the physical body described by Bentov.

To give the reader some idea of what is expected of the would-be yogi in the East where the religious life is a serious vocation, it might be helpful to look at the doctrine of the Eight Limbs of Yoga. (99) This enshrines the Hindu teaching about the way an aspirant prepares himself for liberation through yoga. Some of the 'limbs' have to be developed by the aspirant alone; others can only be properly developed in association with a qualified guru who understands his individual temperament and can handle his training accordingly.

The first limb is a matter of working at oneself until one has the necessary qualities to satisfy a guru that one is ready for the systematic development of higher powers. This first limb is called Yama. It includes enough to keep most of us busy working on ourselves for a life-time and still be modest about our attainments at the end of it. Yama self-discipline involves the acquisition of certain moral attributes. It comprises an oriental equivalent of the Ten Commandments and the Sermon on the Mount. The qualities aimed at require both the practice of avoidances and the positive exercise of virtues. For instance, one must avoid inflicting injury on any creature; one must not covet what others have and one has not; one must avoid excesses of all sorts; one must be prepared to forgo sexual satisfactions. It is because of the first requirement that Hindus and Buddhists are vegetarians and because of the last that, in India, men and women are expected to live full social and family lives before approaching a guru. In the East the spiritual life is a vocation many undertake as a matter of course in the latter half of life. None but the man who can be celibate 'for God's dear sake' becomes a yogi while still young, however important his religion may be to him.

On the positive side one must be truthful, brave, kind and pure. Some of this is reminiscent of St Paul in Corinthians. One must be able to exercise forbearance, bearing all things patiently. One must be merciful. One must be pure in heart as well as in body. One must be simple and live simply. One must be temperate in speech and seemly in behaviour.

The second limb is Niyama and is chiefly a matter of religious practices, though moral qualities such as modesty and shame at wrong-doing are listed as Niyama. It includes purificatory austerities and fasts; belief in Veda; study of the Hindu holy books; making the prescribed sacrifices and worshipping either the Lord or the Great Mother. All these are required of the aspirant under this heading. Charity is also

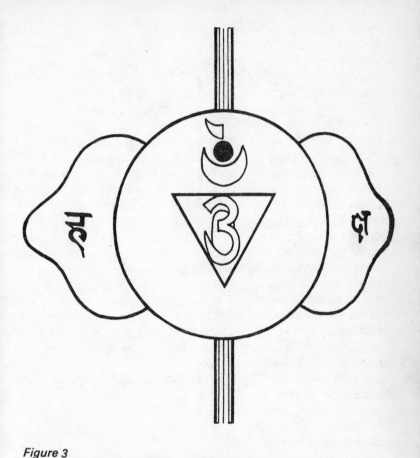

Figure 3
Ajna Chakra   3rd Lingra Chakra   Between eyebrows
Presiding divinities   *Devi*: Hakini; *Deva*: Shambhu
Tattva   Mind (Manas)
Associated senses   Mental faculties
Petals and Letters   Moon white
Pericarp   Bindu and Nada above a crescent moon
Trikona   Linga of the white lustre of lightning flashes
          Bija of Vedas (OM) of a white flame-like radiance

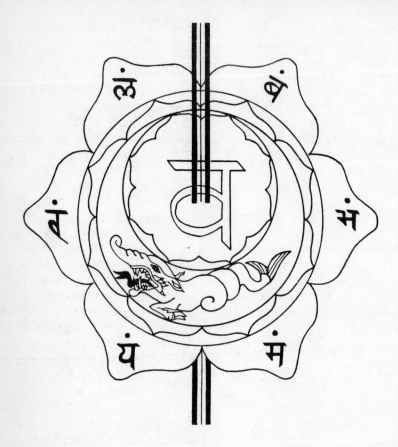

Figure 4
Svadhisthana Chakra   Sacral region
Presiding divinities   *Devi*: Rakini; *Deva*: Vishnu
Tattva   Water (Apas)
Associated sense   Taste
Petals   Vermilion with letters 'shining colour of lightning'
Pericarp   Shining moonlit watery region with
   (1)   Bija - also of Indra - 'White as autumnal moon'
   (2)   Makara, part-alligator part-fish - strength and absorbent
          power of water

expected towards the deserving. Mantras in common religious use should be recited. This stage of preparation for yoga can be made within the community in the East. In the West it tends to be associated with the conventual life.

In the Ashrams of serious teachers of yoga it is only after a sound moral and religious foundation has been laid that postures, Pranayama and exercises to discipline the senses are taught under instruction. These are limbs three, four and five. Six, seven and eight are called 'the inner limbs' because they relate to the interior development of the mind. They are Dharana, concentration of the mind on its object; Dhyana, contemplation of the object; and Samadhi where there is consciousness only of the object, with self dropping away. The object is normally some aspect of the Divine chosen as an avenue to Brahman and so to the Samadhi state proper which is union with Him. Meditation as understood in the West tends to be a combination of five, six and seven in so far as it is done to enrich and develop the mind in order to achieve Samadhi. The kind of meditation which is only directed towards quietening the mind by the repetition of inner sounds without concentrating on their meaning is not meditation in the same sense. It is a Dharana exercise of a negative kind which only becomes a limb of yoga if it is employed in a religious context and practised in association with Yama and Niyama. The question to ask is, 'Why is the mind being steadied?' If it is to deal with anxieties and improve health, it is a good idea but hardly a spiritual exercise. In this connection advocates of Transcendental Meditation as a cure for social ills are trying to promote a course of therapy of a kind which reduces the conflict between surface and subliminal selves and gives the latter a better chance of surfacing. It is a valuable form of exercise but is not a substitute for yoga. Transcendence cannot be assumed to follow automatically upon the steadying of the mind and tranquillising the nervous system, helpful as this is in improving the quality of one's personal life.

This may be a good place to make another distinction, this time between the yogi and the shaman. Puharich has dealt with this subject from a scientific angle in *Beyond Telepathy* (62) and I do not propose to go into it in detail now. I want merely to point out the difference between mediumistic and spiritual forms of ego-transcendence. The shaman is a tribal priest of great social importance and highly developed psychic gifts. He is not a would-be saint whose goal is to rise above both society and himself by entering the Divine. The shaman is a practitioner offering services which can be seen and assessed. The yogi is a contemplative whose contribution is invisible. It cannot be assessed. Indeed, it can be all too readily discounted unless he is also a guru with a notable following.

The Ajna (verses 32-8)

This is the Chakra of the mind which is said to have its anchorage point here as the life-vehicle is anchored in the Anahata and the physical body in the Muladhara. It is called Ajna (command) because it is here that the Sadhaka hears the command of his own inner guru. By virtue of the forces in the heart centre, Shabda, the meaning of things, can be grasped intuitively; in the brow centre these can be formulated in words and organised into sentences. When the subtle bodies are sufficiently purified, the still small voice associated with 'And the Lord said' in so many sections of the Bible can be heard here. This is why meditation begins with disciplining the mind and the senses. The sort of inner chatter that goes on in our heads for much of the time makes it impossible to hear commands so softly spoken and yet clearly not coming from the place in our heads where we normally talk to ourselves. This is why Purnananda says in verse 32 that this Chakra ideally 'shines with the glory of Dhyana (meditation as the state of contemplation of the Divine)'. In all these texts it is the fully developed condition of the Chakras which is being described.

This is a centre illuminated by the light of the moon. It is par excellence the Chitrini Chakra into which the glory of the indwelling sun can be reflected. In most of us, however, it is a personality centre whose energies are almost wholly determined by the socially conditioned ego. This is why its development involves so much self-discipline, for it is here that, if we do not watch out, the mind can be the slayer of the real in spite of all our efforts to see clearly. While there is conflict between the subliminal selves, serving the Jivatman, and the surface selves produced by conditioning, the mind, or Antahkarana, cannot fulfil its proper role as reflector of the true self.

Unlike the other major Chakras, the Ajna is depicted as small. In spite of its common association with the winged sphere on the top of the caduceus, its two petals fill only the span between the eyebrows. Most of its energies are focused inward. It is, of course, the familiar third eye which the West tends to think of as connected with psychic powers. In the East its connections are mainly religious. The priestly caste in India, the Brahmins, paint a spot on their foreheads to mark its position. Originally it was a sign that the Shiva eye, the eye with which the Lord can be seen, was open and His commands could be heard. The Tantrantara Tantra calls this Chakra, for this reason, 'the house of Shiva'.

The Ajna is a very white lotus and the letters on its two petals, though not themselves white, signify whiteness. Its Bija, its seed-mantra, is white. The Linga is white and lies within a silvery white Trikona. The crescent moon above the Trikona is white. All this emphasises the degree of purity which must be achieved before this lotus can fully open, a fact which is made clear in the text. Chitta must be refined. Hakini, the presiding goddess here, represents pure Chitta. Her mind is exalted by the drinking of ambrosia and she is seated on a white lotus.

Verse 33 tells us that Manas and Buddhi 'dwell' in this Chakra. Manas is said to be its prevailing energy as Prana and Apana are the prevailing energies of the Anahata and the Muladhara. This, however, is a subtle form of mental energy, not Manas merely as the selector in and out of sense impressions. In the Ajna Chakra 'constantly shines the excellent Manas, made beautiful by the presence of Shakti Hakini. It is lustrous and has Buddhi, Prakriti and Ahangkara for its adornment' (commentary on verse 40). This Manas selects impressions from all parts of the mind, including presumably those coming in from the Brahman self in its abode in the Sahasrara.

The 'Bija of the Vedas' lies inside the Trikona and is the well-known seed-mantra OM. Its letter is shaped like a 3 and also like a white flame. The importance of the proper use of the OM is that it throws a downward light into the Chitrini Nadi and the Brahmanadi inside it. In other words it operates to carry the effects of the purification of the mind into the lower levels of one's being, so that all parts of the personality share in the general improvement. This is of great assistance in releasing the subliminal self which the surface self overlies and obscures.

We are told in verse 34 that when the Sadhaka is able to meditate on this lotus in such a way that he is nothing but the lotus he becomes 'all-knowing and all-seeing', which is where the idea that this is a 'psychic' centre comes from. 'Full of fame, long-lived, he ever becomes the Creator, Destroyer and Preserver of the three worlds' explains its association with magic. However, all these powers are, for the true yogi, merely secondary by-products of identification with the Brahman self, of 'being Brahman'. Otherwise it would be difficult to distinguish between the yogi and the shaman. 'Being Brahman' means that any use of his heightened powers by the yogi would necessarily be as 'the benefactor of all, and versed in all the Shastras' (verse 34).

Verse 35 deals with the letters of the 'Bija of the Vedas' and the commentary helps to clarify the reasons for its dual form. Purnananda uses the special name given to this Bija, the Pranava. The 'combination of letters which form the Pranava' to which he refers are A, U and M. It is only in the Samadhi state of meditation when subject and object are one that the A and U merge to become O. Presumably the Shabda represented by the Bija can take two forms and operate within the Chakra in different ways at different times. Purnananda specifically relates it to Buddhi as the purified state of the mind at the level of higher intelligence. Its radiance is likened to a flame. It represents the Jivatman at this level. It is both that which enlightens what is below and that which reflects into the conscious mind enlightenment from above.

Chit and Shabda are well represented in this centre for above the Trikona are Nada and Bindu resting in a white crescent moon. Nada, it will be recalled, is the name given to the first movement in cosmic Chit which ultimately eventuates as Shabda or meaningful sound. Bindu is the point — and the word means point — deep within the consciousness of individual entities which receives this movement. It is out of Bindu that the Tattvas arise, from the Shiva-Shakti downwards. In Nada and Bindu all states are still undifferentiated and there is no distinction between Chit-Shiva and Chit-Shakti, the experiencing consciousness and the phenomena experienced. In Bindu all potential forms of awareness and all types of creative activity exist as latencies. Everything is possible but nothing yet exists. This is no doubt what lies behind the statement that the Sadhaka who can live fully in the Ajna can do anything. It is then the AUM becomes the OM, for Manas and Buddhi are now merged with Bodhi, mind with supermind.

The lights which verse 36 tells us surround the pure white flame of the Atma within the Trikona can only be seen by the yogi who has first closed his mind to all outward things, 'closes the house which hangs without support', and who has faithfully served his guru — the one within even more faithfully than the one without. He then achieves the state of no-mind (Umani) where all 'becomes dissolved in this place which is the abode of uninterrupted bliss'. Unless the Sadhaka can reach this state he is not yet fully in yoga.

It is to be noted that this bliss is not that of Moksha or liberation. The latter is not engendered in the Ajna, but accompanies the arrival of Chit-Kundalini at her final destination in the Sahasrara. The Samadhi of the Ajna, however, is the first we read of which is full of light. One is reminded of the text, 'when the eye is single, the body is full of light', which may be a description of what happens when experiencing this state of the Ajna. This light is not only that of the moon. We learn from verse 37 that light also comes into the Ajna from above which is like 'a flaming lamp' and 'lustrous like the clearly shining sun and glows between the sky and the Earth'. This light is that of the Supreme Shiva in the Sahasrara which is reflected down and can be seen by the yogi who is truly an Adhikari in this meditation.

The presence of Nada and Bindu as well as the Trikona and Linga makes it clear that the Ajna governs an area of great potentiality. Its position is intermediate between the crown centre and the Chitrini string of Chakras. It has executive powers over the centres of the body through the mind which it controls. It is also receptive to influences from above which it can transmit downwards. It is able to respond to the command of the inner guru when the mind has been purified and convey it to the inner ear. It plays the moon to the guru's sun, reflecting down from causal levels into the mind the instructions incorporated in the subliminal self so that the Antahkarana operates both as the effect of higher causes and the cause of lower effects. It is, however, also a field of potential conflict for it is here the ego and the true self, Sri Aurobindo's real soul, must come to terms. The work which has to be done through the Eight Limbs of Yoga is aimed at removing the ego sources of conflict which prevent the mind from truly reflecting the mind of the guru, the Lord within. This must also be the work on the Antahkarana about which the Tibetan writes. It is only when the mind is purely an instrument of the true self that there is ego-transcendence in the full meaning of the term. This transcendence is dual. The ego, as a point focusing individuality, transcends the limitations of the mental body and can enter the causal body on the supramental plane. The ego, operating within the subliminal self, can also transcend the limitations of the superficial self and its distorting influence. Once the ego becomes receptive and the true self active, the downflow of forces from the Sahasrara increases and the centre of consciousness is progressively drawn into it.

The Svadhisthana and Manipura Chakra (verses 14-21)

The Svadhisthana is sometimes called the sacral Chakra. It is not one of the Linga Chakras, but its relation with the Muladhara appears to be complementary in a number of respects. Both centres arise in the perineal region. This band of tissue contains the orifices of the bladder, vagina and anus in women, the anus and the roots of the genitalia in men. According to Purananda's account, which is based on masculine physiology, the Muladhara is placed below the genitals

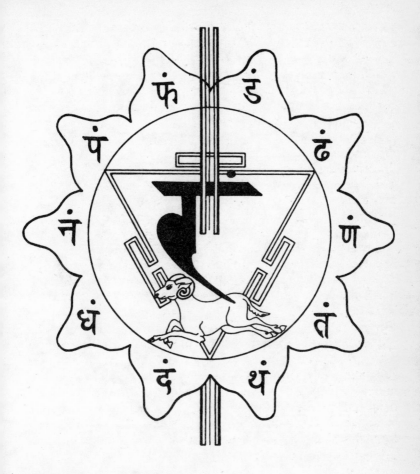

Figure 5
Manipura Chakra   Solar plexus region
Presiding divinities   *Devi*: Lakini; *Deva*: Rudra
Tattva   Fire (Agni Tejas)
Associated sense   Sight
Petals   Colour of heavy rainclouds, with letters the 'colour of the blue
        lotus'
Pericarp   Triangular region with projections to suggest rotation and
        'shining like the rising sun' with
   (1)   Bija of Agni (Fire)
   (2)   Ram associated with Rudra (the presiding Deva of the Chakra)

Figure 6
Vishuddha Chakra   Throat region
Presiding divinities   *Devi*: Shakini; *Deva*: Androgyne Sada - Shiva
Tattva   Ether (Akasha)
Associated sense   Hearing
Petals   Smoky purple with crimson letters
Pericarp   Circular ethereal region colour of full moon with
  (1)   Snow white triangle representing the Shakti
  (2)   Bija and elephant also shining white

and above the anus. It is attached to the mouth of the Sushumna though it does not actually open into it under normal conditions. The Svadhisthana, on the other hand, is 'placed inside the Sushumna'. It is, therefore, one of the Chakras which is strung along the Chitrini Nadi and Chitrini energies can enter it, which is not the case with the Muladhara. However, it shares with the Muladhara a common affinity with the Earth. Its Bija, seed-mantra or essential quality, is a Bija of Earth. It represents a more fluid aspect of the Earth, the element associated with it being water, but both Bijas are Bijas of Indra which is another way of saying they belong essentially to the Earth. Fire, the element associated with the next highest Chakra, is not connected with the Earth in the same intimate way. It enters the Chitrini Nadi at the solar plexus and its natural affinities are with the heart centre, the Anahata Chakra. The energies in the sacral centre will be Apanas, downward-tending Pranas; those in the solar plexus centre will partake more of the nature of the upward-moving Pranas of the heart centre.

The two lower centres would thus seem to reinforce one another in keeping the Jivatman rooted in the dense physical world of matter. The dim forms of consciousness they mediate will be geared to supporting instinctive survival and reproductive patterns of behaviour. The fiery element, associated with the Manipura Chakra at the solar plexus, being less stable and earthbound, is able to facilitate the development of more assertive and emotional responses. The fact that the root Chakra is normally sealed off from forces coming down the Sushumna suggests that, more than any of the other Chakras, it is concerned with keeping physiological processes free from conscious interference. Such modifications as are permissible in the sphere of Mother Earth apparently have to be routed through the Svadhisthana. This is interesting because it is through the genetic and reproductive mechanisms that mutations occur and these fall within the force-field of the sacral centre.

It is noteworthy in this connection that it is only now that we are developing biofeedback techniques that Western physiologists have come to realise that the so-called involuntary processes in the body can be consciously controlled, something fakirs in the East have known for a long time. From a Tantric point of view how wisely we use these techniques will depend on the degree to which our ego-judgments are in line with the body's own best interests. At present far too little is known about how the various bodies work or how they interact in health and disease. Nor do we align ourselves sufficiently with inner sources of knowledge. Though every new discovery starts with an intuition, in science as in life, scientists still look dubiously upon the intuitive method. They are only just beginning to trust their own hunches without apologising for appearing irrational.

It is through intuition that the guru within is contacted, and it is this part of us which knows the answers to all the questions we are likely to ask. To believe in it is to open a door into higher sources of knowledge than the ego can achieve unaided. And yet without the ego this knowledge must remain transcendent. It needs stepping down into the world of space-time and for this to happen without distorting truth two things are needed, a cleansed vision and an unobtrusive ego. For the Sadhaka whose Dharma is science, these are necessary limbs of yoga and intuition is the single most valuable gift with which their exercise can endow him. Only by its means does the Truth-seeker become the Truth-knower.

15
Theosophy and Tantra

Those who are familiar with Theosophical doctrines will by now have seen that there are areas of agreement and disagreement between Tantric and Theosophical theories about both man and nature. As so much of what is known in the West about Eastern religion and science has been filtered through one or other of the Theosophical schools, this means that bridge-building between Tantra and science must involve our making use of bridges between Hinduism and Theosophy which are already in existence.

Some Theosophical theories are readily recast in scientific terminology. Many of their subtle entities can be converted into force-fields without significantly altering their character. The human aura described in visual terms by such clairvoyants as C.W. Leadbeater (38) and Phoebe Bendit (7) can also be considered along the same lines as the phenomena of Kirlian photography. (49) The Theosophical doctrine of 343 cosmological planes, on the other hand, resists such efforts and this leads to derivative difficulties in the psychobiological sphere since the nature of man must conform to the nature of the universe of which he is a part.

For the reader unfamiliar with Theosophy let me try to summarise briefly its main teachings about the planes of nature and the constitution of man. In doing this distinctions between the three major schools will not be drawn beyond indicating that the Steiner school of Anthroposophy tends to theorise more functionally than the Adyar school which has a generally more structural approach. The Bailey and Adyar schools give more schematic accounts of cosmic planes, and the constitution of man in relation to them, than do the Anthroposophists. Steiner approaches both man and the universe as a physiologist rather than an anatomist, with the result that his *Occult Physiology* touches on the Chakras but does not deal with their structural arrangement as, for instance, Leadbeater does in *The Chakras*.

Theosophy (38) divides the cosmos into seven major planes of infinitely fine substance within each of which there are seven lesser planes each diversifying its characteristic substance in various ways. Each lesser plane is further divided into seven sub-planes leading to even greater diversification. In this way a multiplicity of forces are postulated which can also be regarded as modifications of primordial substance. The order of density is from above downwards, the densest plane being the physical, the seven sub-planes of which are composed of solid, liquid, gaseous and four etheric types of matter. The septenary of lesser planes of which the physical is the lowest contains in addition the astral, mental, Buddhic and three Nirvanic planes. The three Nirvanic planes of the Adyar school are more often called spiritual, monadic and divine in the cosmology of Alice Bailey, (3) otherwise the accounts of the two schools coincide in essentials. As in Hinduism all three Theosophies assume creation to have come about as a result of a divine urge towards manifestation and to have comprised the clothing of spiritual essences in increasing densities of matter.

Most of what Theosophy teaches about human nature and all that is said about the Chakras, Prana and Kundalini can be understood without going beyond the highest Nirvanic plane. This is roughly what the Tantras treat as the cosmic manifold. If seven other supracosmic planes exist, the Tantras do not appear to regard their existence as practically relevant. From a scientific point of view postulating them would not only be irrelevant but speculative to an unacceptable degree. Many scientists tend to close their minds to theories as a whole if parts, even relatively extraneous parts, go beyond what they can take seriously. It is hard for many of them to bring mind into the physical universe. To ask them to bring in not only spirit as understood by the Tantrika, but spirit as it may manifest on hypothetical planes several floors higher up, is to ask the impossible.

Following on its cosmological assumptions, Theosophy attributes to man more bodies than is customary in Hinduism. It also uses Sanskrit terms differently in connection with them as has already been indicated. In *Man Visible and Invisible* Leadbeater allocates two bodies to the physical plane, the dense physical and the etheric. The Bailey school takes a similar view. The two schools are also in agreement about the existence of an astral plane and an astral or desire body, and of a mental body and a mental plane. In *Man and His Bodies* Annie Besant gives man two distinct mental vehicles. These operate on two different mental levels, a Rupa level and an Arupa level. Rupa means form or body and these two vehicles are described as mediating concrete and abstract thought respectively. This is in conformity with Leadbeater's distinction in *Man Visible and Invisible* and Alice Bailey's in *A Treatise on Cosmic Fire*. All three place the causal body on the higher mental plane and not on the supramental plane of Bodhi as in the Tantras and in the writings of Sri Aurobindo. They apparently consider abstract mind to be responsible for the creation of concrete forms, though it is not quite clear how this comes about. The placing of the causal body on the plane of mental rather than supramental energies is a definite departure from the position of classical Hindu thought as expounded by the scholars consulted by Sir John Woodroffe. (98) In Hindu psychology the causal or Bodhi body is quite distinct from the Antahkarana or mind body and operates on a truly formless (Arupa) level transcending abstract as well as concrete thought. This level is that of the divine not the human mind and is causal for this reason.

The tendency in Theosophical literature to suggest that levels of ourselves exist in readily distinguishable bodies on the various planes makes it difficult for psychologists like myself to adapt its concepts for use by academic personality theorists. The astral plane presents even greater problems than the mental plane. Both the astral plane and the astral body are referred to constantly by writers dealing with psychic phenomena. For instance, there is a considerable body of work dealing with astral travelling and astral projection. (20, 52, 96) Robert Monroe in *Journeys out of the Body* describes three levels of consciousness in which he was aware of his embodied self behaving in different ways while his physical body lay unconscious on the couch. Clearly he was only out of the body in a limited sense. Nevertheless the body he appeared to be in did not vary. It was the laws governing its behaviour which changed so that he presumed himself to be in different locales rather than in different bodies. *Life after Life*, written by the medical philosopher Dr Raymond Moody, also poses problems which those using Theosophical categories tend to analyse in terms of an astral plane. His book is a collection of case histories of the experiences of patients resuscitated after being thought to have died. Dr Elisabeth Kubler-Ross, who wrote the introduction to Moody's book, did so because she too had come to recognise that there seems to be some sort of body into which the 'I' of apparently dead people can transfer itself and from it can watch its inert physical opposite number as if it belonged to a separate person. Sooner or later academic psychologists must examine these phenomena and try to make scientific sense of them.

According to Theosophical theory such experiences can be accounted for by assuming a transfer of consciousness from the brain to the astral body. This is said to occur not only at death but also during sleep. In sleep the astral body is said to leave its physical counterpart to rest and recuperate while it carries on a life of its own on the astral plane. Some sleepers, like Joan Grant in *Time out of Mind*, (39, 25) claim to be able to bring over into waking consciousness undistorted recollections of their astral adventures. Shamans are said to get much of their knowledge of distant events by astral travelling in trance states.

There is a growing corpus of evidence for the existence of other 'bodies' into which the centre of consciousness can be transferred and which can, in varying degrees, function independently of the dense physical body. This in itself does not necessarily warrant the assumption of an astral plane. This plane is sometimes called the emotional plane and it is assumed that the astral body is the emotional or desire body.

In Theosophical charts of the universe the astral stratum is as wide and distinct as those of the physical and mental layers into which matter is divided.

It is the existence of a realm of emotion *per se* which is the psychologists' sticking point in accepting the astral plane, not journeys out of the body. All the scientific evidence produced so far suggests there is no such thing as pure emotion. Cannon and his successors (15, 17, 100, 71) have demonstrated conclusively the role of physiological processes in determining emotional reactions. Anxiety, aggression, mania and depression can all be produced by manipulating the balance of biogenic amines such as epinephrine and norepinephrine in the bloodstream. Mental components also seem inseparable from emotion. For example, the physiological patterns of fear and rage are indistinguishable. What one actually feels, however, differs widely depending upon the way a situation is perceived. If it is judged to be alarming one feels afraid, but if the same situation is seen as infuriating one responds with anger. The situation is the same, the physiological pattern is the same, but the emotional responses are completely different.

An instance of how quickly thought can alter emotion is one with which we must all be familiar. We are on a visit and asleep in a strange bed. In the night we wake up with the impression that there is someone in the room. We peer through the gloom and see a dim shape by the window which resembles a man. Our hearts thump and we feel a rush of fear which is quite instinctive. As our eyes get used to the dark and our memories remind us where we are we realise that what looked like a man is only our clothes over a chair or some unfamiliar piece of furniture. Instantly, in response to our new assessment of the situation, our fear goes and relief and even amusement takes its place. It seems unnecessary to postulate a physical-astral-mental combination of bodily interactions to account for this. An interaction of physical and mental components would seem sufficient.

To question the existence of an emotional plane is not the same as doubting that there are out-of-the-body experiences just because the adjective 'astral' is so often used in connection with them. Moody's patients' reports resemble one another too closely not to point to an actuality which needs explaining. It is also feasible that the body they find hard to describe has an anatomy and a physiology. If so it is possible that the science of the Chakras may help Western science to arrive at a theoretical framework into which they might fit. In suggesting we might begin by abandoning the idea of an emotional plane I am only applying Occam's razor to a theory of planes which seems to lean on too logico-structural an approach to the energy levels of the universe.

It would not seem to violate any fundamental principle of occult science if, for instance, instead of thinking in terms of stratification, the planes were thought of more flexibly as a band of energies of different wave-lengths interacting as do those of the electromagnetic spectrum. Many phenomena might be more easily explained if the astral and mental planes were seen as part of a continuum of energies out of which subtle entities are constituted. Such entities would operate under different laws from those applying to their physical counterparts but in a way which ensured that the two sets of laws functioned co-operatively to facilitate interaction between energy levels. Such an approach is implicit in Hindu psychobiology which is why I have found it easier to use as an analytic tool than the Theosophical schema. It assumes fewer entities and explains more phenomena more satisfactorily.

When one adds Sri Aurobindo's conception, as described by Sharma, of a bi-polar organisation of the individual round the ego and the true self (79) we also have a much more flexible psychological theory than any at present current in the West. It enables us to include within developmental psychology both the biosocial and psychospiritual effects of evolutionary changes. The notion of the ego being largely an artificial self-portrait fashioned under environmental pressures is now generally accepted by psychologists. To call the organisation of ideas and attitudes clustered round it the superficial self would seem a quite valid description of this area of the personality. The concept of a subliminal self which is not an artefact and of which the ego is largely unaware is not at all clearly envisaged and yet much evidence points in its direction. Something of the sort must exist to explain a whole range of innate responses. These work through mechanisms which generate sensations of well-being or disease which may be physical, mental or emotional. Through them is run a wide gamut of services within the personality. This is done in a thoroughly efficient and realistic fashion in spite of varying degrees of interference from the superficial self. It could explain the surprise of the ego at achieving feats it had thought beyond its competence; and also those intuitive hunches that astonish us by paying off. If we remember past lives it is not with our superficial memories since these are the products of our current life-time. There must be some more permanent part of the self in which more enduring images can be stored. There is no Theosophical equivalent of this personality theory.

Another important distinction between the Tantric and Theosophical accounts of human nature has to do with their common acceptance of the doctrine of reincarnation. In the case of Tantra the embodied spirit drops only the physical body and its supportive life-vehicle between incarnations. As Stevenson describes, it is its retention of an intact subtle body down to the Chitta level which makes sense of the fact that living people appear able to carry with them as their own the memory-banks of individuals who have died before they were born. (82) The 'reincarnating ego' postulated by Theosophy consists of the spiritual self in the causal body on the higher mental plane. (60) This means that between incarnations all thought-forms and memory images garnered during life in the physical body dissolve into formless (Arupa) abstractions. Thus between one life and the next there would be complete erasure of discrete memories and not merely forgetfulness. This view of man makes it far harder to account for the accumulating data suggestive of past life recall. Either this must be pure fantasy or some sort of psychic penetration into history. In the latter event, however, there would be no guarantee that the life recalled has any direct connection with the person who may genuinely feel that what they are remembering is a past life of their own.

In order to bring out the differences between the Tantric and Theosophical approaches to cosmology and the constitution of man I have tried to devise a Tantric tabular

224

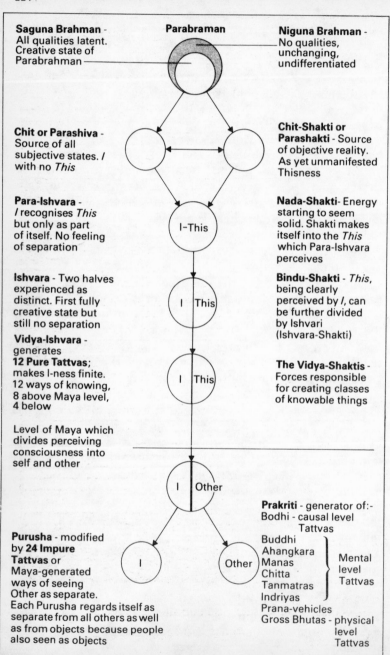

Saguna Brahman - All qualities latent. Creative state of Parabrahman

Parabraman

Niguna Brahman - No qualities, unchanging, undifferentiated

Chit or Parashiva - Source of all subjective states. *I* with no *This*

Chit-Shakti or Parashakti - Source of objective reality. As yet unmanifested Thisness

Para-Ishvara - *I* recognises *This* but only as part of itself. No feeling of separation

I–This

Nada-Shakti- Energy starting to seem solid. Shakti makes itself into the *This* which Para-Ishvara perceives

Ishvara - Two halves experienced as distinct. First fully creative but still no separation

I | This

Bindu-Shakti - *This*, being clearly perceived by *I*, can be further divided by Ishvari (Ishvara-Shakti)

Vidya-Ishvara - generates **12 Pure Tattvas**; makes I-ness finite. 12 ways of knowing, 8 above Maya level, 4 below

I | This

The Vidya-Shaktis - Forces responsible for creating classes of knowable things

Level of Maya which divides perceiving consciousness into self and other

I | Other

Prakriti - generator of:-
Bodhi - causal level
Tattvas

Purusha - modified by **24 Impure Tattvas** or Maya-generated ways of seeing Other as separate. Each Purusha regards itself as separate from all others as well as from objects because people also seen as objects

I   Other

Buddhi
Ahangkara
Manas   Mental
Chitta   level
Tanmatras   Tattvas
Indriyas
Prana-vehicles
Gross Bhutas - physical
level
Tattvas

Figure 7   Suggested Tantric schema

225

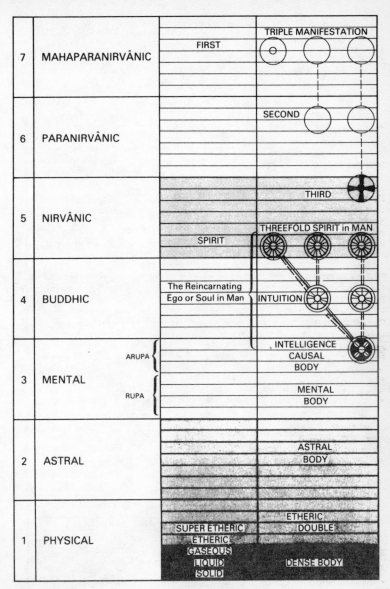

Figure 8
Theosophical schema (Adyar school) after Leadbeater

226

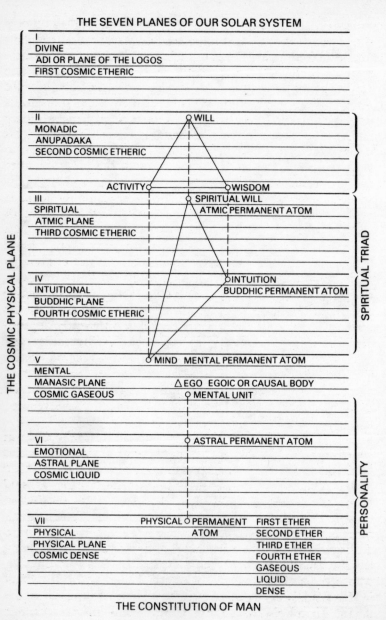

THE SEVEN PLANES OF OUR SOLAR SYSTEM

THE COSMIC PHYSICAL PLANE

| I |
| DIVINE |
| ADI OR PLANE OF THE LOGOS |
| FIRST COSMIC ETHERIC |

| II | WILL |
| MONADIC |
| ANUPADAKA |
| SECOND COSMIC ETHERIC |

ACTIVITY — WISDOM

| III | SPIRITUAL WILL |
| SPIRITUAL | ATMIC PERMANENT ATOM |
| ATMIC PLANE |
| THIRD COSMIC ETHERIC |

| IV | INTUITION |
| INTUITIONAL | BUDDHIC PERMANENT ATOM |
| BUDDHIC PLANE |
| FOURTH COSMIC ETHERIC |

| V | MIND MENTAL PERMANENT ATOM |
| MENTAL |
| MANASIC PLANE | △ EGO EGOIC OR CAUSAL BODY |
| COSMIC GASEOUS | MENTAL UNIT |

| VI | ASTRAL PERMANENT ATOM |
| EMOTIONAL |
| ASTRAL PLANE |
| COSMIC LIQUID |

VII	PHYSICAL PERMANENT	FIRST ETHER
PHYSICAL	ATOM	SECOND ETHER
PHYSICAL PLANE		THIRD ETHER
COSMIC DENSE		FOURTH ETHER
		GASEOUS
		LIQUID
		DENSE

SPIRITUAL TRIAD

PERSONALITY

THE CONSTITUTION OF MAN

Figure 9
Theosophical schema after Bailey

summary to set beside those of the Adyar and Bailey schools shown here, and which I hope readers may be able to adapt for themselves. What needs to be borne in mind is the duality-in-unity which is characteristic of Hindu cosmology. The Tantra, as we have seen, holds that the universe exists because the Divine as intelligent being (Chit-Sat) envisions it and wills its continuance. It is therefore at once a play of unfolding images and processes and something being observed. This means that in order to understand it one must be prepared to study it on two fronts, from the angle of the play of nature and from the standpoint of man as the experiencer of its unfolding action. This separation, however, can only be made as a mental exercise in abstraction and for the purpose of gaining knowledge which is necessarily partial. In reality the experiencer and the experienced are two parts of an integral universe which together they constitute. Tantric cosmology therefore divides the manifested world into Shiva elements and Shakti elements which relate respectively to subjective states and the universe of objects. The Shiva elements are the various Purushas which experience reality differently depending on the level at which consciousness is focused at any given time. The Shakti elements are the forces of Nature (Prakriti) and the entities they create in order that they may be experienced. The cosmos of multiple planes described by the Theosophists would be aspects of Prakriti; the reincarnating ego would be a type of Purusha.

The Theosophical treatment of Kundalini and the Chakras which most nearly approaches that found in the Tantras and Upanishads is that found in the Tibetan books of Alice Bailey. This is perhaps not surprising, as the Tibetan was said to be the abbot of a Buddhist monastery near the Indian border. He would thus have been well versed in Tantric literature on the subject, this having been incorporated into Tantric Buddhism. The teaching of the Adyar school is based largely on the work of the clairvoyant, C.W. Leadbeater, whose book, *The Chakras*, is a basic Theosophical textbook in this field. It does not go into the realm of Kundalini in any detail. Theosophical theories about Kundalini as a cosmic force derive from H.B. Blavatsky's *The Secret Doctrine*. Their most systematic interpretation is contained in Bailey's

A Treatise on Cosmic Fire, where it is treated as a vitalising fire at work in matter and responsible for its rotary motion. At a cosmic level it is called 'logoic kundalini' or 'fire by friction'. This latter usage very graphically conveys the part played by stress in producing changes in the relations of entities in the physical universe. It is the thrust of a dis-equilibrating force which elicits the recoil that re-equilibrates energy fields. Kundalini, as we have seen, is that which uses both thrust and recoil to maintain the harmony of nature as a system of such fields. Tantric scholars tend to emphasise Kundalini's stabilising influence and underplay its role in condoning and controlling the thrust side of power. It is above all the force which keeps things within the bounds of natural law using equilibrium and disequilibrium, action and inaction, equally to this end.

In the teaching conveyed by the Tibetan through Alice Bailey the fires of Kundalini in the body are described as glowing within the centre at the base of the spine where they modify the Pranic fluids coursing through it. Kundalini thus circulates as heat while remaining in the root Chakra as fire. In *A Treatise on Cosmic Fire*, Alice Bailey writes as if there is a constant movement of this modified Prana up the Sushumna Nadi. According to the Tantric texts we have been studying, the Sushumna is normally sealed against ascending forces so that energy from below only reaches it indirectly. There is a discrepancy here. The Tantric texts clearly imply that Prana blended with Kundalini moves out of the Muladhara via Ida and Pingala and the Nadis associated with the arrows of the Prithivi square and the letters on the various petals. They state clearly that the Brahman door into the Sushumna is closed by the head of the sleeping Kundalini. These may seem academic points at this stage, but may prove of more practical significance to research later.

In assessing Alice Bailey's contribution to the science of the Chakras it is germane to remember that the Tibetan never left Tibet and never met this collaborator personally. All his teaching was conveyed telepathically. According to Alice Bailey's *Autobiography*, their first contacts were conversations involving interior speech. The initial instalments of their books were dictated sentence by sentence and transcribed in the usual way. Later, however, ideas were formulated by the Tibetan and, when received, written down by Alice Bailey in her own words. There must have been a good deal of clairvoyance at the teaching end as we are told that the Tibetan was very particular about checking the finished work. He apparently spoke a somewhat old-fashioned and stilted English but understood the language perfectly. Discrepancies between Tantric and Theosophical cosmologies in the Tibetan books of Alice Bailey are thus particularly intriguing and no facile explanation suggests itself. The discrepancies with regard to Kundalini and the Chakras are few. This regarding the Sushumna is one of them. Otherwise it is in this area that I have found the Tibetan's teaching most characteristically Tantric.

The need to revive the science of the Chakras and set it in a context that Western science can assimilate is a very real one. It is, moreover, in the best Tantric tradition to attempt to do this. Indeed, the whole series of Tibetan books dealing with them can be seen as an attempt to bring our knowledge of the Chakras and the Laya process into the twentieth century; to spread it as a knowledge that saves. Their significance for medicine and psychology and, to a lesser extent, for physics, is considerable. For those who hold this Tibetan teacher in great reverence, and I know they are many, I would point out that no Tantrika would want the work of reinterpretation to stand still. We are not only free to try to clarify ambiguities and reformulate doctrines in order to keep pace with changing thought-patterns, we are under an obligation to do so. It is of the essence of Tantra to encourage individuals to think for themselves and to attend above all to the guru within. If I had not read the Tibetan's work, this would be a different book. Nevertheless it would be no real sign of gratitude for the ideas he sparked off not to have gone on to explore for myself this complex and difficult terrain. This is all the more true because I had already encountered the Chakras in the exercise of a healing gift I had found myself to possess.

I had found myself to have this ability in the course of investigating the work of a spiritual healing centre. I wanted to understand what was going on and had been unable to find any book which went into the matter with sufficient detail when I stumbled on *Esoteric Healing* in a Theosophical bookshop. My finding it was serendipitous in the extreme. I was leaving the shop empty-handed when I came across it, the owner having been unable to produce anything but a few slim booklets which I had already seen. It was only because the doorway was blocked that I paused by the shelf on which Alice Bailey's books were displayed and so came on it. It hit my eye at once. I went on from *Esoteric Healing* to *Esoteric Psychology* and what I read in these books made more sense of what I had found myself doing than anything I have read before or since or heard said by any practising healer. What I want to do here is to expatiate on those parts of the Tibetan's teaching which I have verified in my own experience as a psychologist with healing hands. I have said enough about discrepancies and ambiguities for serious students to look out for them and meet them in their own way.

In *A Treatise on Cosmic Fire* the Tibetan discusses Laya yoga, the process of achieving liberation by means of dissolution, in terms of the burning up of impurities in three fires and so freeing the spirit into the Moksha state of Satchitananda. Kundalini he represents as the fire inherent in matter, and calls it fire by friction. The fire generated by mind he calls solar fire and the fire of spirit, rather oddly, electric fire. All these fires are forces and so Shaktis in Tantric parlance. Accompanying them is both light and heat. The light gives this process its Jnana dimension. Light and enlightenment are words used frequently when discussing yoga. Warmth goes with the vital principle and courses with Prana through all living things. Thus at all levels where there is fire there is also light and life. Kundalini only rises into the Sahasrara centre at the crown of the head when all the fires have done their purifying work in the body. This is another way of saying that coiled Kundalini can only rise as Devi Tripura, the Threefold Goddess, when the true self is in full command at all levels of its embodied nature. Or one can say that it only happens when the superficial self has been burned up and the subliminal self is in charge of the personality.

Prior to achieving the purified state one can think of fire

at work at all three levels in interim ways. Kundalini and Prana focus the fires of the Earth and of the solar system and anchor them in individual bodies. From the largest creature to the smallest cell all things are unique individualisations of parts of the Earth and through it of the solar system. They are also transformers of all the energies which pass through them. Evolution is a process of energy exchanges in which the three fires enter into the physical world in varying degrees depending on the capacity of organisms to contain them. The Tibetan appears to associate Kundalini fires with latency, to see them as needing to be activated. This would be to identify them with its coiled aspect which acts through inertia. He tends to connect active physical fires with Prana and this is legitimate provided one recognises that Prana, like all other forces, becomes subject to Kundalini as soon as it enters dense matter. All active forces are presumably activators of Kundalini as soon as they enter the physical realm and are harnessed there. There is a sense in which there is no physical Prana without Kundalini or any physical activity which does not involve Prana. They are correlatives which necessarily modify one another.

The same is true of the fires of mind. As soon as the mind becomes involved with the physical mechanisms through which it gains bodily expression in the world of dense matter, it becomes involved with Prana and Kundalini and their fires blend. When the fires of spirit are able to descend into evolving beings, a new set of energies enters and has to become integrated into the complex system already operating. It is because of the need to incorporate all new energies as harmoniously as possible that evolution is a graduated process. The fiery analogy emphasises that these forces can be powerful to destroy and need to be properly harnessed.

The blending of fires is done largely through the agency of the Chakras which must exist in some form in all creatures. As we have already seen, there is an initial fusing of active Pranic and quiescent Kundalini fires in the centre at the base of the spine, producing, presumably, the combination referred to in the Tantras as Apana-Vayu with which this centre is said to be filled. Some such site of fusion must be present in all vertebrates. The busier animals are and the wider their range of activities the more Prana is needed to provide them with the necessary vitality and to metabolise the greater intake of food. The more active and skilful an animal becomes in the course of evolution, the larger the amount of Pranic fire in the system and the greater the need to call in fires from the mental level. This enhanced activity means livelier contacts between the fires of life and mind and the latent fires of matter. In consequence the Kundalini fires glow more warmly and the chemical fires burn more brightly in the body cells.

In the lower animals all the fires must burn low at first with energy circulating slowly through Nadis and Chakras. One presumes that any mental fire present will be in the form of psychic Prana and in amounts varying with the complexity of the animals' instinctive behaviour patterns. The sensory levels of mental matter would be involved but not the levels mediating self-conscious intelligence.

Unlike the authors of any Tantric text with which I am familiar, the Tibetan refers to a special Pranic centre where solar energy can enter directly into the system modified only by the Earth's planetary field. In man he places this centre between the shoulder blades. Leadbeater does not mention this centre in *The Chakras*, but interestingly enough Brugh Joy describes in *Joy's Way* how he found it when learning to plot the Chakras with his hands. The Tibetan asserts that when the blended Pranas coming up from below meet the pure Prana in this centre an important evolutionary watershed is crossed. He maintains that vitality then pours in, bringing with it the impetus towards more wide-awake states of consciousness. More is noticed, more is responded to, new skills develop. Behaviour becomes generally more flexible. Kundalini responds to this extra-vibratory activity by speeding up the rate of change in cellular processes. Pyro-electricity may well be a manifestation of increased Kundalini fire in the body. The survival rate of organisms rises not only through greater alertness but because the body is better at throwing off infections. In man this phase would represent one of rude health in a physically robust but mentally immature humanity. It is a plateau on which the individual may have to rest for a considerable time while the energy body is prepared for an influx of new fires from the mind into the brain. Evolution is characterised by a number of these plateaux when species must have been undergoing radical energy redistributions. One important one must have preceded the arrival of warm-blooded mammals.

The introduction of Manasic fires, the fires of mind, involve an impingement of the two Pranic streams, the 'pure' and the 'blended', upon the throat Chakra. This system arises in the region of the brain stem at the back of the neck, a spot mentioned by sufferers from the physio-kundalini syndrome as one from which sensations fan out over the back of the head. The Tibetan contends that the throat is a major synthetic force-centre in respect of incoming mental energies. Its job is to see that the influx of Manasic fires merges as smoothly as possible with the fires already in circulation. Incidentally the brain stem is the site of the reticular activating system which Dr R.K. Wallace in 'The physiological effects of transcendental meditation' claims to play a crucial role in the management of stress, operating on the autonomic nervous system below the level of consciousness. (89) The reticular nerves constitute the part of the nervous system we know least about because their fibres are so fine and the number of branching dendrites per cell so numerous that dissecting them out is a matter of extreme delicacy. In their fineness and in the diffuse way their networks are distributed over the body they could be the nerves in the most intimate contact with the minute energy channels of the Nadi system. If so, the reticular formation, their headquarters in the brain stem, and the throat Chakra in the subtle body, could work in very close collaboration. The work of Wallace and his colleagues and that of Bentov (70) are possibly complementary studies of the physiological accompaniments of the blending of the fires in the head and neck Chakras. The Tibetan points out that such energy transfers can cause physical discomfort and malaise. In modern man the nose, throat and chest do indeed seem to be particularly vulnerable to infections. Additional Manasic influxes could be a factor in producing heightened stress over the whole area controlled by the throat centre.

There being no fire without light, enhanced fiery activity

makes for greater illumination. This means not only clearer perception and deeper insight but the light in the cells is said to glow brighter and the whole aura to become more radiant. As a result of the extra work involved in effecting and maintaining new energy arrangements, the Chakras themselves also undergo noticeable changes. In order to cope with the additional Prana entering at shoulder level a vitality triangle is set up involving the spleen and a centre just above the diaphragm as well as the centre between the shoulder blades. This stimulates the Chakras generally and from wheels they become spheres and rotate more rapidly. Even more brightness and speed follow the entrance of the Manasic fires into the throat centre.

This is perhaps a suitable point to say something about the throat Chakra as it is depicted in *The Serpent Power* and dealt with in the Tantric verses translated by Woodroffe. It is called the Vishuddha, which means pure, and is particularly connected with the purification of intelligence at the Buddhi level. This may at first seem surprising since the Ajna is regarded as the Chakra of the mind, as we have seen. I think the importance of the Vishuddha is that it is the highest of the bodily Chakras and the lowest of the head Chakras. Both it and the small Chakra of twelve petals at the root of the palate, the Lalana, are close to the brain stem and its junction with the spinal cord. They are, therefore, intermediate between the subtle counterparts of the spine and brain. The purification with which the throat centre is connected will thus seem to be of those energies in the body which subserve the life of the mind. All those mechanisms in the gross and subtle bodies which mediate sensations from the physical world must be cleansed so that the mind can see clearly with the eyes of the subliminal self. The Tattva of this centre confirms this. It is Akasha or Ether, the finest of the gross Bhutas. Its influence must therefore be on the physical concomitants of mental processes, not on the mind itself. The purification of the mind as such is a matter for the higher forces associated with the Ajna.

As I pointed out earlier, Tantric texts and the Mandalas used to illustrate them deal with the Chakras as they should work. They do not discuss aberrations as does the Tibetan.

They therefore enlarge on the purity of this Chakra. Though less white than the Ajna and the Sahasrara, it has a white central core and the cool white light of the moon shines in it. This has a quietening effect on all the excitable Rajasic forces in the body as well as bringing illumination into the darkness caused by Tamasic unconsciousness. The moon is Sattvic and so brings consciousness and calm. It is therefore more dominant in the higher Chakras where the more spiritual forces operate. This suggests that the fire of spirit, which the Tibetan calls electric fire, burns with a white light.

Alongside the moonlit whiteness of this Chakra is great power. It is symbolised by the images of a number of strong animals. According to the Nirvana Tantra, within its Mandala is a bull and over that a lion-seat on which sits an androgyne Shiva-Shakti clothed in the skin of a tiger. The Bija of the Chakra is set on a snow-white elephant, symbolic of both strength and endurance. The presiding goddess of the Vishudda is Shakini who carries a bow and arrow, a noose and a goad. The commentary refers to her as 'light itself' and in one meditation about her she is described as holding a book and making the gesture signifying knowledge instead of carrying a bow and arrow. The bow and arrow can thus be seen as weapons for use against ignorance. The two meditators are not contradicting one another but rather are illustrating how meditating on the Chakras should be undertaken. The aim is further insight into their meaning, not the generation of sensations and visions by focusing attention on the parts of the body in which they are situated. As muhammad Subuh once said in a group discussion, when discussing the visions sometimes seen by his Subud followers, the descent of the spirit into the body does not need to be sensed. He pointed out that such visions were the by-product of blockages preventing its quiet entry, the sort of impeding condition met with by Sannella's meditators.

In view of the role of Kundalini in controlling the balance of forces at the physical level it is interesting to note the important part played by latency and timing in determining evolutionary advances in bodies. The Tantras assume the Brahman self to be the ever-present context within which personality develops, but until the energy bodies can handle the Manasic fires, its influence remains cryptic. It remains passive in the same sense that a mother is passive while a child grows in her womb. Both are at work though neither seems to be doing anything. Meanwhile Kundalini as Shabdabrahman represents its interests in promoting bodily changes. In this the subliminal organisation and its constituent Shaktis are its active partners. Its passive partner is coiled Kundalini in the root Chakra and it is this which controls timing. It is it which says, 'Now we are ready. Now it is safe to move.' It is when the superficial self thinks it knows better and tries to force the pace that disease and disruption ensue. It is not in this department that the Kingdom of Heaven suffereth violence.

I get the impression that it is on latency and timing that the further development of the nervous system will be found to turn, not on the use we make of our will and our wits. I suspect that all the structures are there but that there are switches still to be turned on. As we saw earlier, the physical switches are enzymes and the formation of enzymes is a matter of putting together molecules. It is the forces behind the organisation of molecules into enzymes which control timing and it is just with these that Kundalini appears to be most intimately concerned.

The great enzyme factories are controlled from the head and the timing of their manufacture and release depends on the nature of the interaction between the Chakras in the body and those in the head. This is another reason why the bridge centre at the throat is so important if bodily mechanisms are to develop in phase with the evolving mind and stand up to the pressures put upon them by descending spiritual energies. It is worth noting that during the last fifty years more and more secretions have been isolated in the pituitary gland, which is said to be the gland which works in closest association with the Chakra between the eyebrows. It is currently thought that the pituitary and its powerful neural partner, the hypothalamus, are probably in overall control of all the enzyme switches at present working in the body. The thyroid gland at the throat, with which it has close functional links, may once have been dominant but is now definitely lower in the metabolic hierarchy. Whether glandular dominance can be transferred in the same way that neural control can be is not known, but it violates no principle of developmental biology to assume the possibility. If it can there are grounds for postulating that metabolic and neural transfers may follow energy transfers in the Chakra system and not vice versa.

The centre between the eyebrows is primarily responsible for the development of the intellect and of the capacity of the personal self to order its life with discipline and fore-sight. Intuition is apparently not in its gift. This is related to the activities of the crown centre, the Shiva centre or the Sahasrara. Intuition in its ultimate form is the faculty of direct insight into the true nature of things. When in a permanent state of enlightenment it is the Chit element in Satchitananda. What we call intuition is sporadic and unpre-dictable and may not even be true intuition at all, but at least it gives us an intimation that there is a part of us beyond the personal self and glimpses of another way of working.

What the Tibetan calls the soul in contradistinction to the spiritual self is probably what Sri Aurobindo meant by the subliminal self. It is said that the soul is our archetypal form, a sort of multidimensional living blueprint of what we are to become. Its existence is one long meditation aimed at creat-ing us and being incarnated through us. It is set this task by the spiritual self which, at the core of our being, has willed to incarnate and willed the blueprint. It wills the soul and the soul meditates us.

Meditation from this point of view is a creative process in the course of which the soul builds forms in mind-stuff which, in their turn, solidify into the things we know. There is latency and timing in this meditation. There is the saying so often quoted: When the pupil is ready the Master appears. Something of the same sort could be said of meditation: when the soul is ready we are prompted to meditate. Equally it could be said that if we attended to our souls we would know not only when but how to meditate. Unfortunately we are seldom wise enough at the outset to have the right kind of patience. Going with Tao instinctively does not come naturally to us in the West where 'waiting upon the Lord' is too often a phrase sadly without meaning.

Moreover, meditation alone is not enough, as we have seen. There must be a seeking which will not be denied and an orientation towards goodness. The enlightened are also the saints and if one is not both one is neither, whatever anyone may say of us or we may claim for ourselves. I mentioned earlier the emphasis placed by the Tibetan upon building the Antahkarana and the notion I had that the Antahkarana was a bridge. In a sense a bridge has to be built, not only one between the ego and the spiritual self but one in the energy bodies between the body and the head. Our working on the one would seem to facilitate the formation of the other. We ourselves, however, can only work with Manasic fires to dissolve the phoney superficial self. Spiritual fires work on us and Kundalini fires on our bodies. All three fires must blend fully before Kundalini can uncoil and in her Tripura Devi form rise up to meet Shiva in the Place of Nectar.

16
Developmental stresses in the Chakras

In *Esoteric Healing* and *Esoteric Psychology* Bailey's Tibetan deals at length with what he describes as disorders associated with discipleship, but I have found his theories apply equally well to many people who are not consciously following any spiritual discipline. This is presumably because we are all evolving whether we think of ourselves as maturing spiritually or not. The treatment which most helps such people is to set their disabilities in a developmental rather than a medical context. Enabling them to modify their self-portraits, and to adjust their aims to conform better with the needs of their subliminal selves, can lower psychosomatic stresses remarkably quickly in some cases. It was in aiding one to reason from the sites of physical dis-ease to the Chakras possibly involved, and from there to the developmental crises being undergone, that I found the Tibetan books most valuable. They are indeed Tantras in that their healing intention is to spread the knowledge that saves in a practically useful way. They are not really books to be argued about in so far as their medical and psychological theories are concerned. They should be put to the test of practice. What proves valid can be used; what does not work can either be discarded or re-evaluated.

Before going into some of these theories in greater detail let us briefly go over some points again.

The science of the Chakras cannot be divided into two parts, one dealing with their anatomy and physiology and the other with their psychological roles. Hindu traditional medicine is psychosomatic for the same reason that traditional yoga is a series of inner exercises inseparable from a code of conduct. Both recognise the dual nature of the mechanisms through which spirit incarnates into and evolves through the physical world. Man, like God, is seen as essentially spirit whether this is thought of as reality, consciousness, energy or life. Matter is not merely that which can be covered by chemistry and physics. These deal only with the most densely embodied spiritual essences. Incarnation is a progressive precipitation of spirit into life and life into form, the final precipitate being the universe of modern physics. Evolution is the movement of events through time whereby incarnated spiritual essences progressively ensoul and refine the forms they have engendered.

From this point of view there would seem to be an involutionary phase showing a gradual reduction of the spiritual content of structures until we arrive at mineral forms which appear exclusively material. Seen by the naive spectator this process can hardly go further. Men have never spoken more of matter and less of spirit; never before have societies been so deeply materialistic. We live in the first civilisation with no instinctive belief in a life after death. Never until now have our eyes so lost their vision that learned men can sit down in solemn conclave to decide whether or not such phenomena as telepathy and clairvoyance actually exist.

So thoroughly are we now embedded in matter that there can be no further development for man unless he can free himself from some of its dead weight. The involutionary arc having reached its nadir the evolutionary drive must turn upwards. If so we can anticipate that forms will begin to lose some of their material content while their life and consciousness aspects expand in increasingly more spiritual directions. Perhaps it is a premonition of something of this sort which is behind two popular tendencies among the young that so disturb their parents, their use of consciousness-enhancing drugs and their refusal to join the rat-race for material success. The yoga craze and the Jesus movements are parts of this drive towards a more spiritually orientated society. Their social conditioning by a greedy and self-seeking older generation, however, often shows. They want too much too soon. Some religious variant of egalitarianism also seems to be at work so that they believe that what one has all can have.

As I hope to show, there are inevitable discomforts and stresses in all progress whether on the involutionary or evolutionary arcs. What one would like to see is more recognition of the individual differences between people, what they can realistically expect of themselves and the rates at which each can advance. Bentov and Sannella are, of course, right. The times are urgent and we must be prepared to take some risks in order to enhance the quality of our contributions if our world is not to go up in smoke. But far too many of the casualties of drugs and Kundalini experiences have been out for kicks and panaceas or dared into them by pushers and profiteers. Proportionately far too few have fallen fighting to save our embattled race.

According to the gurus there should be no Kundalini syndrome. The disorders of spiritual growth are less related to movements of Kundalini than to changes in the balance of forces in the Chakras during transformational processes. Some illnesses have patterns which only really make sense when interpreted in this way. The Tibetan's books deal exclusively with these. They are associated with the hazards of occult development as the bodies of 'probationers and disciples treading the Path' try to keep pace with the demands of the spiritual taskmaster within. There is a sense in which sooner or later we must all tread this path and be subject to its evolutionary stresses. Discomforts cannot be avoided even when under skilled supervision and when all attempts to accelerate matters are kept strictly within bounds. But the Kundalini syndrome apparently should not be among them. It suggests mismanagement and premature interference with the fires of matter with consequent gaps and rents in the vital shields which guard the orifices of the Chakras. These are designed to keep their force-fields apart until such time as they can safely overlap. So seriously can the protective mesh of Nadis be damaged that, we are told, no further spiritual progress is possible in this life-time. Efforts can only exacerbate the burning sensations, headaches and other symptoms associated with such rents. I have come across cases of the repair of a Chakra ruptured by shock, but I do not know of any instance where this has happened to a person damaged by unwise quests for premature Samadhi. Those seeking enlightenment are presumably expected to show good judgment and common sense or pay for the lack of them.

According to the Tibetan, much of the illness of the present time is necessary. This is because energies which have so far been concentrated in the centres below the diaphragm are being enticed under evolutionary persuasion into their opposite numbers above it. Only the crown and root Chakras are at present exempt from involvement in this transference operation. This is why disturbances should not affect coiled Kundalini at this stage. These centres represent the two extremes between which man is extended, spirit and matter. For a long time their roles are passive, the one mainly concerned with keeping man incarnate and the other keeping him open to his cosmic environment at spiritual levels. It is the job of the intermediate centres to mediate the integration of forces so that evolution finally produces a human being whose body, personal ego and subliminal soul can work together as well as Plato's charioteer and his two horses.

It is important to allocate the role of the charioteer to the immortal, subliminal self and not to the transitory superficial ego. As I learnt from many closed doors, there is a senior partner within who sees further and knows better. However wise and far-seeing one tries to be, the personal self is blinkered and, like the horses, its vision does not extend very far in any direction. Sri Aurobindo (30) speaks of two of the three spinal pathways as not merely positive and negative but as specifically carrying forces either up or down. He envisages this up-and-down traffic as primarily responsible for wakening Kundalini and the Chakras. He tells us that we do not have to will the opening of the Chakras. They open of themselves under the influence of descending forces.

This is not an assertion to take lightly in view of the wisdom and saintliness of this great yogi. It is, however, one which needs pondering, since it runs counter to the views expressed by others. It seems likely that he is talking about a phenomenon of a later stage of Chakral development when spiritual as well as Manasic fires are active in the subtle bodies. As we have seen, the Chakras do not start off fully functional as does the stomach, for instance. They mature in phases like the nervous system whose nerves are not all operational from birth. The descending order of their final flowering may be associated with the lead-up to enlightenment, a sort of benison from on high in anticipation of the consummation which could never come about without them. If so, Sri Aurobindo's pupils must have been well advanced spiritually to be opened in this way. For most of us there must still be a lot of purification of ascending forces remaining to be done. As we shall see our patterns of illness all tend to confirm this.

The Tibetan (6) contends that as man moves towards greater self-awareness the first pair of Chakras to be stirred is that of the sacral and throat centres, both of which are concerned with creativity and self-expression. A lot of activity is going on between these centres in many people at the present time. This is reflected in the current vogue for exotic and varied new art forms and the prevailing promiscuity among the young some of whom are finding the problems of adolescence very hard to handle. When energy reserved by nature for millennia for the production of new generations comes under pressure from a spiritual magnetic centre to rise up and create forms of a less substantial kind, there is bound to be stress of a generalised and complex kind. The sacral vortex, which has been positive in relation to a negative one at the throat, becomes agitated under the influence of forces bent on reversing this age-old polarity. It goes temporarily out of kilter while the throat centre has to contend with the extra energy load to which it has to adapt. Not surprisingly the organs in their vicinity, and forming part of their energy fields, tend to share in the upheaval. Not only psychological sex difficulties can be expected, but trouble in the reproductive organs themselves. Menstrual irregularities, fertility problems and tumours are often attendant upon what are basically developmental changes at the energy levels of personality. It is the same in the throat area. Disorders of the thyroid and parathyroid glands and pulmonary upsets can have their origins at energy as well as tissue levels.

The solar plexus and heart Chakras are another functional

pair. They, too, are much involved in transformation processes at this time. The solar plexus centre is not only concerned with digestive functions but also with emotional self-protective reactions. Psychologically speaking personalities focused here are ego-centred and defensive. Many of us do our living and thinking from this centre, unflattering as this may sound. This is why we can be so easily influenced by the media into buying everything in sight in order to keep up with the Joneses. It is also why we can so readily get caught up into the panics and violence of mass responses to a crisis. It makes us manipulable through fear which is why evil men use terror and assassination as political tools with so much success.

As our true self gains a stronger hold our feelings undergo changes in the direction of social justice and compassion. We begin to identify with causes and pursue less selfish goals. This is because energy is being transferred via ascending pathways from the solar plexus to the heart Chakra. The physical troubles that ensue at this stage are most likely to affect the digestive tract or the heart and blood vessels. There is, however, another set of troubles connected with this phase which can be seen bedevilling society in a big way. These result from our thinking too much with our hearts and too little with our heads.

By and large we still live pretty much through the Chakras in the body. The head centres play less part in our thinking than most of us would like to believe. A wise man once said that more harm was done by the wrong sort of idealism than by downright wickedness. This is something it might be sensible to ponder in all its political implications. We can be manipulated not only through our fears but also through our generosity and compassion. The soft-centred man is not the best of champions on any battlefield in the hard world of today. This is why good teachers of meditation ask their pupils to focus their consciousness in their heads first, raising it consciously from below if necessary.

In general there are rather too many devotees among meditators. In their enthusiasms, whether religious or social, people tend to be insufficiently critical. There is too much experimentation and too little healthy self-examination in choosing the groups we join and the courses we follow. What suits our best friends may not suit us and we should have enough common sense to sort out how best our developmental needs and our friendships can be reconciled. A bit more gentle scepticism would not do us any harm either. It can save us from being conned by false prophets as well as pressure-salesmen. It can also protect us from the all or nothing kind of emotional attitudes which lead to fanaticism and misplaced loyalties.

There is another reason why it is valuable to raise the focus of consciousness into the head at the outset of a meditation period. This is because the centre between the eyebrows, the Ajna Chakra, exercises a synthetic function. As we have seen, it can harmonise the energies from all the Chakras once they have been raised into it. If this is done successfully mental energies can enter in and modify the quality of the whole Nadi system and through it the responsiveness of nerves and tissues. The role of the brow Chakra in this regard is not surprising since its sphere of influence covers not only the frontal lobes of the cerebral cortex but also the pituitary gland and the hypothalamus. These last two constitute the body's major centres for the manufacture of the hormones which control its chemical thresholds and hence our emotional responses.

The brow Chakra can come under considerable pressure while the centre of personality is being raised into the head, and the capacity for abstract thought is increasing. We all know what headaches one can get working out knotty problems and preparing for stiff examinations. All sorts of head troubles can arise at this stage. More blood has to be drawn up against gravity; new nerve paths have to be opened up. All this means that energy flows can run into blockages and stagnant pools can form. Brain and optical nerve tumours may develop as well as disorders of overstimulation such as migraine. Tumours and clots may be quite evanescent, remitting spontaneously. This is because the Chakras, Nadis and glands have between them managed to get the energy flowing again, pools evaporating and excess tissue dispersing, waste products being carried away automatically by the body's scavenger cells.

It is because so many of the ills we suffer from are secondary to abnormalities in the energy systems of the body's subtler sheaths that so-called spiritual healers can effect cures. I say so-called advisedly because the energy transactions are seldom carried out at such lofty levels. What those of us with healing hands most probably do is use our energy body hands to tease out congestions in the patient's Nadi system — an unusual kind of massage rather than a demonstration of spiritual powers at work. By such temporary intrusions into another person's force-field we can presumably sometimes induce a healthier state which his own mechanisms can then maintain. If this is correct, should the patient be unable to preserve the field-state produced for him by the healer, the symptom may well recur or some new symptom arise in its place. I have known this happen. It is a situation which exactly parallels that resulting when fever-reducing drugs fail to get temperature mechanisms back to normal and the fever re-asserts itself. Healers will have noticed that such secondary breakdowns do not always occur in the same place and may even produce what looks like a different disorder. What can happen in such cases, if we are dealing with a true secondary, is that a new blockage arises somewhere else but nevertheless within the same Nadi circuit. Similar reactions occur with imperfectly absorbed blood clots. Secondary infarcts can occur anywhere in vessels along the same line of flow.

As the physical and subtle bodies and the life-vehicle are overlapping force-fields, there will be many areas of energy interchange other than the major Chakras. There must be a great many smaller centres transducing and distributing energy in more specialised ways. Acupuncture points may prove to be nodal sites of this kind.

There must also be two basic and distinguishable systems interacting at all levels, a Shiva system and a Shakti system. The former will be responsible for the recording of experience on behalf of the Purusha. The latter, the Prakriti system of Shaktis, will be responsible for the day-to-day management of the structures within which the organs of perception are set. The Chakras must handle the energies of both systems much as mixed nerve centres re-route somatic and psychosomatic impulses impartially. The polarity between the crown and root Chakras must play an important part in controlling the interrelations between the Purusha set of forces and the Kundalini-Prakriti set. This conforms with the idea that energies move up and down through the Chakras and suggests that Sri Aurobindo's ascending and descending forces are operative throughout evolution, but that in the early stages the ascending forces are dominant.

This would give primacy to the centres below the diaphragm during the phase when the Chakras appear only as rotating discs, which is consistent with the Tibetan's developmental theory that there are reversals of polarity going on during the whole course of evolution with the Kundalini-Shakti pole finally becoming negative and the Shiva pole positive. This would be the consummation of the evolutionary process seen as an exercise in the spiritualising of matter. Thus the ultimate goal of Kundalini is to work herself out of a job.

This she cannot do without the aid of human beings as transformers. It is perhaps some dim perception of this fact which leads us to feel we should play a more active role in our relations with her when times are urgent. Our mistake is in thinking this means ego interference with her forces rather than altering polarities within ourselves. It is the activating of the Sahasrara we should be aiming at by improving the quality of our Purusha side, for when the Shiva pole becomes active great changes supervene. Something appears to happen which converts the whole body into a single magnetic field generated in a higher order of substance. This is possibly what the Tantras are telling us through the imagery of a permanent reunion of Shiva and Shakti through the agency of the risen Kundalini. The whole material envelope in which the real self is embodied becomes transformed, its various energies spiritualised. That this may be true even of dense matter is suggested by the stories told of the bodies of saints which remain uncorrupted after death. Something of this sort may explain the marks on the shroud in which the dead Jesus is said to have been wrapped and which are currently puzzling scientists.

Not only subtle but all matter can apparently be lifted out

of our space-time under special circumstances. Presumably for this to happen all three aspects of Kundalini must be equally involved and 'rise' together. Such a movement would not be ego-controlled but organised from the causal level since it is only there that the individual's destiny can be seen as an enfolded and unfolding tale within the cosmic story of enfolded and unfolding Brahman.

In his poetic description of his Kundalini experiences and his search for 'Mount Kailas' where truth was to be found 'kept in one place', Miguel Serrano brings out clearly both the way the ego keeps taking over and the elusiveness of the true self within. In *The Serpent of Paradise* he tells us that he first encountered the Serpent in childhood and from the beginning felt himself related to it in a special way. For him also there were sensations in the feet and legs as well as in the spine as with the subjects of the Sannella study. His experiences, however, usually took place at night between sleeping and waking. In some respects they were more akin to those of Monroe in his out-of-the-body states than to those of Sannella's meditators. For instance, the objects round him became related to him in a new way and he seemed to move into a different time. 'I could see myself moving and acting at a tremendous speed, and inside my head thousands of words would gush forth at an increasing tempo.' And again, 'I would have the feeling that a switch had been turned which made me lose control of myself.' Unlike Monroe, however, he seems not to have had sensations of leaving his physical body and finding himself in another one. 'I would feel dizzy and helpless,' he writes, 'and the only way I could escape was to fall into deep sleep.'

Unlike Gopi Krishna, Miguel Serrano seems to have been born into these experiences. Tantrika would probably say that he was continuing a development begun in an earlier life. The onset of these experiences was not associated with any spiritual exercises nor, in his native Chile, was there any framework of ideas into which he could readily fit them. He also differed from Gopi Krishna in that, in his attempt to understand them, he never seems to have regarded them as anything but subjective. His close friends and advisers in these matters were people like Jung and Hermann Hesse,

Nehru and the Dalai Lama. His whole approach was that of a poet and a mystic who was only incidentally a man of action. His struggle was between his ego and his true self and it seems to have been conceived by him as a battle rather than a prospective merger, which also seems to have been the case with Jung. (33) If Muhammad Subuh is right in saying that elaborate imagery can be a by-product of conflict between an insistent spirit and a resistant conscious mind, this may account for the symbolic richness of their inner lives and the religious context of much of their writing.

Serrano became aware early of the inadvisability of interfering with the course taken by his 'dawn fainting spells'. He writes, 'I would sometimes try to direct the process and to control the sequence. The result was always catastrophic, however; for while part of me was in one realm the other part was in another, and the two always clashed violently. With my conscious ego awake in the middle of the process, I would remain in a halfway or neutral state. The vibrations which had begun to rise from my feet would begin to distribute themselves about my body, but the terrible music would never reach my brain, because there I was conscious and trying to hold on to daily reality. And so I would be caught between two worlds, unable to experience either satisfactorily.'

This could be what Sannella's Western meditators may also have been doing, consciously or unconsciously. The physio-kundalini cycle may, in that case, be traceable to the psychosomatic effects of conflicting frames of reference; the Western one which produces our ego-oriented social outlook, and that of the seeker struggling to establish a way of seeing more in keeping with the values of the true self and its latent but powerful subliminal organisation. Certainly this is what Serrano's description seems to suggest.

Such ego-influenced partial risings cannot be connected with coiled Kundalini or Kundalini-Prithivi. This, as we have seen, only leaves the root Chakra at death when the forces which have kept the dense body in manifestation return to the common pool of physical energy I have called Mahakundalini. If we could pull coiled Kundalini out of the Muladhara and put it back whenever we wished, we could be recurrently dying and coming alive again, risking brain damage every time we mismanaged the manoeuvre. The Mahayogi is said to be able to will his own death once he is truly Adhikari (competent). This is because, through identification with the true self, the Lord within, he knows his proper time and mode of departure. When he goes, however, coiled Kundalini finally departs also for no one who is completely liberated ever needs a gross body again. The experience of patients resuscitated after seeming dead, like that of the posturing Indian who nearly died, are probably instances of the partial dislocation of Kundalini mechanisms. The ability of Kundalini-Prithivi to re-establish its hold on the dense body if it is not the person's proper time for dying indicates not only its intrinsic power, but also that of the Jivatman who wants coiled Kundalini to stay in place until it gives the word.

What then are the ways in which we can interfere with the operations of Kundalini if we are unwise enough to try? In the first place it must be through Chit-Kundalini since we use our conscious selves to direct thought here and there in order to manipulate forces at subtle levels. Thus we can visualise streams of energy coming up the spine or behaving in this way or that in the various Chakras. As a result of this sort of Chit activity we can do either of two things. We can create thought-forms which stimulate the Indriyas and Tanmatras to produce inner sensations sometimes so vivid that we imagine they represent actual physiological happenings. Or we can direct our thoughts so intently towards the body that we upset it physically by loading the areas concerned with abnormal amounts of psychic Prana. In the former case Chit-Kundalini forces are operating mainly in the subtle body and affecting the Purusha at the level of the Antahkarana. In the latter event they are being pushed into the life-vehicle in a way which disturbs the normal balance of physical and psychic Prana. If this is done too often it interferes with the working of Kundalini-Shabdabrahman, the causal form of Kundalini responsible for maintaining all bodily structures in their proper state. If we force Chit-Kundalini in this way all we do is disorganise our energy systems and so lay ourselves open to secondary disorders in our physical health. It must be noted, however, that in none of these sometimes injurious and often fruitless activities is Kundalini-Prithivi, coiled Kundalini, directly affected. From a Tantric point of view the various psychological and physiological phenomena described by the contributors to the Kundalini issue of *Human Dimensions* would seem to be associated with either Chit-Kundalini alone or with the combined forces of Chit-Kundalini and Kundalini-Shabdabrahman.

One can see why truly competent gurus advise us to set to work on our egos and leave Kundalini in our bodies to organise its own ways and means of rising. Kundalini in nature as a whole, however, is something to which we could well devote more attention. Doing so could lead to new and important insights into the working of the body of our planet and how its forces circulate and interact.

If we presume for the purposes of argument that ultimately physical substances dissolve into spin and that Kundalini is the energy which, acting causally on dense matter, differentiates it in terms of spins generated within it, this makes Kundalini the basic physical principle. Gravity, which eludes our efforts to integrate it into the electromagnetic spectrum, does not so easily slip out of the Kundalini system of forces. It is as much a product of spin as magnetism. This can be seen when we consider centrifugal force which is an induced form of gravity. Indeed, scientists are considering the possibility of a centrifugal force-field round spacecraft in order to counteract the adverse effects of weightlessness on health. If they can do this they can produce a localised gravity which will enable astronauts' bodies to behave normally. The main difference between gravity and magnetism would seem to be that gravitational forces introduce a contractive influence into magnetic fields.

The prevalence of the spiral form in nature is becoming increasingly obvious the more one studies the movement of forces. The winds spiral as also do the great ocean currents, the stars in their courses, whirlpools and climbing plants. Structures also spiral. There are spiral convolutions in the intestines of cattle. The muscle fibres controlling the contractions of the vital left chamber of the human heart produce a spiral movement. As Theodor Schwenk points out in *Sensitive Chaos*, (72) the human heart is a spiral both as a form in space and a movement in time.

The whole universe is a pattern of spins from the tiny neutrino to the wheeling galaxies. The Tantrika would see this as inevitable since the spiral is the form through which Mahakundalini works and all physical structures are expressions of its action in dense matter.

It is an interesting thought that life on Earth developed in the great oceans when they were vast bowls of 'primal soup', for if serpentine forms rule supreme anywhere it is in water. And it is known that the great oceanic currents and the winds they generate in the atmosphere above them either circulate horizontally or form clockwise and anti-clockwise north-south spirals flowing in symmetrical but opposing senses in the two hemispheres into which the central equatorial current divides the Earth. (61) This serpentine form, so characteristic of the element out of which life sprang, may well have stamped itself on all spawned within it. The double helix found in all replicating cells may have arisen in the DNA molecule as the most natural form for life to take in a world ultimately organised by Kundalini.

Earth may indeed be the most advanced product of Kundalini so far. In the known universe at least this seems to be so. If the Kundalini spectrum of forces can be studied in detail anywhere it is here and, in view of the pollutants we are pouring into the seas which are Earth's cleansing areas, the time to do so is surely now.

Glossary

Adhikara competence, capacity; readiness for training for yoga

Adhikari one who is already competent

Agama Tantra as a teaching to be listened to; from a word meaning 'to listen'

Ahangkara (Ahamkara) element in mental matter which confers I-ness; ego idea

Ajna Chakra force centre between the eyebrows mediating subtle body energies

Akasha the least dense form of gross matter dealt with by physics

Anahata Chakra force centre in the heart region of the subtle body

Ananda bliss, delight, the joy inherent in creation; the self-delight characteristic of transcendental and infinite Beingness

Ananda-kanda Chakra small centre just below the Anahata Chakra of particular importance in Bhakti yoga, the yoga of devotion

Antahkarana the mind as a generic term inclusive of all forms of mental matter; mind conceived as a causal agent

Apana Prana with a downward tendency; downward breath

Apas water

Artha a phenomenal object; the thing perceived as an entity, mentally or sensibly

Arthavaveda Veda from which the magical lore of the Tantras was derived

Arupa without form

Asanas yogic postures

Ashram school or community gathered round a particular guru

Atman the self; the divine essence of individuality; the individualising aspect of Brahman

Avidya absence of the knowledge of the Oneness of things; partial knowledge; sometimes translated as ignorance

Bhakti devotion

Bhutas things having physical magnitude and composed of one or more of the five major bhutas, earth, water, fire, air and ether

Bija a seed-mantra; the significant sound associated with the characteristic working of an energy-field (Shakti or force)

Bindu point; creative centre; starting point of a manifestation

Bodhi supramental matter; causal level in the production of forms

Brahma, Brahmani, Brahman masculine, feminine and neuter versions of the name of God, the Absolute, the Divine; ultimate reality

Brahma-dvara Brahman gate; orifice leading from the basal Chakra into the Sushumna, normally closed by the head of coiled Kundalini

Brahmanadi channel within the Chitrini Nadi which remains empty until the rising of Kundalini in her threefold form

Brahmarandhra fissure at crown of head in the subtle body through which Prana leaves the dense body at death

Brahma Vidya Brahman knowledge; true wisdom; knowledge of Brahman as the One and the All

Buddhi form of mental matter mediating intelligence

Chakra (Cakra) force vortex in the subtle body; circle round a teacher

Chela disciple; pupil attendant upon a guru

Chit (Cit) consciousness as pure intelligence; an aspect of the Divine nature

Chitrini (Citrini) the inner of the two Nadis lying inside the Sushumna Nadi

Chitta (Citta) form of mental substance mediating memory and the formation of habits

Dakini presiding goddess of the Muladhara Chakra at the base of the spine

Deva god; godhead

Devata divinity of either gender

Devi goddess

Dharana concentration of the mind on its object; exercises to improve concentration

Dharma law governing world order; world and individual destiny; literally that which holds things together and which one lays hold on

Dhyana meditation, contemplation of an object of spiritual worth

Diryabhava divine or spiritual (Sattvic) quality in a person's disposition

Granthi knot; junction of a group of energy streams in the subtle body

Guna qualifying attribute; the three major gunas are inertia, activity and equilibrium

Guru teaching yogi. Inner guru — name given to true or Brahman self in a person

Hakini presiding goddess of the Ajna Chakra

Hangsa (Hamsa) one of the names of the Jivatman in its Purusha aspect

Hatha yoga system using physical exercises as a means to yoga

Ida spinal Nadi arising at the base of the spine and passing to the left outside the Sushumna; terminates in the region of the right nostril

Indra an Earth god associated with Prithivi as Earth goddess

Indriyas the senses as mental faculties distinct from the sense-organs

Ishvara God; the Lord; the creative aspect of the Divine

Ista Devata one's own personal divinity

Jappa repeated recitation of mantras

Jiva the individual as a human being

Jivatman the individual as an embodied spirit

Jnana knowledge in a general sense; understanding

Jnanamayapurusha the self as knower

Kakini presiding goddess of the Anahata Chakra

Kamamayapurusha desire self

Kanda a powerful force centre at the base of the spine in the subtle body from which all the 72,000 Nadis originate

Karana causal

Karma action; work; the power which relates the causes and effects of action and so influences the circumstances governing the soul's earthly existence

Lalana Chakra a secondary force centre in the subtle body in the region of the brain stem

Laya dissolution. Laya yoga — discipline stressing dissolution of the ego-self

Linga phallus as symbol of Shiva, the male partner in the Shiva-Shakti Tattva. Sometimes spelt lingam

Maha great

Mahakundalini Kundalini as a cosmic force

Mahayogi yogi who is fully competent (Adhikari)

Manas (adjective) **Manasic** — that which thinks (**Man**); sensory level of mind-stuff

Manipura Chakra force centre in the subtle body in the solar plexus region

Mantra thought as a force which operates as a cause; creative power of thought

Maya the phenomenal world as that which is experienced

Mayapurusha the experiencing aspect of personality

Moksha liberation (see also Mukti)

Mudra ritual gesture

Mukti liberation; freedom of the soul

Mula root

Muladhara Chakra root Chakra at base of spine in the subtle body from which the spinal Nadis rise and which supports the Chakras

Nada the first produced movement in cosmic consciousness at the transcendental level which eventuates in Shabdabrahman, sound as a divine creative force

Nadi force channel in the subtle body

Nirguna without gunas or qualities

Nirvana liberating annihilation; individual extinction; a state beyond Mukti since there is no return from it

Niyama disciplines which qualify one for acceptance for yoga training

Nyasa Tantric ritual of 'giving life' to the image of one's Ista Devata

Panchatattva the Tantra dealing with 'the Secret Ritual' regarded by some as obscene

Para supreme

Parabrahman supreme Brahman, transcendental and without qualities

Pashubhava term used to describe man who is in bondage to his instincts; animal nature dominant (Pashas — bonds)

Pingala spinal Nadi arising on the right at the base of the spine in the subtle body and terminating in the region of the left nostril

Prakriti objective nature as the multidimensional universe

Pralaya interval between two breaths of Brahman during which time the universe goes out of existence

Prana vital energy; breath Prani — living things or breathing creatures

Pranava special name given to the Mantra OM

Pranayama forms of breathing associated with yoga training and practice

Prithivi Earth both as a Shakti and as a form of gross matter

Purusha self as percipient; as subject not agent

Rajas guna with quality of activity

Rishi holy man, seer or sage

Rupa form; manifested in a recognisably distinct way

Sadhaka (Sadh — to strive) — one who follows a discipline. Sadhika — feminine form of the term. Yoga only one such discipline (Sadhana)

Sa'ham 'I am She' said in relation to the goddess who is one's Ista Devata

Sahasrara Chakra Chakra at the crown of the head in the subtle body; the thousand-petalled lotus

Samadhi ecstasy associated with yogic trance state

Samskara the world of Maya; the realm governed by Karma in which the reincarnating soul experiences joy and suffering, birth and death

Sankhya Hindu philosophy as an analytical system

Sat Being

Satchitananda Divine state of Being in which there is self-awareness and self-delight in one's Brahman nature

Sattva (adjective **Sattvic**) equilibrium and forces conducive of harmony and spiritual consciousness

Shabda sound; idea and the language in which it is expressed

Shabdabrahman sound as a creative force carrying the Divine intention into manifestation; generator of significant forms; cosmic sound

Shakini presiding goddess of the Visuddha Chakra at the throat

Shakti the feminine aspect of the Divine in manifestation; power or force; creative energy at work in nature (Prakriti); active partner in the Shiva-Shakti Tattva

Shangkara (Samkara) founder of the Advaitu school of Hindu philosophy

Sharira (Sarira) body

Shastra scripture; holy book

Shiva (Siva) masculine aspect of the Divine in manifestation; receptive consciousness; creative energy mediating experience (purusha); passive partner in Shiva-Shakti Tattva

Shudra (Sudra) untouchable; member of this caste

So'ham 'I am He'

Spanda movement

Sthula gross, dense, heavy

Suksma subtle, fine

Sushumna (Susumna) major spinal Nadi in the subtle body

Svadisthana Chakra force centre in the subtle body in the sacral region

Svarupa the inherent nature of a thing; a thing as it is in itself and not as perceived by the Jiva

Tamas (adjective **Tamasic**) guna with the quality of inertia and unconsciousness

Tanmatra sensory category dividing sense experience into classes as sight, hearing, taste, etc. at the mental level; a universal in the

Platonic sense

Tantras sacred writings prescribing a wide range of religious practices aimed ultimately at yoga; the beliefs underlying these practices

Tantrika a member of one or other Tantric discipline and way of worship

Tapas literally heat but used also for energy

Tattva one of the thirty-six modifications of the Divine nature out of the interactions of which the multidimensional universe came into being

Tejas fire

Triguna composed of all three gunas

Trikona triangle symbolising the threefold nature of Shakti

Tripura threefold

Umani literally no-mind; beyond all concepts and percepts

Upanishad literally inner knowledge; a class of Hindu Shastras

Vajra a Nadi within the Sushumna associated with Rajasic energy

Vayu breath of life; air; wind

Veda earliest Hindu scripture

Vedanta philosophy and practices based on the Upanishads and Veda

Vidya true spiritual knowledge of the underlying unity of things

Vijnana knowledge of the divine based on direct experience

Vishuddha Chakra force centre in the subtle body in the throat region

Vishnu the Divine as preserver

Virabhava a person in the heroic class; of a heroic disposition in tackling one's spiritual shortcomings

Yama practices aimed at moral self-control and mastery of the passions and egoism

Yoga literally union; practices aimed at union with the Divine and liberation from Karma and the need to reincarnate into physical existence

Bibliography

1. Aurobindo, Sri (1976), *The Synthesis of Yoga*, Sri Aurobindo Ashram Trust, Pondicherry, 6th edn (first published in 1955).
2. Aurobindo, Sri (1977), *The Life Divine*, 2 vols, Sri Aurobindo Ashram Trust, Pondicherry, 10th edn.
3. Bailey, Alice A. (1925), *A Treatise on Cosmic Fire*, Lucis Press, London and New York.
4. Bailey, Alice A. (1942), *Esoteric Psychology*, Lucis Press, London and New York.
5. Bailey, Alice A. (1947), *An Unfinished Autobiography*, Lucis Press, London and New York.
6. Bailey, Alice A. (1953), *Esoteric Healing*, Lucis Press, London and New York.
7. Bendit, P.D. and Bendit, L.J. (1957), *Man Incarnate*, Theosophical Publishing House, London.
8. Besant, Annie (1896), *Man and his Bodies*, Theosophical Publishing House, London.
9. Bird, Christopher (1978), *Divination*, Macdonald & Janes, London.
10. Blavatsky, H.P. (1893), *The Secret Doctrine*, Theosophical Publishing House, London.
11. Brahma, N.K. (1939), *Causality and Science*, Allen & Unwin, London.
12. Burr, H.S. (1947), 'Field theory in biology', *Science Monthly*, vol. 64, pp. 217-25.
13. Burr, H.S. (1972), *Blueprint for Immortality*, Neville Spearman, London.
14. Calder, N. (1977), *The Key to the Universe*, BBC, London.
15. Cannon, W.B. (1915), *Bodily Changes in Pain, Hunger, Fear and Rage*, Appleton, New York.

16. Capra, F. (1975), *The Tao of Physics*, Wildwood House, London; Fontana, London, 1976.

17. Carlsson, A. et al. (1957), *Psychotropic Drugs*, Elsevier, Amsterdam.

18. Chardin, T. de (1959), *The Phenomenon of Man*, Collins, London; Harper, New York.

19. Coe, M.R. Jr. (1959), 'Does science explain poltergeists?', *Fate*, July, pp. 79-90.

20. Crookall, R. (1964), *The Techniques of Astral Projection*, Aquarian Press, London.

21. Duch, W. (1978-9), 'Science explains reincarnation', *New Humanity Journal*, nos 23-7.

22. Eitel, E.J. (1873), *Feng-Shui*, Trubner, London.

23. Gardner, M. (1967), *The Ambidextrous Universe*, Allen Lane, London.

24. Gauquelin, M. (1970), *Astrology and Science*, Peter Davies, London.

25. Grant, J. (1956), *Time out of Mind*, Arthur Barker, London.

26. Grant, J. and Kelsey, D. (1967), *Many Lifetimes*, Doubleday, New York.

27. *Gray's Anatomy* (1973), Longman, London.

28. Hasted, J. (1978), 'Speculations about the relations between psychic phenomena and physics', *Psychoenergetic Systems*, vol. 1.

29. Hasted, J. (1981), *Metal Benders*, Routledge & Kegan Paul, London.

30. *Human Dimensions*, vol. 5, no. 3: 'Kundalini: catastrophe or creative consciousness'.

31. Joy, W. Brugh (1979), *Joy's Way*, Tarcher, Los Angeles.

32. Jung, C.G. (1958), *Psychology and Religion: West and East*, Routledge & Kegan Paul, London.

33. Jung, C.G. (1963), *Memories, Dreams, Reflections*, edited by A. Jaffe, Collins and Routledge & Kegan Paul, London.

34. Karagulla, S. (1967), *Breakthrough to Creativity*, De Vorsa, Los Angeles.

35. Kilner, W. (1911), *The Human Atmosphere or Aura made Visible by Chemical Means*, University Books, London; reissued as *The Human Aura*, University Books, New York, 1965.

36. Krippner, S. and Rubin, D. (eds) (1973), *Galaxies of Life*, Gordon & Breach, New York.

37. Krishna, G. (1971), *Kundalini: The Evolutionary Energy in Man*, Shambhala, Boulder, Co.

38. Leadbeater, C.W. (1902), *Man Visible and Invisible*, Theosophical Publishing House, Wheaton, Ill., Madras and London.

39. Leadbeater, C.W. (1908), *Invisible Helpers*, Theosophical Publishing House, Wheaton, Ill., London and Madras.

40. Leadbeater, C.W. (1927), *The Chakras*, Theosophical Publishing House, Wheaton, Ill., London and Madras.

41. Lockyer, Sir N. (1909), *Stonehenge and Other British Stone Monuments Astronomically Considered*, 2nd edn., Macmillan, London.

42. Long, M.F. (1936), *Recovering the Ancient Magic*, Rider, London.

43. Long, M.F. (1948), *The Secret Science behind Miracles*, Kosmon Press, Los Angeles.

44. Meek, G.W. (1973), *From Seance to Science*, Regency Press, London and New York.

45. Michell, J. (1969), *The View over Atlantis*, Sago Press, London; Abacus, London, 1973.

46. Monroe, R.A. (1972), *Journeys out of the Body*, Souvenir Press, London; Doubleday, New York.

47. Moody, R.A. (1975), *Life after Life*, Mockingbird Books, St. Simon's Island, Ga.; Bantam, 1976.

48. Moss, T. (1973), 'Bioenergetics and radiation photography', Proceedings of the International Conference of Psychotronics.

49. Moss, T. and Johnson, K. (1972), 'Is there an energy body?', *Osteopathic Physician*, October.

50. Motoyama, H. (1972), *Chakra, Nadi of Yoga, Meridians and Points of Acupuncture*, Institute of Religious Psychology, Tokyo.

51. Muldoon, S. and Carrington, H. (1951), *The Phenomenon of Astral Projection*, Rider, London.

52. Muldoon, S. and Carrington, H. (1956), *Projection of the Astral Body*, Rider, London.

53. Northrop, F.S.C. and Burr, H.S. (1935), 'An electro-dynamic theory of life', *Quarterly Review of Biology*, vol. 10, pp. 322-33.

54. Orgel, L. (1980), radio talk in the *Science Now* series, BBC, London.

55. Ostrander, S. and Schroeder, L. (1973), *Psychic Discoveries behind the Iron Curtain*, Abacus, London.

56. Payne, P. and Bendit, L.J. (1943), *The Psychic Sense*, Faber, London.

57. Planck, M. (1950), *A Scientific Autobiography*, Williams & Norgate, London.

58. Playfair, G.L. and Hill, S. (1978), *The Cycles of Heaven*, Souvenir Press, London.

59. Powell, A.E. (1925), *The Etheric Double*, Theosophical Publishing House, London.

60. Powell, A.E. (1928), *The Causal Body and the Ego*, Theosophical Publishing House, London.

61. Press, F. and Siever, R. (1974), *Earth*, W.H. Freeman, San Francisco.

62. Puharich, A. (1962), *Beyond Telepathy*, Darton, Longman & Todd, London.

63. Radha, Swami Sivananda (1978), *Kundalini Yoga for the West*, Timeless Books, Porthill, Idaho; Shambhala Publications, Boulder, Colorado.

64. Ravitz, L.J. (1959), 'Application of electrodynamic field theory in biology, psychiatry and hypnosis', *American Journal of Clinical Hypnosis*, vol. 1, no. 4, April.

65. Russell, E. (1971), *Design for Destiny*, Neville Spearman, London.

66. Ryall, E.W. (1974), *Second Time Round*, Neville Spearman, London.

67. Ryzl, M. (1962), 'Training the psi faculty by hypnosis', *Journal of the Society for Psychical Research*, vol. 41, no. 711, pp. 234-52.

68. Ryzl, M. (1966), 'A method of training in ESP', *International Journal of Parapsychology*, vol. 8, no. 4.

69. Sagan, C. (1981), *The Cosmos*, Macdonald, London.

70. Sannella, L. (1976), *Kundalini — Psychosis or Transcendence*, Dakin, San Francisco.

71. Schildraut, J.J. and Kety, S.S. (1969), 'Biogenic amines and emotion', in K.H. Pribram (ed.), *Brain and Behaviour*, vol. 1, Penguin, Harmondsworth.

72. Schwenk, T. (1965), *Sensitive Chaos*, Rudolf Steiner, London.

73. Scott, Mary (1962), 'Releasing the individual', conference paper, Centre for Spiritual and Religious Studies, Brighton.

74. Scott, Mary (1969), 'Meditating through our actions', *Science of Thought Review*, November.

75. Scott, Mary (1974), 'How far can humanness extend?', *Human Dimensions*, vol. 3, no. 2.

76. Scott, Mary (1975), 'Science and subtle bodies: towards a clarification of issues', College of Psychic Studies, Paper No. 8.

77. Scott, Mary (1976), 'More about science and subtle bodies', *Research Centre Journal*, vol. 20, no. 4, Theosophical Society in

England.

78. Serrano, M. (1974), *The Serpent of Paradise*, Routledge & Kegan Paul, London.

79. Sharma, R.N. (1960), 'The Philosophy of Sri Aurobindo', Ph.D. thesis, Lucknow University.

80. *Some Unrecognised Factors in Medicine* (1949), Transactions of the Theosophical Research Centre, London.

81. Steiner, R. (1932), *An Occult Physiology*, Rudolf Steiner, London.

82. Stevenson, I. (1966), *Twenty Cases Suggestive of Reincarnation*, University of Virginia Press.

83. Stewart, A.J. (1970), *Falcon: The Autobiography of His Grace James the 4, King of Scots*, Peter Davies, London.

84. Thomas, Lewis (1974), *The Lives of a Cell*, Viking Press, New York.

85. Tyler, F.C. (1939), *The Geometrical Arrangements of Ancient Sites*, Simpkin Marshall, London.

86. Underwood, G. (1972), *Patterns of the Past*, Abacus, London.

87. Van der Post, L. (1961), *The Heart of the Hunter*, Hogarth Press, London; Penguin, Harmondsworth, 1965.

88. Vasiliev, L.L. (1963), *Experiments in Mental Suggestion*, Institute for the Study of Mental Images, Church Crookham, Hants.

89. Wallace, R.K. (1970), 'The physiological effects of transcendental meditation', doctoral dissertation, University of California, Los Angeles.

90. Wallace, R.K. and Benson, H. (1972), 'The physiology of meditation', *Scientific American*, February.

91. Watkins, A. (1922), *Early British Trackways*, Simpkin Marshall, London.

92. Watkins, A. (1925), *The Old Straight Track*, Methuen, London.

93. Welch, H. (1957), *The Parting of the Way*, Methuen, London.

94. White, G.S. (1969), *The Finer Forces of Nature*, Health Research, Mokelumne Hill, Cal.

95. White, S.E. (1945), *The Betty Book*, Robert Hale, London.

96. Whiteman, J.H.M. (1961), *The Mystical Life*, Faber, London.

97. Wilhelm, R. (1931), *The Secret of the Golden Flower*, Routledge & Kegan Paul, London.

98. Woodroffe, Sir J. (Arthur Avalon) (1919), *The Serpent Power*, Ganesh, Madras; Dover, New York, 1974.

99. Woodroffe, Sir J. (Arthur Avalon) (1920), *Shakti and Shakta*, Ganesh, Madras.

100. Woolley, D.W. (1962), *The Biochemical Bases of Psychoses or the Serotinin Hypothesis about Mental Disease*, Wiley, New York.

Index

acupuncture, 26, 61, 107-8, 246
Adhikara, *see* competence
Ahangkara, 34-5, 37, 38, 39, 40, 54, 61, 79, 171, 174, 211
Ajna Chakra, 147, 152, 163, 164, 194, 210, 234, 237, 245; Mandala of, 210-14; and pituitary gland, 147, 236, 245
Akasha, 51-3, 234; *see also* space
ambrosia, 150, 162, 203, 211
Anahata Chakra, 152, 194, 197, 205, 206, 210; Mandala of, 204-10; Prana and Vayu in, 205, 206-7, 211
Ananda, 42, 45, 150; *see also* bliss; Satchitananda
Ananda-kanda Chakra, 204, 206
Anderson, Carl D., 69
Antahkarana, 59, 137, 192, 197, 210; Hindu view of, 40, 137, 169, 171, 174, 175, 197, 214; Tibetan's view of, 40, 174-5, 214, 238
Anthroposophy, *see* Steiner
Apana, *see* Prana; Vayu
aquastats, *see* geodetic lines
artefacts: prehistoric, 90, 98, 107, 113, 114-15; astronomical significance of, 104, 115; on geodetic lines, 99, 102, 103-4; on ley lines, 111
Artha, 159-60
Asanas, 11, 22
astral body, 219-20
astral plane, 219-22
astral projection, 28, 62-3, 65, 66, 72, 73-4, 129, 220-2
astrology, 89, 124-5

astronomy, 88-9, 90-1, 104, 115, 116
asymmetry, 67, 68, 69, 113, 119
Atma, 140, 142, 143-4, 213; *see also* spirit
Atman, 30, 35, 42, 58, 77-8, 80, 85
atmosphere, 46, 47-8, 49, 105-6, 122
aura, 60, 106, 107, 150, 217, 234
Aurobindo, Sri, 10, 14, 25, 51, 178 et passim; on ascending and descending forces, 157, 158, 176-8, 190, 242-3, 247; on Avidya and Vidya, 31-2, 80; on dual selves, 170-5, 189, 214, 222; on mental matter, 36-7, 38-9, 174
Avalon, Arthur, *see* Woodroffe
Avidya, 29, 31-2, 45, 56, 80, 144

Bailey, A.A., 2, 3, 217, 218, 228; Tibetan writings of, 40, 174-5, 179, 192, 227-9, 230-4
Becoming, 31, 91, 138; evolution a cycle of, 54, 136
behaviour, 38, 41, 46, 56; adaptive, 73, 74, 93, 149; Chakras and, 136, 149, 157, 173, 215, 232; conscious, 41, 172, 215; instinctive, 54, 61, 74, 149, 215
Being, 142-3; bodies qualify, 144; Brahman as pure, 54, 55, 91, 138, 159; Vidya as knowledge of true, 31
Bentov, I., 95, 109, 182-91 passim, 207, 233, 241
Besant, Annie, 219
Bhutas, 52-4, 79, 135, 234
Bija, 23, 161, 200, 205, 211-15 passim, 235

Bindus, 151, 152, 212-13
biology (gists), 6, 7, 27, 39, 61, 76, 91, 97, 237; implications of Kundalini for, 85-6, 162-3, 164-6; Kundalini and laws of, 186; *see also* Mahakundalini
biophysics, 127
Biot, Jean-Baptiste, 68
blind springs, 102-3, 105, 106, 109, 112, 115, 128, 136; as Kundalini coils, 105, 109, 116, 127, 148; *see also* geodetic lines
bliss, 11, 29, 45, 143, 144, 161, 197; font of Eternal, 203, 206; types of, 150-1, 169, 213
Bodhi, 33-4, 203, 213
Bodhi body, 33-8 passim, 137, 161, 166, 171, 214, 219
body (ies), 40, 73, 74, 93, 96, 138, 151, 231, 235; alignment of, 62, 242; central in Kundalini yoga, 43; dual at all levels, 170, 240; an integral multi-level field, 135, 136, 191, 246, 247; interlocking mechanisms in, 63-5, 73, 127; Kundalini threefold in, 152; qualify consciousness, 43, 144, 163; refining matter of, 33, 36, 75, 210, 230, 234, 247; Shabdabrahman in, 24, 79, 86, 153, 162, 163-6; Shiva-Shakti Tattva in, 196-7; 'subliminals' in, 173, 192; Theosophical theory of, 60, 62, 219-22
Brahman, 22, 54, 58, 78, 169, 172, 186; Absolute, the One and the All, Para-, 29, 32, 41, 54, 78, 89, 91, 130, 176; the Divine, God, 14, 17, 21, 22-4, 28-9; emanations of, 30-42, 51-4, 58, 77-81; evolution a breath of, 44-6, 51-2, 81, 83, 86; as first cause, 29, 30, 44, 54; identification with, 17, 22-3, 130, 150-1, 212; Jivatman as agent of, 33, 38, 55, 137-8; known only in experience, the Many, 29, 91, 159; in man, 22, 88, 248; polarities within, 77, 86, 88; Satchitananda as knowable, 41; Sound-, 78, 158-9; Tao and, 106; threefold in manifestation, 151; universe as immanent, 24, 44, 81; void as unknowable, 41, 54, 106, 158
Brahman self, *see* Jivatman

Brahmanadi, 148, 149, 165, 194, 200, 202, 203, 212
Brahmin, Brahminism, 17, 20, 211
brain, 59, 72-3, 128, 132, 149, 178, 220, 234, 245; physio-kundalini cycle and, 184-5, 189, 190, 233; *see also* nervous system
Buddhi, 34-8, 39, 51, 54, 61, 74, 79, 128, 174, 234; in Ajna, 211, 212, 213; in Theosophy, 37
Buddhism, 12, 18-19, 20, 29, 108; Mahayana, 21; Tantric, 18, 169, 227; Taoist, 18; Zen, 4-5, 13, 109
Burr, H.S., 48, 49, 59, 60, 61, 68

Cady, P., 118
Cannon, W.B. 221
causal body, *see* Bodhi body
cell(s), 26-7, 43, 46-7, 50, 234, 252; embryonic, 164-5; memory, 39, 61
Chakra(s), 14, 24, 28, 33, 61, 87, 92, 93, 136, 161, 180, 242; as adapters, 136, 147, 148, 236; Chitrini, 148, 149, 194, 196, 210, 214-15; developmental stress in, 173, 180, 233-4, 241-2, 243; equipotentiality of, 136, 246; evolution of, 157, 177, 179-80, 233-4, 243-8; force-fields of, 177, 241; glands and, 147, 178, 236, 245; Linga, 152, 194, 196-214; a multilevel system, 136-7, 169; as objects of meditation, 5, 25, 93, 161, 204, 206, 212, 213; perceived by sensitives, 26, 61, 169; polarities between, 88, 146, 153, 177, 180, 206-7, 343-4, 247; psychosomatic entities, 61-2, 93, 156, 173, 179; as transducers, 129, 136, 147, 148, 177, 178, 199, 246; *see also* Chakral centres; *and under individual Chakras*
Chakral centres, 137, 176, 207, 232; basal, root, 33, 92, 96, 109, 135, 137, 146, 165, 215; brow, between eyebrows, 178, 210, 237; crown, head, 33, 137, 214, 233, 237, 244; heart, 152, 163, 180, 204, 206, 210; sacral, 180, 214-15, 243; solar plexus, 180, 215; throat, 180, 233, 236, 243
Chardin, T. de, 39, 136, 137-8
chemistry (ical), 16, 39, 48, 63, 68, 74, 86, 90, 91, 120, 240, 245; body,

93, 97, 131
Chien Shuing, Mme, 70
Chit, 41, 148-9, 150, 178, 191; in
    Ajna, 212, 213; Atma and, 140,
    143-4; as consciousness, 140-3; as
    intelligence, 143-6; -Kundalini,
    145-6, 164, 192, 197, 250-1;
    moon and, 150, 206, 212; role in
    Kundalini system, 145-6, 148-51,
    164, 197-8, 250-1; in Satchitananda,
    237; Shabda and, 212; -Shiva,
    145-6, 213; as ultimate reality,
    140-3
Chitrini Nadi, 148-50, 162, 178, 190
Chitta, 51, 53, 62, 74, 128, 174, 211;
    at death, 42, 223; and memory,
    38-9, 42-3, 61, 79
Christianity, 11-13, 30, 137-8, 153
clairvoyance, clairvoyants, 24, 26,
    60, 61, 83, 112, 169, 217, 229,
    240
Coe Jnr, M.R., 132, 134
competence, 14, 22, 146; of Mahayogi,
    197-8, 250
consciousness, 2, 3, 4, 11, 31, 41, 54,
    66, 144, 177, 205, 242; Chakras
    and, 145, 146, 147, 152-3, 163-4,
    194, 196-214 passim, 232; Chit
    and, 140-3, 148-9, 178, 197-8, 203;
    cosmic, 43, 54, 78-9, 80, 160, 175,
    177; dissociated states of, 29, 62-3,
    66-7, 129, 220; ego-, self-, 34, 38,
    171, 179; ergo- 79, 82, 91; evolu-
    tion of, 32, 44-5, 54, 80-1, 91,
    148-9, 163-4, 190-1, 240; Gunas
    and, 148-9; intelligence and, 143-6,
    149; levels of, 55, 66, 67, 73, 74,
    134, 214; Maya and, 31-2, 41, 54-5,
    171; Shabda and, 163; as ultimate
    reality, 140, 141; in Western
    psychology, 141-2, 152
cosmology, 81, 82, 83, 85, 91, 168;
    Theosophical, 217-19, 229; see also
    Hinduism, cosmology of; physical
    world; universe
creation, 12, 31, 41, 43, 44, 45, 54,
    56, 169; from above, 78, 178;
    Chit and, 143-4; role of perception
    in, 163; a single operation, 81-2;
    work of Shaktis, 163, 186
currents, 71, 111, 132, 178; dragon,
    90, 106-7, 111, 112, 127, 133;
    Earth, geodetic, 90, 91, 97, 105-6,
    109

Curry, M., 118

Dakini, 92-3, 96, 132, 149, 200
death, 42, 74, 79, 151, 207, 220, 223,
    249-50
Devas, 22, 25, 31, 194
Devata, 17, 23, 92, 201, 205, 206
Devi, 22, 31, 32, 86
Dharma, 15, 92, 198
Dhyana, 11, 22, 209, 210; see also
    meditation
dichotomy, see dualism
Dirac, P.A.M., 69
divination, 87, 111, 112, 117; see also
    dowsing
divinities, see Devata
dowsers, 87, 90, 98-9, 101, 116, 121,
    123, 126, 133
dowsing, 88, 98, 102, 111, 116,
    117-19, 121; researches of Under-
    wood, 98-104
dualism, 6, 28-9, 30, 85, 87, 131, 134,
    141, 142

Earth, 45, 47, 49, 51, 53, 90, 105,
    122, 252; Chakras of, 88, 92, 200,
    215; forces, 87, 88, 96, 97, 104,
    106-7, 109, 113, 116, 127, 231;
    force-fields of, 97, 103, 105, 109,
    128; a living being, 45-6, 50-1,
    89, 106, 121, 136; -Moon complex,
    104, 112-13, 115, 119; solar
    influences on, 88, 90, 113, 115-16,
    231
ego, 25, 35, 38, 39, 40, 129, 144, 156,
    174, 176; as centre of awareness,
    34, 141, 169; -consciousness and
    Ahangkara, 34, 40, 171; a con-
    struct, 40, 171-2, 174, 176, 210;
    -distortions, 171, 173, 174, 175,
    188; reincarnating, 223; -reinforc-
    ing attitudes, 172, 173, 249; resis-
    tance to true self, 171, 188, 192, 214
    249; subliminal self and, 161-2,
    216, 222-3, 238; -transcendence,
    13, 15, 25, 36-41 passim, 109, 151,
    172, 174, 210, 214
electromagnetism, see magnetism
elementary particles, see particles
embryo (logy), 163, 164-6, 203
emotion, 180, 220-2, 245
enlightenment, 5, 7, 8, 13, 15, 25, 33,
    45, 109, 130, 156; Chit and, 144,
    149, 237; common-sense and, 32,

42; an embodied state, 11, 28, 29, 36, 109, 197

environment, 27, 39, 48, 49, 131; cosmic, 7, 242; created by living things, 47, 73, 96; internal, 179, 192; mental pollution of, 122

enzymes, 48, 91, 145, 236; see also molecules

ether, 41, 60-1, 64; as Akasha, 51, 53, 234

evolution, 40, 72, 90, 131-2, 170, 179, 233, 247; of bodies, 45, 235; Brahman knowledge in, 79; of consciousness, 44-5, 54-5, 80, 81, 91, 148-9, 163-4, 190-1, 240, 242; controlled from above, 55-6, 58-61, 79, 137; as a cycle of Becoming, 54; of the ego, 40, 41, 109; of forms, 44-5, 240; Hindu theory of, 40, 44-6, 54-6; Jivatman and, 137-8; micro-organisms and, 46-7; of nervous system, 73, 96, 149; patterning and, 48, 131

extrasensory perception (ESP), 26, 27, 83, 117

Fall, the, 170

Feng Shui, 111, 112, 113, 114, 116

fields, 50, 58-9, 168, 177, 179, 191, 241, 246; Kundalini qualifies all physical, 128; life, L-, 48, 49, 59-64, 74, 86, 106; patterning by force-, 48, 58, 97, 106; Prana, 59, 128; terrestrial, 97, 105, 109, 128; thought, T-, 59-64, 74, 86, 106

fire, 129; as a Bhuta, 53; as a Tattvic image, 89, 151, 152, 215; Tibetan's three, 228, 230-4, 236, 238, 241

flame, 186, 203, 206, 212-13

food-sheath, see gross body

force(s), 30, 31, 42, 84, 116, 129, 131, 133, 151, 152, 180, 185; ascending, 156, 177-8, 190, 247; cosmic, 30, 77, 133; descending, 156-7, 158, 162, 176-8, 190, 214, 247; Earth, geodetic, 96, 97, 105-7, 116-17, 120, 178, 200, 251-2; non-physical, 50, 51, 56, 65, 84, 120, 178, 200, 251-2; nuclear, 64-5, 70, 71, 72, 84, 86, 91, 129, 131; Kundalini co-ordinates all, 33, 87-8, 92, 127, 133, 135, 167, 178-9; Shaktis as specific, 51, 83, 196,

230; thought as a, 65, 134-5, 154, 160, 163, 165-6; undifferentiated, 42; unknown to science, 97, 99, 104; see also gravity, magnetism

forms, 31, 38, 41, 42, 43, 65, 77, 142, 205; agents of differentiation, 42, 144; ergoconscious, 83, 84-5; evolution of, 44-5, 52, 132, 177, 240; intelligence inherent in, 93, 145; Kundalini and stability of, 39, 77, 86, 149, 178-9, 186; Kundalini threefold in all, 151; needs prior to, 81; Pranas differentiated by, 42; purpose implicit in, 143, 159; Shabda and, 52, 86, 88, 158-60, 186, 205; thought-, 23, 134-5, 154, 159, 172, 250; see also patterning

Freud, S., 56, 173

Gardner, M., 71

geodetic lines, 98, 99-102, 103, 105-6, 107, 120, 126, 127, 133; and ley lines, 98, 111, 115, 116; Prana in, 116, 128

geomancy, geomancers, 106-7, 111, 116, 128; see also Feng Shui

gland, glandular system, 190; Ajna and pituitary, 147, 178, 236, 245; Vishudda and thyroid, 236

God, gods, see Brahman; Devata

Granthi, 147, 148, 165, 192, 200-1

gravity, 57, 59, 76, 84, 86, 91, 107, 133, 251

gross, physical body, 33, 35, 37, 39, 40, 52, 60, 73, 88, 147, 169; anchored in Muladhara, 186, 197, 199, 205, 210; in astral projection, 62, 63, 129; as chemical body, 93, 97, 131; as food-sheath, 89, 93, 97, 128, 137, 152; Kundalini and survival of, 186, 193, 249-50; in Kundalini yoga, 28, 43; physical Prana in, 41, 61; and self-portrait, 171-2; synthesis of forces in, 84, 178-9

Gunas, 148-9, 151, 152, 177, 178, 190, 191, 235

guru, 21, 24, 25, 145, 160, 207, 241, 251; role of, 8, 11, 13-14, 130, 173-4; within, 8, 210, 213, 214, 216, 229

handedness, 67-72, 99-103 passim,

112, 127-8
hallucinations, 54
Hartmann, E., 118-19
Hasted, J., 61, 87
Harvalik, Z.V., 119
healers, healing, 61, 87, 155, 169, 171,
    174, 187-8, 246; Chakras and,
    229-30; Kundali system and, 177,
    181, 194-5
heat, 48, 49, 228, 230; conceived
    spatially, 52, 53
Hinduism, cosmology of, 28-43;
    Brahmanic emanations in, 30-42,
    51-4; deviant views of Maya in, 29,
    31; evolution in, 40, 44-6, 54, 56,
    163-4; forces personalised in, 30;
    levels of matter in, 33-5, 37, 38-9,
    44, 55, 58, 82; monotheism of, 30,
    78-9; multidimensionality in, 31,
    43, 51; origin of life in, 48, 88; a
    phenomenological system, 29, 31,
    51-4, 79-80, 83, 160, 167, 227;
    physical universe in, 51-4, 81, 83-5,
    89; Shiva-Shakti Tattva in, 78-81,
    91, 162, 227; space in, 52-5, 81-2;
    and Theosophy, 217-19, 229;
    see also Hinduism: Tantric
Hinduism, psychology of, 28-43
    passim; Antahkarana in, 40, 137,
    169, 171, 174, 175, 197, 214;
    bodily death in, 42, 74, 79, 151,
    207, 223, 249-50; memory in,
    38-9, 42-3, 74; mind-body relation
    in, 22, 30, 32, 39, 96, 129, 134-5;
    reincarnation in, 42-3, 223; Shiva-
    Shakti Tattva in, 137-8, 152, 191,
    196-9, 213; theory of perception
    in 51-4, 159-60, 163-4; types of
    awareness in, 29, 31-3, 36-8; types
    of body in, 33, 62; see also Jivatman;
    Kundalini system; Purusha
Hinduism, Tantric, 16-24, 32, 43, 227;
    Avidya and Vidya in, 29, 31-2, 45,
    55-6, 80; a body-affirming system,
    11, 23, 28; enlightenment in the
    flesh in, 28, 29, 36, 109, 197;
    Theosophy and, 217-39
Hoyle, Fred, 49
hypnosis, 37, 54, 66-7, 75

Ida Nadi, 146-7, 148, 150, 178, 190,
    228
illusion, 28-9, 31, 35, 81; see also

Maya; Shangkara
individual differences, 54, 241; among
    meditators, 5; in spiritual develop-
    ment, 7-8, 157
Indriyas, 37, 52-4, 79, 135, 250
inspiration, 150, 162, 176
Integral Yoga, see yoga
intellect: rational, 18, 130-1, 162
intelligence, 85, 87, 92, 96, 134, 150,
    166; carriers of the pure, 92, 132,
    143, 144, 145, 149, 200, 205;
    Chit-Shakti as, 143-6, 148-9, 178,
    212-13; consciousness and, 143-6,
    198; inherent in matter, 92-3;
    qualified by bodies, 145
intuition, 3, 6, 45, 176, 195; inspira-
    tion and, 150, 162; reason and,
    130-1, 162, 237; in science,
    237
Ishvara, Ishvari, 30, 36, 85; Shaktis
    as, 79, 158, 159-60, 162, 186,
    196

Jivatman, 25, 55, 136, 152, 197, 205,
    206, 211, 212; agent of Brahman,
    33, 38, 55, 137-8; Atman in man,
    30, 143-4; beyond Maya, 171;
    Chit in, 143-4; Kundalini and incar-
    nation of, 43, 153, 165-6, 250;
    Kundalini works under, 33, 85,
    109, 146, 161-2, 250; personality
    controlled from, 34-5, 38, 137-8,
    157, 165-6, 169, 170, 235-6;
    Shabda and, 203; uniqueness of
    each, 30, 40; 'wears' energy bodies,
    161, 165; yoga as union with,
    14-15
Jnana, 32, 150, 230; see also yoga;
    Jnana
Joy, W.B., 156, 176-7, 193, 232
Jung, C.G., 6, 7, 93, 122, 130, 134,
    139, 173, 249

Kanda, see Granthi
Karagulla, S., 26
Kilner, W., 60
Kirlian photography, 26, 60, 217
knots, see Granthi
knowledge, 31-3, 36-8, 55-6, 130,
    150, 202, 235; Brahman, 32, 37,
    79, 204; intuitive, 162, 216; lost,
    25; partial, 29, 56, 80, 227; see also
    Jnana; Vidya

Krishna, Gopi, 5-6, 8, 24, 248
Kundalini, 7, 26, 92, 127, 152-3,
  168, 182, 228; basic physical principle, 43, 93, 97, 167-8, 185, 251;
  Brahmanic agent, 32, 43, 186;
  Chit-, 145-6, 148-51, 164, 250-1;
  coiled, 96, 105, 109, 128, 151,
  164, 197, 200-4, 230-1, 242;
  confusion about, 11, 24-5, 108,
  129; co-ordinator of forces, 33,
  87-8, 92, 127, 133, 135, 167,
  178-9; dangers of manipulating,
  14, 25, 81, 84, 207, 250-1; a de-
  limiting force, 83-4, 186, 228;
  an Earth force, 96, 106-7, 109,
  193, 251-2; as fire of matter,
  129, 230-4, 241; insight and, 36,
  164; intelligence inherent in, 92,
  166, 168; -Prakriti, 186; -Prithivi,
  249-51; risen form of, 109, 137,
  230, 238, 247-8; rises progressively,
  36, 194; role in yoga, 36, 80;
  serpentine, spiral formations of, 69,
  85, 106; -Shabdabrahman, 24, 79,
  86, 88, 153, 158, 161, 166, 169,
  186, 192, 250-1; a stabilising
  agency, 77, 83, 86, 97, 127-8, 149,
  168, 178, 192, 228; a threefold
  Devi, 146, 151-2, 167, 197-9,
  201, 230, 238; works under
  Jivatman, 33, 85, 109, 146, 161-2,
  250; see also physical world;
  Shakti
Kundalini arousal, 5, 14, 25, 130,
  134-5, 158, 182, 189, 242;
  accidental, 5, 198-9, 207
Kundalini cycle, see physio-kundalini
Kundalini experiences, 2, 5, 95, 135,
  182, 183, 241; of Krishna, G.,
  5-6, 8, 24, 248; of Serrano, M.,
  248-9
Kundalini science, see science, Eastern
Kundalini syndrome, see physio-
  kundalini
Kundalini system, 24, 28, 33, 89, 129,
  138-9, 152, 245; Chit roles in,
  145-6, 148-51, 164, 197-8, 250-1;
  disturbances in, 180, 194, 241-2,
  243, 249-51; evolution of, 146,
  194, 230-4, 243-8; polarities in,
  88, 137, 146, 153, 180, 206-7,
  243-4, 247; Prana in, 86, 87-8,

127-35, 178, 186, 193, 201, 228,
  231-4; Sahasrara-Muladhara axis of,
  138, 146-53; Shabda in, 153,
  162-3, 165-7, 203, 205; Shiva-
  Shakti Tattva in, 246-7; two Nadi
  systems in, 146-50, 151, 162; up
  and down forces in, 97, 157, 158,
  162, 164, 176-8, 180, 190, 242,
  247; see also Kundalini; nervous
  system
Kundalini yoga, 10, 11, 14, 24, 33, 40,
  88, 129, 138, 146, 156, 207;
  bliss in, 11, 45, 197; growth of
  insight in, 36, 144; enlightenment
  in the flesh in, 28, 197; a Laya
  yoga, 151; Mantras in, 22, 161;
  reunion of Shiva and Shakti in, 36,
  138, 144; role of body in, 43, 146;
  three Kundalinis in, 197-9; see also
  yoga

Lalana Chakra, 234
latency, 36, 179, 213, 231, 235-6,
  237
laws: of life, 50, 82; natural, 97, 166,
  168, 186, 228; of physics, 50, 65,
  66, 71
Laya, 151; centre, 4; process, 229;
  yoga, 230
Leadbeater, C.W., 217-18, 219, 227,
  232
letters, 159, 161, 162, 200, 201, 205,
  211, 212, 228; see also sound,
  lettered
ley line network, 98, 112, 113-16, 119,
  120, 128; see also geodetic lines;
  telluric emanations
liberation, see Moksha
life, 50, 73, 82, 85, 86, 131, 199, 230,
  240; after death, 240; as evolute of
  matter, 65; -fields, 48, 49, 59-64,
  74; -forces, 41, 90, 96; -forms, 47,
  49, 50, 121; -mind frontier, 71;
  origin of, 47-50, 73, 88; Prana and,
  41, 42, 44, 87, 152; -principle,
  163, 201
life-vehicle, 39, 41, 55, 59, 62, 86, 93,
  128, 131, 169, 246, 250; anchored
  in Anahata, 197, 210; at death, 42,
  223
light, 90, 159, 166, 167, 213, 230,
  233-4; conceived spatially, 52, 53;

polarised, 67, 68-9
Linga, 96, 109, 138, 152, 197-211
passim; see also Chakras, Linga
Livingston, J., 123-4
Lockyer, Sir N., 114, 116
lotus: Chakral, 61, 150, 159, 199-200,
204-6, 211-12; with no form, 176;
thousand-petalled, 144, 162, 176,
206; twelve-petalled, 138-9, 146,
153, 162, 176

magnetism (tic), 57, 58-9, 64, 70, 86,
128, 177, 180; electro-, 48, 60-1,
84, 85, 105, 107, 120, 129, 133,
167, 251; fields, 58, 69, 103, 128,
183-4, 187, 189, 191, 247, 251;
psycho-, 64
Mahakundalini, 77-94 passim, 106,
120, 133, 249, 252; as geodynamic
force, 96, 105, 106; implications
for science, 81-91
Mahayogi, 29, 81, 85, 176, 197, 198-9,
250
man, mankind, 22, 45, 85, 89, 104,
163; dual nature of, 227, 240;
as Earth's nervous system, 46;
Theosophy on nature of, 217;
as transformer of matter, 137,
151, 247
Manas, 39, 51, 53, 61, 74, 79, 128,
174, 238; in Ajna, 211, 213; forces
of, 61, 233, 242; in Theosophy, 37
Mandala(s), Ajna, 210-14; Anahata,
204-10; as biological statements,
97; Manipura, 215; Muladhara,
92-3, 96, 97, 128, 161, 199-204,
205; as objects for meditation,
5, 25, 93, 161, 204, 206, 212, 213;
Svadisthana, 214-15; Vishudda,
234-5
Manipura Chakra, 215
Mantra, 14, 22, 149, 153, 154-5;
as formative force, 24, 158, 160-2,
163, 165-6
Mantra Vidya, 14, 16, 23, 153, 154,
160
matter, 6, 21-2, 26, 41, 44, 93, 130,
137, 142, 163, 240; Akasha as
physical, 51; anti-, 69, 72, 73, 76;
ergoconscious, 84, 88, 127, 166;
fires of, 129, 230-4, 241; frontier
between physical and mental, 42,
64, 70, 72, 76, 93; interlevel

mechanisms in, 66-74, 127; Kundalini and dense, 43, 93, 96-7,
231, 251-2; levels of, 33-9, 44, 55,
58, 82, 135, 166, 240; particles
and states of, 64, 69-72; patterning
of, 36, 48, 64, 131, 159; Prana and,
41-2, 231; refining of, 33, 44, 45,
90, 137, 151, 163, 247; in Theosophy, 218; thought and, 134
Maya, 15, 32, 35, 41, 170; -density,
-thickness, 38, 43, 45, 82, 197;
deviant views of, 29, 31; as illusion,
28-9, 31, 81; partial knowledge
and, 29, 32, 81; as phenomenal
universe, 29, 31, 81; -purushas, 32,
35, 36, 39, 55; as consciousness,
31, 32, 41, 54, 78; thinning veils
of, 44-5, 176; see also Avidya
medicine, 16, 53, 61, 141, 166, 181,
229, 240
meditation, 2, 7, 14, 22, 29, 130,
158, 183, 245; body in, 155-6, 210;
Chakras as objects of, 5, 25, 93,
161, 204, 206, 212, 213; as creative
process, 237-8; difficulties with, 3,
5, 155, 235; relaxation and, 187-8;
Samadhi state of, 209, 212; Transcendental, 109, 187, 209; in the
West, 209
meditators, 84, 85, 134, 135, 154,
155-6, 160, 244; Kundalini
experiences of, 95, 134, 182, 189,
235, 249; soul as, 237
memory, 40, 61; Hindu theory of,
38-9. 42-3. 74; particle theory of,
75-6; of past lives, 42, 74-5, 223;
personal identity and, 43, 74,
mental body, see Antahkarana
Mermet, Abbé, 117
metal bending, 62, 133, 134, 160
microbiology, 26, 46
micro-organisms, 26, 46-7, 48, 50-1,
68
Miller, S., 47-9
mind, 3, 22, 26, 37, 41, 48, 82, 152;
Chakra of mind, 199, 214, 234;
-body relation, 22, 29-30, 39, 71,
96, 127, 129, 134-5, 141, 185;
common unconscious as cosmic,
122, 134, 167, 175; fires of, 230-4;
as instrument, 40, 215-16; -life
frontier, 71; of Lord within, 214;
-matter dualism, 6, 87, 141, 142;

-matter frontier, 72; in physics, 120-1, 167, 181; purification of, 212, 213, 214, 234; sensory, 37-8, 39, 66; super-, 155, 175, 213; Tattvas of 34-40, 79

mitochondria, 46, 50, 165

Moksha, 7, 14, 15, 176, 187, 201, 204-5, 208, 213, 230

molecules, 42-50 passim, 63, 71, 89-90, 92, 236; handedness of, 67, 68, 90; spiral formations in 65, 68

Monroe, R.A., 63, 65-6, 72, 73, 220, 248

Moody, R., 220, 221

Moon, 89, 104, 112-13, 115-16, 119

moon: as Tattvic image, 89, 150, 151, 152, 206, 210, 211, 235

Motoyama, H., 61, 183

movement, see Spanda

Mudras, 207

Mukti, see Moksha

Mula Mantra Chakra 149, 153, 162, 164

Muladhara Chakra, 92-3, 105, 138, 162, 197; anchors Jivatman physically, 186, 197, 249-50; body's form centre, 205; coiled Kundalini in, 148, 186, 193, 197, 200-4, 230-1, 242; Kundalini and Prana in, 87-8, 186, 201, 205, 211; Mandala of, 92-3, 96, 97, 128, 161, 193, 199-204, 205; -Sahasrara axis, 138, 146-53, 158, 177, 191; Shiva in, 200, 202; three Kundalinis in, 202-4; see also Chakras; Kundalini system

mysticism, mystics, 6, 13, 29, 156, 166, 177

Nada, 212-13

Nadi(s), 28, 33, 87, 89, 136, 148, 241; Chitrini system, 146-7, 148, 151, 162, 178, 190-1, 215; Ida-Pingala system, 147-50, 151, 178, 190, 200, 228; nervous system and, 147, 149, 177; single source of all, 148, 163, 192-3; see also Kundalini system

natural selection, 48, 50

nature, 31, 39, 45, 47, 48, 89, 106, 153, 185; controlled from above, 55-6, 163; intelligence implicit in,

79, 93; Kundalini and laws of, 166, 186, 228; a multi-dimensional hierarchy, 46, 51, 56, 58, 109; spiral formation in, 251-2; a system of induced fields, 58-9, 228

nectar, 150, 151, 162, 178, 205, 238

nervous system, 37, 73, 74, 105-7, 117, 128, 243; evolution of, 2, 73, 96, 149, 188, 236; physio-kundalini cycle and, 183-5, 187-8, 189-91; Prana and, 207; see also Kundalini system

Nirvana, 8, 28, 176

Northrop, F.S.C., 49, 59

Nyasa, 23

Omega, 137-8 see also Chardin, T. de

Orgel, L., 50

out-of-the-body experiences (OOBE), see astral projection

parapsychology, 32, 123, 132, 154

parity, 69-70

particles, 6, 46, 50-1, 72-3, 85, 133, 167; anti-, 65, 69, 70, 72, 73; elementary, 63-5, 69-73; handedness in, 69, 70; interdimensional transactions of, 69, 71, 82-3; mentoid, 39, 76, 79; origin of, 64; psychomagnetic entities, 64, 132, 133; and states of matter, 64, 69-72; theory of memory, 75-6

Pashu, 15-16

Pasteur, L., 48, 67, 68, 70, 71

patterning, patterns, 31, 36, 61, 67, 72, 74, 91, 131, 188, 190; energy, 106, 116, 135, 155, 198-9; evolutionary role of, 48, 132; by force-fields, 48, 58, 97, 106; of illness, 241, 243; and origin of life, 48, 131; by Shabda, 158-9, 166; stability of, 83, 91, 122; stress-relieving, 187; by thought, 134

Pearson, K., 64, 69

perception, 39, 61, 83, 163, 173, 246; clarifying, 32, 80, 216, 234; emotion and, 221; Hindu theory of, 51-4, 159-60, 163-4; see also Hinduism: psychology of

personality, 39, 180-1, 188, 191, 210, 212; controlled from Jivatman, 34-5, 38, 137-8, 235-6; in Western psychology, 219, 222-3; see also

psychology
petals: Chakral, 150, 159, 162, 199, 200, 204, 205, 211, 228
Peyre, F., 118, 119
philosophy, 12, 28-9, 151; of science, 6, 141; see also Hinduism
photosynthesis, 46, 90, 129
physical world, 40, 43, 58, 59, 92-3, 127, 132, 234, 240; conceived perceptually, 51-4; created by cosmic thought, 163; Kundalini Shakti of, 77-94 passim, 106, 133, 138, 153, 161, 163, 168, 228; natural law in, 168, 185, 228; purpose in, 92, 132; stability of, 77, 97, 168, 186; see also nature; universe
physics, 6, 7, 39, 43, 69, 76, 77, 84, 91, 119, 132, 141, 240; Chakras and 229; geodetic system and, 97, 104, 116; Hindu, 53, 55; implications of Kundalini for, 81-5, 86-9, 91, 127, 129, 167; mind in, 120-1, 167, 181; and origin of life, 50; and Prana, 120; telluric emanations and, 119-20; void of, 78, 81
physio-kundalini, 95, 182, 183, 198, 207; cycle, 95, 96, 97, 109, 182-94 passim, 249; syndrome, 6, 96, 191, 193, 207, 233, 241-2
physiology, 27, 67, 135, 166, 215, 221; of physio-kundalini cycle, 182-94 passim; occult, 63, 222; Tantric, 62-3, 87, 185-7, 190-1, 192, 193-4, 239
Pingala Nadi, 146-7, 148, 177, 178, 190-1, 228
Planetary Magnetic Grids, 118-20; see also telluric emanations
polarity(ties), 30, 77, 107, 129, 185, 189; Apana-Prana, 206-7; Chakral, 88, 146, 153, 177, 180, 206-7, 243-4, 247; changes of, 192-4; cosmic, 78, 86, 88, 141; in Earth's magnetic field, 103; Earth-Moon, 112-13; mind-matter, 141; Shiva-Shakti, 33, 137, 146, 191; spirit-matter, 137, 141, 242; Sun-Earth, 88-90
Ponnamperuna, C., 49
Prakriti, 31, 35, 45, 58, 73, 84, 146, 163; Chit and, 198; -density, 43, 44; generates all lesser Tattvas, 79;

as multidimensional nature, 51, 79; as phenomenal world, 31, 51, 54, 80, 89, 138, 185-6, 227; -Purusha distinction, 31, 35, 41, 42, 54, 78, 227, 246-7; sets Kundalini's limits, 79
Prana(s), 39, 41, 42, 60, 74, 87, 147, 174, 228, 250; in astral projection, 62-3, 129; at death, 42, 86; as electromagnetism, 60, 120,129; in geodetic and ley lines, 116, 128; in Kundalini system, 77, 86, 87-8, 127-35, 178, 186, 193, 201, 228, 231-4; and life, 41, 42, 44, 51, 230; in life-vehicle, 39, 41, 42, 59, 131; physical and psychic, 41, 61, 72, 93, 127, 152, 178, 250; in Theosophy, 41, 60, 230-4; Vayu and, 201, 205, 231
Prana sheath, see life-vehicle
Pranayama, 11, 147, 207
Prithivi, 53, 55, 96-7, 105, 132, 249; as the Earth, 43, 45, 88, 193; in Muladhara Mandala, 92-3, 200, 201; as physical level of Prakriti, 185
projections, 173, 175-6
psychobiology, 5, 7, 30, 42, 132, 217
psychokinesis (PK), 132, 133-4
psychology, 10, 56, 76, 92, 171, 219, 220, 222; Chakras and, 229-30, 239-52 passim; Chinese, 130, 133-4, 173; consciousness in Western, 141-2, 143, 145; ego in, 40, 171-2, 173-4, 176, 210, 222; emotion in, 221; inadequacies of Western, 188-89; see also Hinduism, psychology of
psychosomatic disorders, 5, 97, 173, 175, 188, 249; and Chakral development, 180, 192, 239, 241-6
psychotherapy(ists), 173, 174, 181, 187-8
Purnananda, Swami, 201, 202, 204, 210, 212, 214
Purusha(s), 31, 45, 56, 91, 146, 250; aspects of Shiva, 32, 33, 35, 78, 80, 137, 146, 152, 194, 205, 206; Brahman as experiencer, 33-41 passim, 146, 227; evolution of, 45, 55, 164, 194; Para-, 32, 35, 55, 80, 194; -Prakriti distinction, 31, 35, 41, 42, 54, 78, 80, 227, 246-7;

types of, 32, 35, 36, 39, 66

Radha, Swami Sivananda, 150
Rajas(sic) 148, 149, 177-78, 190, 235; see also Guna
Ravitz Jnr, L., 66
reality, 22, 26, 55-6, 71, 72, 73, 167, 172, 174; illusion and, 28-9, 80; Satchitananda as, 142, 161; Shiva-Shakti aspects of, 91, 227; ultimate, 29, 34-5, 80, 130, 140-3, 144
reincarnation, 12, 42-3, 65, 74-5, 223
religion, 12, 13, 14, 18, 19, 22, 29, 30, 154, 174, 207-9; see also Tantric religious practices
Romain, L., 119
Ryzl, M., 26

Sadhaka, 11, 14, 15-16, 22, 144, 151, 161, 213
Sadhana, 14-16, 18, 21, 23, 146
Sahasrara Chakra, 138, 150, 162, 176, 211, 237, 247; as abode of Shiva, 32, 80-1, 137, 237; descending forces from, 162, 164, 214; -Muladhara axis, 138, 146-53, 158, 177, 191; reunion of Shiva and Shakti in, 138, 144, 194; see also Chakras; Kundalini system
Samadhi, 11, 17, 18, 32, 130, 150, 242; Anahata and, 206; ecstatic states and, 150-1, 213; in the flesh, 36, 201; as a limb of yoga, 209, 212
Sankhya, 18; see also Veda
Sannella, L., 95, 96, 109, 134, 182-94 passim, 198, 235, 248, 249
Sanskrit terms, 53, 139-40, 141, 154; misuse of, 11, 185; in Theosophy, 24-5, 37, 219
Satchitananda, 41, 45, 142-3, 144, 161, 169, 171; Chit in, 142, 150, 237; experienced in the flesh, 146, 176, 230
Sattva(vic), 148, 149, 177, 190, 235; see also Gunas
science: Eastern, 62, 80, 124, 130, 160, 222; Kundalini, 10, 87, 96, 106, 113, 136, 145, 239; Tantric, 33, 40, 42, 85, 90, 92, 95, 127
science, Mantric, see Mantra Vidya
science, Western, 6, 32, 43, 53, 56, 63,
79, 90, 131, 222, 251; dismissive attitudes in, 117, 118, 122-3, 183, 218; forces unknown to, 97, 99, 104; Hinduism and, 7, 13, 30, 80; inadequacies of, 9, 32, 57, 76, 85, 89, 168; intuition in, 133, 181, 216; Kundalini and, 25, 182; mind in, 87, 120-1, 127; narrow energy spectrum in, 85, 120; philosophy of, 6, 141; Theosophy and, 217, 221-2; value of Hindu models for, 56, 59, 62, 83, 87, 120-1, 217, 222
self, selves, 7, 13, 35, 36, 38, 40, 41, 134, 247; -awareness, 34-5, 40; conflict within, 161, 171, 173, 179, 180, 188, 191-2, 209, 211, 214, 249; conscious, ego-, 8, 134, 142, 150, 156, 171, 174, 242, 250; divine, spiritual, 30, 40, 56, 237, 238; greater, higher, wiser, 4, 8, 156, 176; lesser, personal, 13, 161, 188, 237; non-alignment of, 191; -portrait, 171-2, 173, 222, 239; subliminal and surface, 170-5, 212, 214, 222-3, 234-42 passim; true, 35, 40, 55, 144, 162, 174, 211, 214, 230, 244, 247
sensitives, 26-7, 176, 181, 183; see also clairvoyants
serpentine formations, 83, 93, 111, 252; in geodetic system, 99, 101, 105, 127-8; Kundalini and, 69, 85, 106, 127, 146; see also blind springs; spirals
Serrano, M., 248-9
Shabda, 52, 78, 79, 83, 149, 154, 166, 210, 212; as a formative force, 24, 86, 158-66 passim; in Kundalini system, 153, 162-3, 165-7, 203, 205; lettered, 159, 162
Shabdabrahman, 158, 162-5, 166, 192, 205; in the body, 79, 162, 163-6, 186, 197; causal, 96-7, 133, 161, 163, 167, 186, 203; embodies divine intention, 86, 88, 158-9, 166, 204, 236; and integrity of forms, 86, 186, 250; as Sound-Brahman, 24, 78, 158-9
Shaktis, 17, 24, 31, 158, 196; agents of Brahman, 30-1, 51, 55; cosmic role of, 78, 83, 91, 133, 137, 186, 196; each a specific force, 51;

functional duality of, 91, 144; a
multidimensional continuum, 82-3;
in balance when coiled, 77, 86; reunion with Shiva, 36, 81, 137,
144, 194, 247; spectrum, 58, 59,
82, 136; see also forces; Tattvas

shaman, 209-10, 212, 220

Shangkara, 18-19, 28-9, 31, 55, 80

Shiva, 33, 36, 97, 158, 205; Brahman
in souls, 32-3; centre in head, 33,
80, 137, 191; Chit and, 144, 197-8;
cosmic role of, 78, 91, 137; -Linga,
197, 199, 201, 202, 206; Para-,
Supreme, 32, 80, 194, 213; reunion
with Shakti, 36, 81, 137, 144, 194,
247; Tattva: see also Purusha

Smith, R.A., 98, 104

soul, 44, 237; Aurobindo's Real,
170-5 passim, 180, 214; desire-,
171

sound, 53, 78, 154, 155, 160, 166,
167; lettered, 159, 161, 205;
and movement, 153, 159,
unlettered, 159

space(s), 43, 51, 69-72, 83; Akasha as,
51, 53; grain in, 70, 72; multiple,
58, 65, 69, 81-2; -time, 43, 61, 63,
73, 131, 137-8, 168

Spanda, 52, 159, 167; -Brahman, 79

spectrum, 56, 120, 131, 133, 222;
electromagnetic 58, 60, 120, 129,
183, 251; Kundalini, 252; scientific, 85, 120; Shakti, 58, 59, 82,
136

spin, 64, 69-72, 167, 177, 251-2

spirals, 68, 69, 106, 251; in geodetic
lines, 98-105 passim, 112; in Kundalini movements, 106, 127-8,
150; at mind-matter frontier, 71,
72, 73, 93

spirit, 13, 44, 45, 137, 144, 170;
fires of, 230; paths, 111, 112; as
ultimate reality, 140, 240

Steiner, Rudolf, 217-18

Stevenson, I., 43, 74, 223

Sthula Sharira, see gross body

Stone Age monuments, see artefacts:
prehistoric

stress, 97, 187-9, 193, 228; developmental, 179-80, 194-5, 233, 241-6;
psychosomatic, 239, 245-6; spiritual, 174, 178, 182, 192

subliminals, the, 173, 192

subtle body, 24, 33, 35, 37, 40, 41,
52, 60, 73, 93, 97, 107, 128;
in astral projection, 62-3, 129;
deathless, 42, 62; psychic Prana in,
41, 42, 61, 152, 250; up and down
forces in, 156-7. 162, 176-8, 180,
192, 246; see also body; Hinduism, psychology of

Subuh, Muhammad, 235, 249

suffering, 13, 14, 22, 33, 45, 170,
171, 175

Suksma Sharira, see subtle body

Sun, 90, 113, 115

sun: as Tattvic image, 89, 151, 152,
210

Sushumna, 138, 139, 146-50, 163,
164, 178, 190-1, 197, 215, 228;
see also Kundalini system; Nadi

Svadisthana Chakra, 214-15

symmetry, 67-8, 70

Tamas(ic), 148, 149, 178, 191, 235;
see also Gunas

Tanmatras, 37, 52-4, 79, 135, 250

Tantras, 10, 15, 17, 31, 135, 138,
140, 185, 196, 211, 235; essence
of, 16-17, 229; importance of the
body in, 11, 23, 28; misunderstanding of, 16-21; reformulations of
Vedas, 20; science and medicine in,
16; Theosophy and, 217-38

Tantric religious practices, 18, 19-24,
154, 208-9

Tantric science, see science, Eastern

Tantric yoga, see Kundalini yoga

Tao, Taosim, 16, 106-8, 109, 121,
133-4, 237

Tattvas, 35, 78-81, 91, 137, 152, 162,
196-8, 213, 234

telekinesis, 51, 154, 160

telepathy, 51, 60, 87, 154, 159, 209,
228-9, 240

telluric emanations, 117-18, 120, 133

Theosophy, 24-5, 31, 37, 60, 219, 223;
bodies in, 60, 62, 219-22; Chakras
in, 61, 218, 227, 228-9, 231-4; Hinduism and, 217-38; Kundalini in,
227-9, 230-4; manas in, 37; planes
in, 217-22; Prana in,41, 60, 228,
231-4; reincarnation in, 223; schools
of, 3, 217-18; and science, 217

Thomas, Lewis, 46, 89

Thompson, W., 124

thought, 34, 37, 123, 130, 134; effect
on body, 95-6, 173; emotion and,
92, 221; -fields, 59-64, 74; as a
force, 65, 134-5, 163, 165-6;
-forms; 23, 159, 172, 250; Mantric
use of, 23, 95-6, 160-2, 163;
see also Mantra

Tibetan, the, 2, 3, 174-6, 177, 227,
228-9, 239; Antahkarana of, 40,
174-5, 214; on Chakral polarities,
243-4, 247; on developmental
stress, 241-2; on three fires, 228,
230-4, 236

timing, 178-9, 235-6, 237

track lines, see geodetic lines

trance, 14, 220

Trikona, 96, 138, 151, 152, 197-212
passim

Tyler, F.C., 115

Umani, 213

unconscious: common, 122, 134

Underwood, G., 111-16 passim, 120,
133; dowsing researches of, 98-104,
105-6, 118, 126; geodetic theory
of, 104-5, 108, 116, 127, 128,
136, 200

universe, 24, 29, 30, 31, 45, 77, 86,
127, 168; evolution of, 44, 45,
54-6; genesis of, 29, 30-1, 33-43,
51-4, 78, 81, 159, 227; handedness throughout, 67-72; a
hologram, 31, 42, 43, 65, 167;
immanent Brahman, 22, 31; a
pattern of spins, 252; a phenomenological system, 29, 31, 51-4,
79-80, 83, 160, 167, 227; see also
Hinduism, cosmology of; physical
world

Upanishads, 10, 17, 20, 21, 31, 139,
196

Vajra Nadi, 148, 150, 178, 191

Vasiliev, L.L., 59-60

Vayu, 53, 201, 205, 207, 231; see also
Prana

Veda, Vedanta, 16, 17, 18-19, 20, 21,
208

Vidya, 29, 31-2, 45, 55, 80; see also
knowledge

Vijnana, 13, 32, 37; see also knowledge; Brahman

Vishudda Chakra, 234-5

void, the, 36, 44, 79, 86, 159; of
physics, 78, 81; as unknowable
Brahman, 41, 54, 106, 158

water, 49, 98, 99, 252; as a Bhuta,
53, 215; underground, 98,
104-5, 116, 117-18, 120, 124;
see also dowsing

Wallace, R.K. 233

Watkins, A., 111, 113, 116, 128

White, G.S., 103

Wilhelm, R., 130

Wittman, S., 118, 119

Woodroffe, Sir J., 10-21 passim, 51,
92, 93, 142, 151, 219; on Kundalini system, 138-9, 146-7, 185,
194, 199, 234; on Mantra, 160,
162; on mental matter, 37, 38; on
ultimate reality, 140

yoga, 3, 7, 8, 11, 25, 43, 108, 144,
160, 172, 230, 240; of action
(Karma), 7, 12, 13; aims of, 14-15,
35, 80, 130, 149, 151; competence
for, 14, 22, 146, 179; of devotion
(Bhakti), 12; as ego-transcendence,
13; Eight Limbs of, 207-9, 214;
Hatha, 11-12, 14; ideas common
to all, 11, 13; Integral, 14, 25, 32;
of knowledge (Jnana), 7, 12, 13,
14, 55-6; Laya, 151, 230; of
mastery, 214; as union, 8, 11,
14-15, 169; of withdrawal, 14

Zen, see Buddhism